Gender in Physical Culture

This book outlines existing research relating to gender in physical culture. The introductory chapter uses Lamont and Molnàr's (2002) idea of 'boundaries' as visible and invisible socially constructed borders that create social differences, as the theoretical framework for the book. Seven empirically driven case studies follow which, on the one hand, demonstrate how boundary 'work' has taken and is taking place at the level of media, institutions, communities, and individuals, and on the other hand, show how individuals, groups of individuals, and organisations challenge and change dominant gender discourses and practices. The wide variety of rich case materials reveal how gender ideals not only normalise, but are actively and purposefully negotiated and transformed to create individualised and inclusive physical culture contexts. The final chapter explores how the book builds on and extends existing gender and physical culture research. This book was originally published as a special issue of the journal *Sport in Society*.

Natalie Barker-Ruchti is an Associate Professor at the Department of Food and Nutrition, and Sport Science, University of Gothenburg, Sweden. She researches elite sport contexts in relation to gender, learning, career development, and sustainability. She works with longitudinal research methodology and prefers alternative data presentation techniques, including narrative writing.

Karin Grahn is a Senior Lecturer at the Department of Food and Nutrition, and Sport Science, University of Gothenburg, Sweden. She researches youth sports from a gender perspective, including sport coaching textbooks, gender relations in co-educated sports, and body ideals among competitive athletes. Grahn works with diverse qualitative methods and employs a discourse analytical framework.

Eva-Carin Lindgren is an Associate Professor at the Department of Food and Nutrition, and Sport Science, University of Gothenburg, Sweden, and at the School of Health and Welfare, Halmstad University, Sweden. Her current research interests focus on how coaches construct children's team sports, how coaches maximise participation in youth sport, and how top-level coaches construct sustainable sport for elite athletes. She adopts perspectives of gender, alternative intersectionality and health promotion, and works with different qualitative methods.

Sport in the Global Society: Contemporary Perspectives

Series Editor: Boria Majumdar, *University of Central Lancashire, UK*

The social, cultural (including media) and political study of sport is an expanding area of scholarship and related research. While this area has been well served by the *Sport in the Global Society* series, the surge in quality scholarship over the last few years has necessitated the creation of *Sport in the Global Society: Contemporary Perspectives*. The series will publish the work of leading scholars in fields as diverse as sociology, cultural studies, media studies, gender studies, cultural geography and history, political science and political economy. If the social and cultural study of sport is to receive the scholarly attention and readership it warrants, a cross-disciplinary series dedicated to taking sport beyond the narrow confines of physical education and sport science academic domains is necessary. *Sport in the Global Society: Contemporary Perspectives* will answer this need.

For a complete list of titles in this series, please visit https://www.routledge.com/series/SGSC

Recent titles in the series include:

Gender in Physical Culture
Crossing Boundaries – Reconstituting Cultures
Edited by Natalie Barker-Ruchti, Karin Grahn and Eva-Carin Lindgren

DIY Football
The Cultural Politics of Community Based Football Clubs
Edited by David Kennedy and Peter Kennedy

A Social and Political History of Everton and Liverpool Football Clubs
The Split, 1878–1914
David Kennedy

Football Fandom in Italy and Beyond
Community through Media and Performance
Matthew Guschwan

Numbers and Narratives
Sport, History and Economics
Wray Vamplew

Sex Integration in Sport and Physical Culture
Promises and Pitfalls
Edited by Alex Channon, Katherine Dashper, Thomas Fletcher and Robert J. Lake

A Social and Cultural History of Sport in Ireland
Edited by Richard McElligott and David Hassan

Football and Health Improvement: An Emergent Field
Edited by Daniel Parnell and Andy Pringle

Gender in Physical Culture
Crossing Boundaries – Reconstituting Cultures

Edited by
Natalie Barker-Ruchti, Karin Grahn and
Eva-Carin Lindgren

LONDON AND NEW YORK

First published 2017 by Routledge

2 Park Square, Milton Park, Abingdon, Oxfordshire OX14 4RN
52 Vanderbilt Avenue, New York, NY 10017

Routledge is an imprint of the Taylor & Francis Group, an informa business

First issued in paperback 2018

Copyright © 2017 Taylor & Francis

All rights reserved. No part of this book may be reprinted or reproduced or utilised in any form or by any electronic, mechanical, or other means, now known or hereafter invented, including photocopying and recording, or in any information storage or retrieval system, without permission in writing from the publishers.

Notice:
Product or corporate names may be trademarks or registered trademarks, and are used only for identification and explanation without intent to infringe.

British Library Cataloguing in Publication Data
A catalogue record for this book is available from the British Library

ISBN 13: 978-1-138-74034-1 (hbk)
ISBN 13: 978-0-367-14260-5 (pbk)

Typeset in MinionPro
by diacriTech, Chennai

Publisher's Note
The publisher accepts responsibility for any inconsistencies that may have arisen during the conversion of this book from journal articles to book chapters, namely the possible inclusion of journal terminology.

Disclaimer
Every effort has been made to contact copyright holders for their permission to reprint material in this book. The publishers would be grateful to hear from any copyright holder who is not here acknowledged and will undertake to rectify any errors or omissions in future editions of this book.

Contents

Citation Information vii
Notes on Contributors ix

1. Shifting, crossing and transforming gender boundaries in physical cultures 1
   Natalie Barker-Ruchti, Karin Grahn and Eva-Carin Lindgren

2. The illegal transgression: discourse analysis of the media perception of the transgressive aesthetic of performance and display in top-level sports 12
   Sandra Günter

3. Approaching a gender neutral PE-culture? An exploration of the phase of a divergent PE-culture 26
   Suzanne Lundvall

4. History of Swiss feminine gymnastics between competition and feminization (1950–1990) 39
   Grégory Quin

5. 'It has really amazed me what my body can now do': boundary work and the construction of a body-positive dance community 53
   Joanne Hill, Rachel Sandford and Eimear Enright

6. Gendered body ideals in Swedish competitive youth swimming: negotiating and shifting symbolic boundaries 66
   Karin Grahn

7. Health-related gender boundary crossing in youth elite sport 81
   Astrid Schubring and Ansgar Thiel

CONTENTS

8 Hanging up the shirt: an autoethnographic account of disengaging from a social rugby culture 97
   Dean Barker and Natalie Barker-Ruchti

9 Gender and the 'cultural turn' in the study of sport and physical cultures 112
   Susan J. Bandy

Index 123

Citation Information

The chapters in this book were originally published in *Sport in Society*, volume 19, issue 5 (June 2016). When citing this material, please use the original page numbering for each article, as follows:

Chapter 1
Shifting, crossing and transforming gender boundaries in physical cultures
Natalie Barker-Ruchti, Karin Grahn and Eva-Carin Lindgren
Sport in Society, volume 19, issue 5 (June 2016) pp. 615–625

Chapter 2
The illegal transgression: discourse analysis of the media perception of the transgressive aesthetic of performance and display in top-level sports
Sandra Günter
Sport in Society, volume 19, issue 5 (June 2016) pp. 626–639

Chapter 3
Approaching a gender neutral PE-culture? An exploration of the phase of a divergent PE-culture
Suzanne Lundvall
Sport in Society, volume 19, issue 5 (June 2016) pp. 640–652

Chapter 4
History of Swiss feminine gymnastics between competition and feminization (1950–1990)
Grégory Quin
Sport in Society, volume 19, issue 5 (June 2016) pp. 653–666

Chapter 5
'It has really amazed me what my body can now do': boundary work and the construction of a body-positive dance community
Joanne Hill, Rachel Sandford and Eimear Enright
Sport in Society, volume 19, issue 5 (June 2016) pp. 667–679

CITATION INFORMATION

Chapter 6
Gendered body ideals in Swedish competitive youth swimming: negotiating and shifting symbolic boundaries
Karin Grahn
Sport in Society, volume 19, issue 5 (June 2016) pp. 680–694

Chapter 7
Health-related gender boundary crossing in youth elite sport
Astrid Schubring and Ansgar Thiel
Sport in Society, volume 19, issue 5 (June 2016) pp. 695–710

Chapter 8
Hanging up the shirt: an autoethnographic account of disengaging from a social rugby culture
Dean Barker and Natalie Barker-Ruchti
Sport in Society, volume 19, issue 5 (June 2016) pp. 711–725

Chapter 9
Gender and the 'cultural turn' in the study of sport and physical cultures
Susan J. Bandy
Sport in Society, volume 19, issue 5 (June 2016) pp. 726–735

For any permission-related enquiries please visit:
http://www.tandfonline.com/page/help/permissions

Notes on Contributors

Susan J. Bandy is a Senior Lecturer, Ohio State University, Columbus, OH, USA. She earned a PhD in Sport History and Philosophy from Arizona State University. Her research interests pertain to sport literature, art, and film and gender and the sporting body.

Dean Barker is a an Associate Professor of Physical Education and Health, University of Gothenburg, Sweden. His current research focuses on learning in interaction and the development of movement capability.

Natalie Barker-Ruchti is an Associate Professor at the Department of Food and Nutrition, and Sport Science, University of Gothenburg, Sweden. She researches elite sport contexts in relation to gender, learning, career development, and sustainability. She works with longitudinal research methodology and prefers alternative data presentation techniques, including narrative writing.

Eimear Enright is a Lecturer and the Bachelor of Health, Sport and Physical Education Program Convenor in the School of Human Movement and Nutrition Sciences, University of Queensland, Australia. She teaches, researches, and writes primarily about youth voice and young people's participation and learning in, through and about physical culture.

Karin Grahn is a Senior Lecturer at the Department of Food and Nutrition, and Sport Science, University of Gothenburg, Sweden. She researches youth sports from a gender perspective, including sport coaching textbooks, gender relations in co-educated sports, and body ideals among competitive athletes. Karin works with diverse qualitative methods and employs a discourse analytical framework.

Sandra Günter is a Professor of Sociology and History of Sports at the Leibniz University of Hanover, Germany. Her primary areas of research are social construction of gender in sports, theory of the body, ethnicity, inequality, and postcolonial studies. Her qualitative social research is focused on dispositive and discourse analysis. She teaches: sociology of sport, sociology of the body, 'Gender Studies', and qualitative social methods.

Joanne Hill is a Lecturer in physical education and sport sociology, University of Bedfordshire, UK. Her research is on the impact of the social construction of the body,

NOTES ON CONTRIBUTORS

gender, and ethnicity on physical activity and sport engagement and on learning for and about social justice and socio-cultural issues in higher education and physical culture.

Eva-Carin Lindgren is an Associate Professor at the Department of Food and Nutrition, and Sport Science, University of Gothenburg, Sweden, and at the School of Health and Welfare, Halmstad University, Sweden. Her current research interests focus on how coaches construct children's team sports, how coaches maximise participation in youth sport, and how top-level coaches construct sustainable sport for elite athletes. She adopts perspectives of gender, alternative intersectionality, and health promotion, and works with different qualitative methods.

Suzanne Lundvall is an Associate Professor at the Swedish School of Sport and Health Sciences, Stockholm, Sweden. Her main research interests are young people's participation and attitudes to sport, physical activities, and the school subject physical education and health. Her research also includes cultural and aesthetic dimensions of physical culture.

Grégory Quin is a Senior Lecturer at the Sport Science Institute from the University of Lausanne, Switzerland. He currently works to document Switzerland's sport history through systematically gathering documents from the country's news archives. He recently published several books on football and university sports.

Rachel Sandford is a Lecturer in young people and sport in the School of Sport, Exercise and Health Sciences, Loughborough University, UK. Her research interests centre on young people's experiences of, attitudes towards and participation in physical education, physical activity and youth sport with a focus on youth voice, positive youth development, and youth identity formation.

Astrid Schubring is a Senior Lecturer at the Department of Food and Nutrition, and Sport Science, University of Gothenburg, Sweden. Her research focuses on social dimensions of health and illness, youth sport, and career development and coaching in elite sport.

Ansgar Thiel is a Professor for Social and Health Sciences in Sport, and the Director of the Institute of Sport Science, University of Tübingen, Germany. His research focus lies at the intersection between sociology and psychology in sport. One of his main research areas is health in elite sport. He is one of the speakers of a multi-centre study about health management in adolescent elite sports (GOAL study).

Shifting, crossing and transforming gender boundaries in physical cultures

Natalie Barker-Ruchti, Karin Grahn and Eva-Carin Lindgren

Department of Food and Nutrition, and Sport Science, University of Gothenburg, Gothenburg, Sweden

ABSTRACT
At the 2013 conference "Gender in Physical Culture" of the 'Transnational Working Group for the Study of Gender and Sport', held at the University of Gothenburg, a number of presentations related to how individuals, groups of individuals and organizations challenge and change dominant gender discourses and practices. Several of these presentations have come to form this volume on 'Gender in Physical Culture: Crossing Boundaries – Reconstituting Cultures'. To begin the volume, the following article outlines how the seven contributions are connected. We present Lamont and Molnàr's (2002) idea of 'boundaries', which they consider as visible and invisible socially constructed borders that create social differences. Such boundaries are, however, malleable. We propose that this flexibility means that 'gender boundaries in physical cultures' can be shifted, crossed and transformed. The case studies included in this edition present concrete examples of how this is possible.

The idea that gender shapes societies is well established (Bordo 1993; Butler 1999; Connell 1987). Much research demonstrates how gender norms and ideals create dominant symbols and belief systems that influence social structures, institutions, practices, relationships and individual thinking and behaviour. Contemporary forms of human movement – sports, exercise, (adapted) physical activities and dance – are considered particularly powerful in gendering social realities (Bordo 1993; Hargreaves 1994; Markula 2005; Thorpe 2010; Vertinksy 1990). This influence continuously creates inequalities between participants (Chimot and Louveau 2010; Gard 2006) and leaders (Hartmann-Tews and Combrink 2006; Hartmann-Tews and Pfister 2003; Pfister and Radtke 2005; Werthner 2005), and between communities (Pfister 2012; Waitt 2008) and organizations (Hoeber 2007; Shaw and Penney 2003; Shaw and Slack 2002). Gender, however, is also being negotiated. Research demonstrates how individuals or groups/communities of individuals challenge and transgress gender norms and practices including, for instance, through individuals participating in activities considered gender inappropriate (Chimot and Louveau 2010; McGrath and Chananie-Hill 2009; McGuffey and Rich 1999; Theberge 2003) and adopting explicit gender-divergent behaviours (Gill 2007).

Despite such advances, however, gender inequality persists (Dashper and Fletcher 2013). Reasons for this perseverance are manifold and complex, but two important factors that research continuously demonstrates are the resilience of hegemonic gender ideologies (Donnelly 1996) and the limitedness of transgressions in transforming sociocultural realities (Travers and Deri 2010). Indeed, existing Western constructions of gender have been postulated powerful and a change of these slow (Lorber 2001). Moreover, examples of gender unsettling may actually have counter-productive effects, with perceived deviant gender orientations or behaviours being sanctioned (e.g. forms of exclusion from sport) and reinforcing the traditional binary gender model (Barker-Ruchti 2009; Buyesse and Embser-Herbert 2009; Daddario and Wigley 2007). The Caster Semenya case is a recent and telling example in this regard and illustrates how perceived gender deviancy is being disciplined by questioning and removing her eligibility to compete (Schultz 2011) and with negative stereotyping in media texts (Nyong'o 2010). In doing so, the disciplining measures reinforce traditional gender discourses, and thus the traditional binary gender model.

In understanding these limitations, we propose a move away from employing a deficit approach that focuses on gender inequalities and disadvantages to the study of concrete examples of how gender is being challenged and transformed at the micro-level. While we acknowledge that a transformation of gender discourses may be difficult to capture due to its subjective and longitudinal nature, we propose that knowledge of micro-level processes is vital to recognize how power dynamics affect individuals and groups of individuals in creating and maintaining, and negotiating and transforming, dominant gender discourses (McGuffey and Rich 1999). We postulate that such 'stories' of change and transformation can provide and strengthen visions of and ideas for alternative ways of being and doing.

The purpose of this volume is to add to the emerging body of literature on gender shifting and transformation. The contributions provide case studies of how individuals, groups of individuals and organizations negotiate, challenge and transform gender discourses in human movement settings. To connect these contributions, the cases are embedded within the notions of 'physical cultures' and 'gender boundaries'. With regard to physical cultures, several scholars have suggested that this concept is useful as it (a) incorporates today's multitude of human movement forms and (b) provides ways to relationally theorize a wide range of sociocultural issues (Kirk 1999). This second point fits well with the notion of gender boundaries. Figuratively speaking, gender boundaries are visible and invisible socially constructed borders that create social differences; yet, such boundaries, similar to membranes, are malleable (Lamont and Fournier 1992; Lamont and Molnár 2002). For this volume, the nature and processes of 'gender boundaries in physical cultures' are examined on the individual micro-level (e.g. thoughts and actions), communal meso-level (e.g. communities, spaces and locations) and social macro-level (e.g. power, discourses and knowledge).

In the following, we begin by introducing the concept 'physical cultures' and then draw on existing research to outline how human movement forms construct and negotiate gender. We then proceed to present how gender boundaries can be understood and how they can be negotiated and transformed. Lastly, we suggest three areas of research within which the examination of gender transformation has been proposed to be generative and which the contributions to this volume consider.

The construction and negotiation of dominant gender discourses in physical cultures

Historically, physical culture can be associated with practitioners of Danish-Swedish in particular (Kirk 1996, 1999), and systems of Turnen and gymnastics of the nineteenth and early twentieth centuries (Eichberg 1996; Krüger 1996; Pfister 2003; Trangbæk 2000). It was a concept that was used to describe a way of life associated with various forms of exercise and physical activities common at that time. Physical culture was, however, more than mere physical movement; it was a lifestyle that was embedded in beliefs, knowledge and broader individual and social and political practices (Kirk 1999), which reflected contemporary assumptions about men's and women's social roles, moral obligations, relationships and practices and gender discourses (Barker-Ruchti 2006; Kirk 2000; Pfister 1997).

As gymnastics systems, today's movement forms (e.g. physical activities, exercise and all forms of sport) are socioculturally constructed (Kirk 1999). With regard to gender, a large body of literature argues that physical cultures were created from biological determinants, in particular women's physical unsuitability to cope with (strenuous) exercise (Hargreaves 1994; Lorber 1993). Historically, this view splits physical cultures into masculinising practices that were seen to cultivate men's strength and aggression (Light and Kirk 2000; Wellard 2007; Woodward 2007) and feminising practices that were believed to develop artistry and grace (Markula and Pringle 2006a, 2006b). Such gendering has been found to occur through life-course normalization beginning in early child movement activities (Bilden 2002; Giess-Stüber, Voss, and Petry 2003), and continuing in primary school physical education (Bhana 2008; Olynyk 2014), and child and youth (Eliasson 2009; Fundberg 2003; Larsson 2001; Messner 2000) and adult sport (Adams, Anderson, and McCormack 2010; Pike 2012). The idealization and (re)production of such heterosexual masculinity marginalizes femininities and other types of masculinities, and thus 'others' those individuals that do not or cannot conform (Connell and Messerschmidt 2005). At the micro-level, this has been found to exclude and alienate individuals and groups of individuals (Adams, Anderson, and McCormack 2010; Bartkowski and Read 2003; Fundberg 2003; Tischler and McCaughtry 2011).

Gender discourses, however, are not fixed. They can and have been negotiated, transgressed and transformed. Certainly, a number of examples of individuals and events, mainly by women in women's sports, have challenged and changed expected gender norms and practices (e.g. Barker-Ruchti, Grahn, and Annerstedt 2013; Pfister 2001a, 2001b). Contemporary examples also relate to boys/men participating in non-traditional male sports and physical activities (Chimot and Louveau 2010), the co-training of girls and boys/women and men (Grahn and Berggren Torell 2014; Wachs 2005), and the creation of alternative corporeal (and) gender ideals (Anderson 2012; Azzarito 2010; Kelly, Pomerantz, and Currie 2006; Ross and Shinew 2008; Thorpe 2009) and sexuality (Ravel and Rail 2006; Travers and Deri 2010). Further, many scholars have worked with sporting organizations and groups of individuals to positively affect gender equality (Lindgren, Patriksson, and Fridlund 2002; Olofsson 2007; Vertinsky 1992).

Conceptualizing gender boundaries in physical cultures

The concept 'boundaries' is described to recently have impacted social science scholarship in anthropology, history, social psychology, geography and sociology (Lamont and Molnár 2002). Such work has focused on the migration of people (Cushing and Poot 2004;

Skenderovic 2003; Wimmer 2008), lifespan narratives (Albert and Ferring 2013; Grenier 2007), race and ethnicity (Duemmler, Dahinden, and Moret 2010; Wimmer 2011) and sexuality and gender (Pachucki, Pendergrass, and Lamont 2007; Thorne 1986). With regard to physical cultures, the idea of boundary work has been taken up, however, only in terminological ways and without conceptualizing what boundaries are, how they are constructed and, importantly, how they may be negotiated and transformed (Cheska 1984; McGuffey and Rich 1999; Pronger 1998; Silk and Andrews 2001).

In order for this volume to conceptualize and study gender boundaries, we draw on Lamont and Molnár's (2002) theory of 'symbolic and social boundaries'. Their conceptualizations of 'boundary shifting', 'boundary crossing' and 'boundary transformation' help understand how boundaries emerge, what they consist of, how they operate, how they are perceived and how they might be shifted, crossed and transformed.

Symbolic and social boundaries

Metaphorically, boundaries are socially constructed lines or borders that define particular patterns of likes and dislikes or of what is 'in' and what is 'out' (Lamont, Pendergrass, and Pachucki 2001). Such distinctions are evident in what individuals think and do, and how organizations operate. Some such borders are more tangible than others (e.g. compare qualification policies in sport with a coach's personality preferences and sporting federation's distribution of funds). Lamont and Molnár (2002) distinguish between symbolic and social boundaries. Symbolic boundaries represent tools that social actors employ to categorize objects, people, communities, practices, spaces and time. While distinguishing, this process involves negotiation and struggle over what and who fit and what and who do not fit a particular ideal (Bowker and Star 1999). Certainly, they generate feelings of similarity and difference, and through this, opportunities of identification and membership, status and access to resources. Social boundaries, in contrast, are more fixed, or 'objectified forms of social differences' (Lamont and Molnár 2002). They emerge from symbolic boundaries and are manifested in concrete inequality.

How are symbolic boundaries drawn in physical cultures and how may they develop into social boundaries? The common assumption that traditional team sports are more appropriate for boys than for girls exemplifies how behaviours and actions are constructed to define how sports are being understood. It is, thus, perhaps of little surprise that social boundaries in terms of governmental, financial, spatial and expertise resources are distributed unequally between men's and women's sports (Adriaanse and Schofield 2013; Gilenstam, Karp, and Henriksson-Larsén 2008; Müller and Boucherin 2008). It demonstrates how a symbolic boundary has become institutionalized and acts as a social boundary.

Boundary shifting, crossing and transformation

Although both symbolic and social boundaries have been documented as generally solid (Lamont and Fournier 1992; Lamont and Molnár 2002; Lamont, Pendergrass, and Pachucki 2001; Pachucki, Pendergrass, and Lamont 2007), which indeed can be said for gender and physical cultures (Pronger 1998; Travers and Deri 2010), boundary shifting, crossing and transformation are possible and do occur. Conceptually, Lamont and Molnár's (2002) adoption of Star and Griesemer's (1989) proposal that boundaries act as *interfaces*, or membranes, is useful to theorize how boundaries are permeable. At the interfacing points, boundaries adjoin with the membranes of other communities, spaces, objects, (organizational) practices and procedures, and norms and ideas. As they touch, 'boundary objects', as Star and Griesemer (1989) define the interfaces, provide possibilities for communication, exchange, bridging and inclusion, and indeed for the coordination of social action that might lead to boundary transformation (Bowker and Star 1999).

We propose that the ideas of shifting, crossing and transformation occur on a continuum of possible alteration. The three levels we envisage – shifting, crossing and transforming – may build on each other progressively, but also feed into one another. With regard to *shifting boundaries*, we assume that this form of change involves perceptual changes that indicate possible alternative ideas and definitions of phenomena. A shift may occur in relation to perceived norms and ideals, or definitions of an activity or role, and in this sense, occurs more on a perceptual or intelligible level. It may be the beginning of a boundary losing its strength or salience. To illustrate such change and with reference to physical cultures, ideas about which physical and sporting activities women were thought suitable for shifted several times. While it initially centred on physical suitability (Barker-Ruchti, Grahn, and Annerstedt 2013; Hofmann 2012), as women progressively became more integrated in a multitude of sports, the idea of women as athletes became more accepted. Their movement into traditional male sports became easier.

With regard to *crossing boundaries*, we consider a more concrete action to take place (i.e. women's movement into sports). Boundaries may also be crossed by boys/men participating in traditionally women's sport, women being leaders in sport or for institutions to adapt their participation policies and create what Pachucki, Pendergrass, and Lamont (2007) call 'subgenres'. Subgenres might relate to a diverse population taking part in sports and physical activities or diverse performance standards (e.g. outcome-, pleasure-, and self-improvement-oriented) being practiced and celebrated. Such diversification may provide individuals, groups of individuals, institutions and physical cultures with opportunities to cross boundaries and create what Pronger (1998) calls, a 'post-sport'. Indeed, examples from research into physical cultures illustrate such postmodern subgenres, including mixed sport settings (Grahn and Berggren Torell 2014; Wachs 2005), alternative equestrianism, dance and physical education practices (Hedenborg and Hedenborg White 2012).

Lastly, in terms of *transforming boundaries*, we consider such change to refer to an outcome of boundary shifting and crossing. The membrane that previously defined the 'inside' and 'outside' has been transformed, meaning that the components of a membrane have been altered. This changed border redefines its interior and that which is on the outside. While this is likely to begin with internal challenges of symbolic boundaries, their saliency is affected and will eventually 'take the place of social boundaries' (Lamont and Molnár 2002). Although, as acknowledged above, the capturing of such transformation may be difficult, an example of such a process is provided by Travers and Deri's (2010) study on transgender participants in lesbian softball leagues. Their research findings show how the study's transmen and lesbian player communities were segregated by their, respectively, assumed biological commonalities, but how through their playing softball (a type of membrane touching) the characteristics of their particular ideals became infiltrated by a shared cultural affinity. Similar findings of gender transformation have been found in various and starkly different fields, including snowboarding (Thorpe 2005, 2009, 2010), skateboarding (Kelly,

Pomerantz, and Currie 2006), rodeo (Adelman and Becker 2013), roller derby (Murray 2012), rugby (Gill 2007), disabled sport (Apelmo 2012) and dance (Wade 2011).

Examining gender boundary transformation in physical cultures

In order to extend insight into micro-level processes of gender boundary shifting, crossing and transformation in physical cultures, the contributions of this volume focus on the properties of boundaries, mechanisms of shifting and crossing boundaries and perceptions of those included or excluded by boundaries. In particular, the volume is structured to demonstrate how boundary 'work' has taken and is taking place at the level of media, institutions and communities, as well as by individuals. In particular, Sandra Günter (2015) examines how Swiss media, in particular newspaper articles representing South African runner, Caster Semenya, pluralize gender boundaries. Suzanne Lundvall (2015) analyses how one Swedish physical education institution worked to change the national PE culture from being separated along gender boundaries to a gender-neutral culture. In a similar vein, Grégory Quin (2015) outlines how Switzerland's Women's Gymnastics Federation employed its autonomy during the 1960s and 1970s to create a number of innovative changes that challenged gender boundaries. Joanne Hill, Rachel Sandford and Eimear Enright (2015) explore how one dance school transforms gender boundaries through its inclusion policy and teaching practices. Karin Grahn (2015) provides insight into how Swedish youth swimmers negotiate gendered body ideals, and Astrid Schubring and Ansgar Thiel (2015), examining a similar age population in Germany, demonstrate how a female handball player and a male biathlete challenge gendered self-health practices. In the last contribution, Dean Barker and Natalie Barker-Ruchti (2015) reconstruct Dean's involvement in and distancing himself from a New Zealand homosocial sporting community to illustrate how this transformed gender boundaries at a personal level. In conclusion of the volume, Susan Bandy (2015) comments on the volume by demonstrating how the contributions included build on and extend existing gender and physical culture research.

The volume sets out to demonstrate how gender boundaries can be shifted, crossed and transformed. Each of the case studies presented in this volume demonstrates how gender boundaries can be negotiated to be less determining and disadvantageous. We suggest that these findings are generative for future scholarly analyses, and, importantly, offer ideas for how gender boundaries can be negotiated to be more gender inclusive.

References

Adams, A., E. Anderson, and M. McCormack. 2010. "Establishing and Challenging Masculinity: The Influence of Gendered Discourses in Organized Sport." *Journal of Language and Social Psychology* 29 (3): 278–300.
Adelman, M., and G. Becker. 2013. "Tradition and Transgression: Women Who Ride the Rodeo in Southern Brazil." In *Gender and Equestrian Sport*, edited by M. Adelman and J. Knijnik, 73–90. New York: Springer.
Adriaanse, J. A., and T. Schofield. 2013. "Analysing Gender Dynamics in Sport Governance: A New Regimes-based Approach." *Sport Management Review* 16 (4): 498–513.
Albert, I., and D. Ferring. 2013. *Intergenerational Relations*. Chicago, IL: The Chicago University Press.
Anderson, E. 2012. *Inclusive Masculinity: The Changing Nature of Masculinities*. New York: Routledge.
Apelmo, E. 2012. "Falling in Love with a Wheelchair: Enabling/Disabling Technologies." *Sport in Society: Cultures, Commerce, Media, Politics* 15 (3): 399–408.

Azzarito, L. 2010. "Future Girls, Transcendent Femininities and New Pedagogies: Toward Girls' Hybrid Bodies?" *Sport, Education and Society* 15 (3): 261–275.

Bandy, S. 2015. "Gender and the 'Cultural Turn' in the Study of Sport and Physical Cultures." *Sport in Society*.

Barker-Ruchti, N. 2006. "'Stride Jump – Begin!': Swedish Gymnastics in Victorian England." *Sporting Traditions* 22 (2): 13–29.

Barker-Ruchti, N. 2009. "The Media as an Authorising Practice of Femininity: Swiss Newspaper Coverage of Karin Thürig's Bronze Medal Performance in Road Cycling." In *Olympic Women and the Media: International Perspectives*, edited by P. Markula, 214–231. New York: Palgrave.

Barker-Ruchti, N., K. Grahn, and C. Annerstedt. 2013. "Moving towards Inclusion: An Analysis of Photographs from the 1926 Women's Games in Gothenburg." *The International Journal of the History of Sport* 30 (8): 871–891.

Barker, D., and N. Barker-Ruchti. 2015. "Hanging up the Shirt: An Autoethnographic Account of Disengaging from a Social Rugby Culture." *Sport in Society*.

Bartkowski, J. P., and J. G. Read. 2003. "Veiled Submission: Gender, Power, and Identity among Evangelical and Muslim Women in the United States." *Qualitative Sociology* 26 (1): 71–92.

Bhana, D. 2008. "'Six Packs and Big Muscles, and Stuff Like That'. Primary School-aged South African Boys, Black and White on Sport." *British Journal of Sociology of Education* 29 (1): 3–14.

Bilden, H. 2002. "Geschlechtsspezifische Sozialisation [Gender-Specific Socialization]." In *Handbuch der Sozialisationsforschung*, edited by K. Hurrelmann and D. Ulrich, 279–301. Weinheim-Basel: Beltz Verlag.

Bordo, S. 1993. *Unbearable Weight: Feminism, Western Culture and the Body*. Berkeley: University of California Press.

Bowker, G. C., and S. L. Star. 1999. *Sorting Things Out: Classification and its Consequences*. Cambridge: MIT Press.

Butler, J. 1999. *Gender Trouble: Feminism and the Subversion of Identity*. New York: Routledge.

Buyesse, J. M., and M. S. Embser-Herbert. 2009. "Constructions of Gender in Sport: An Analysis of Intercollegiate Media Guide Cover Photographs." *Gender and Society* 18 (1): 66–81.

Cheska, A. T. 1984. "Sport as Ethnic Boundary Maintenance: A Case of the American Indian." *International Review for the Sociology of Sport* 19 (3–4): 241–257.

Chimot, C., and C. Louveau. 2010. "Becoming a Man While Playing a Female Sport: The Construction of Masculine Identity in Boys Doing Rhythmic Gymnastics." *International Review for the Sociology of Sport* 45 (4): 436–456.

Connell, R. W. 1987. *Gender and Power: Society, the Person, and Sexual Politics*. Stanford: Stanford University Press.

Connell, R. W., and J. W. Messerschmidt. 2005. "Hegemonic Masculinity: Rethinking the Concept." *Gender and Society* 19 (6): 829–859.

Cushing, B., and J. Poot. 2004. "Crossing Boundaries and Borders: Regional Science Advances in Migration Modelling." *Papers in Regional Science* 83 (1): 317–338.

Daddario, G., and B. J. Wigley. 2007. "Gender Marking and Racial Stereotypig at the 2004 Athens Games." *Journal of Sports Media* 2 (1): 29–51.

Dashper, K., and T. Fletcher. 2013. "Introduction: Diversity, Equity and Inclusion in Sport and Leisure." *Sport in Society* 16 (10): 1227–1232.

Donnelly, P. 1996. "Approaches to Social Inequality in the Sociology of Sport." *Quest* 48 (2): 221–242.

Duemmler, K., J. Dahinden, and J. Moret. 2010. "Gender Equality as 'Cultural Stuff': Ethnic Boundary Work in a Classroom in Switzerland." *Diversities* 12 (1): 19–37.

Eichberg, H. 1996. "Body Culture and Democratic Nationalism: 'Popular Gymnastics' in Nineteenth-Century Denmark." In *Tribal Identities: Nationalism, Europe, Sport*, edited by J. A. Mangan, 108–124. London: Frank Cass.

Eliasson, I. 2009. *I Skilda Idrottsvärldar: Barn, Ledare och Föräldrar i Flick- och Pojkfotboll* [In Different Sports Worlds. Children, Leaders, and Parents in Girls' and Boys' Football]. Umeå: University of Umeå.

Fundberg, J. 2003. *Kom Igen, Gubbar!: Om Pojkfotboll och Maskuliniteter* [Come on Guys!: About Boys' Football and Masculinities]. PhD thesis, Stockholm: University of Stockholm.

Gard, M. 2006. *Men Who Dance: Aesthetics, Athletics and the Art of Masculinity*. New York: Peter Lang.
Giess-Stüber, P., A. Voss, and K. Petry. 2003. "GenderKids – Geschlechteralltag in der frühkindlichen Bewegungsförderung [GenderKids – Gender Everyday Life in Early Childhood Movement Programs]." In *Soziale Konstruktion von Geschlecht im Sport*, edited by I. Hartmann-Tews, P. Gieß-Stüber, M.-L. Klein, C. Kleindienst-Cachay, and K. Petry, 69–108. Opladen: Leske u. Budrich.
Gilenstam, K., S. Karp, and K. Henriksson-Larsén. 2008. "Gender in Ice Hockey: Women in a Male Territory." *Scandinavian Journal of Medicine and Science in Sports* 18 (2): 235–249.
Gill, F. 2007. "'Violent' Femininity: Women Rugby Players and Gender Negotiation." *Women's Studies International Forum* 30 (5): 416–426.
Grahn, K. 2015. "Gendered Body Ideals in Swedish Competitive Youth Swimming: Negotiating and Shifting Symbolic Boundaries." *Sport in Society*.
Grahn, K., and V. Berggren Torell. 2014. *Barndom och Genus i Idrottslyftsprojekt på Skoltid* [Childhood and Gender in School Sport]. Stockholm: Riksidrottsförbundet.
Grenier, A. M. 2007. "Crossing Age and Generational Boundaries: Exploring Intergenerational Research Encounters." *Journal of Social Issues* 63 (4): 713–727.
Günter, S. 2015. "The Illegal Transgression. A Discourse Analysis of the Media Perception of the Transgressive Aesthetic of Performance and Display in Top-Level Sports." *Sport in Society*.
Hargreaves, J. 1994. *Sporting Females*. London: Routledge.
Hartmann-Tews, I., and C. Combrink. 2006. "Soziale Strukturen und Geschlechterordnung in den Führungsgremien von Sportverbänden [Social Structures and Gender Order in Corporate Boards of Sports Clubs]." *Spectrum* 18 (2): 64–76.
Hartmann-Tews, I., and G. Pfister. 2003. *Sport and Women: Social Issues in International Perspective*. New York: Routledge.
Hedenborg, S., and M. Hedenborg White. 2012. "Changes and Variations in Patterns of Gender Relations in Equestrian Sports During the Second Half of the Twentieth Century." *Sport in Society: Cultures, Commerce, Media, Politics* 15 (3): 302–319.
Hill, J., R. Sandford, and E. Enright. 2015. "'It has Really Amazed Me What My Body Can Now Do': Boundary Work and the Construction of a Body-positive Dance Community." *Sport in Society*.
Hoeber, L. 2007. "Exploring the Gaps between Meanings and Practices of Gender Equity in a Sport Organization." *Gender, Work and Organization* 14 (3): 259–280.
Hofmann, A. 2012. "Ein hürdenreicher Weg: Die olympische Frauen-Leichtathletik vor dem Zweiten Weltkrieg [A Path Full of Hurdles: Olympic Women's Track and Field Before the Second World War]." In *Willibald Gebhardt und seine Nachfolger. Sport und Olympia in Deutschland bis 1933*, edited by U. Wick and A. Höfer, 163–179. Aachen: Meyer and Meyer.
Kelly, D. M., S. Pomerantz, and D. Currie. 2006. "Skater Girlhood and Emphasized Femininity: 'You Can't Land an Ollie Properly in Heels'." *Gender and Education* 17 (3): 229–248.
Kirk, D. 1996. "Educational Reform, Physical Culture and the Crisis of Legitimation in Physical Education." *Discourse* 19 (1): 101–112.
Kirk, D. 1999. "Physical Culture, Physical Education and Relational Analysis." *Sport, Education and Society* 4 (1): 63–75.
Kirk, D. 2000. "Gender Associations: Sport, State Schools and Australian Culture." *The International Journal of the History of Sport* 17: 49–64.
Krüger, M. 1996. *Körperkultur und Nationsbildung: die Geschichte des Turnens in der Reichsgründungsära: eine Detailstudie über die Deutschen* [Body Culture and the Construction of a Nation: The History of 'Turnen' During the Formation of an Empire. A Detailed Study about Germans]. Schorndorf: Hofmann.
Lamont, M., and M. Fournier. 1992. *Cultivating Differences: Symbolic Boundaries and the Making of Inequality*. Chicago, IL: University of Chicago Press.
Lamont, M., and V. Molnár. 2002. "The Study of Boundaries in the Social Sciences." *Annual Review of Sociology* 28: 167–195.
Lamont, M., S. Pendergrass, and M. C. Pachucki. 2001. "Symbolic Boundaries." In *International Encyclopedia of Social and Behavioral Sciences*, edited by N. J. Smelser and B. Baltes, 15341–15347. Oxford: Elsevier.

Larsson, H. 2001. *Iscensättningen av Kön i Idrott: En Nutidshistoria om Idrottsmannen och Idrottskvinnan* [The Staging of Gender in Sport. A Contemporary History About the Sportsman and the Sportswoman]. PhD thesis, Stockholm: University of Stockholm.

Light, R. L., and D. Kirk. 2000. "High School Rugby, the Body and the Reproduction of Hegemonic Masculinity." *Sport, Education and Society* 5 (2): 163–176.

Lindgren, E.-C., G. Patriksson, and B. Fridlund. 2002. "Empowering Young Female Athletes through a Self-Strengthening Programme: A Qualitative Analysis." *European Physical Education Review* 8 (3): 230–248.

Lorber, J. 1993. "Believing is Seeing: Biology as Ideology." *Gender and Society* 7 (4): 568–581.

Lorber, J. 2001. *Gender Inequality*. Los Angeles, CA: Roxbury.

Lundvall, S. 2015. "Approaching a Gender Neutral PE-Culture? An Exploration of the Phase of a Divergent PE-Culture." *Sport in Society*.

Markula, P. 2005. *Feminist Sport Studies: Sharing Experiences of Joy and Pain*. Albany: State University of New York Press.

Markula, P., and R. Pringle. 2006a. *Foucault, Sport and Exercise: Power, Knowledge and Transforming the Self*. London: Routledge.

Markula, P., and R. Pringle. 2006b. "Knowledge and Truth. Discursive Construction of the Fit and Healthy Body." In *Foucault, Sport and Exercise*, edited by P. Markula and R. Pringle, 51–71. London: Routledge.

McGrath, S. A., and R. A. Chananie-Hill. 2009. "'Big Freaky-Looking Women': Normalizing Gender Transgression through Bodybuilding." *Sociology of Sport Journal* 26 (2): 235–254.

McGuffey, C. S., and B. L. Rich. 1999. "Playing in the Gender Transgression Zone: Race, Class, and Hegemonic Masculinity in Middle Childhood." *Gender and Society* 13 (5): 608–627.

Messner, M. 2000. "Barbie Girls versus Sea Monsters: Children Constructing Gender." *Gender and Society* 14 (6): 765–784.

Müller, C., and B. Boucherin. 2008. *Geschlechtsspezifische Budgetanalyse der Abteilung Jugend und Sport im BASPO* [Gender-Specific Budget Analysis of the Department 'Youth and Sport' of the Federal Office of Sport]. Magglingen: Eidgenössisches Büro für die Gleichstellung von Frau und Mann, Bundesamt für Sport.

Murray, M. G. 2012. *The Unladylike Ladies of Roller Derby?: How Spectators, Players and Derby Wives Do and Redo Gender and Heteronormativity in All-female Roller Derby*. PhD thesis, New York: The University of York.

Nyong'o, T. 2010. "The Unforgivable Transgression of Being Caster Semenya." *Women & Performance: A Journal of Feminist Theory* 20 (1): 95–100.

Olofsson, E. 2007. "The Swedish Sports Movement and the PE Teacher 1940–2003: From Supporter to Challenger." *Scandinavian Journal of Educational Research* 51 (2): 163–183.

Olynyk, I. 2014. *Att Göra Tudelning. Om att Synliggöra och Diskutera Ämnet Idrott och Hälsa För de Yngre Åldrarna ur ett Genusperspektiv* [Making Dichotomy. About Making Visible and Discussing Physical Education for the Younger Ages from a Gender Perspective]. Licentiate. Malmö: Malmö Högskola.

Pachucki, M. A., S. Pendergrass, and M. Lamont. 2007. "Boundary Processes: Recent Theoretical Developments and New Contributions." *Poetics* 35 (6): 331–351.

Pfister, G. 1997. "Sport – die Befreiung des weiblichen Körpers oder die Internalisierung von Zwängen? [Sport – The Freeing of the Female Body or the Internalization of Compulsions?]" In *Die Zivilisierung des weiblichen Ich*, edited by G. Klein and K. Liebsch, 206–247. Frankfurt am Main: Suhrkamp.

Pfister, G. 2001a. "Breaking Bounds: Alice Profé, Radical and Emancipationist." *The International Journal of the History of Sport* 18 (1): 98–118.

Pfister, G. 2001b. "Die grossen Frauen in der FSFI Alice Milliat und Eliott Lynn – zwei aussergewöhnliche Sportlerinnen-Biographien [The Big Women of the FSFI. Alice Milliat and Eliott Lynn – Two Extraordinary Athlete Biographies]." In *Olympisches Spiele. Bilanz und Perspektiven im 21. Jh.*, edited by M. Krüger, 138–145. Münster: Lit Verlag.

Pfister, G. 2003. "Cultural Confrontations: German Turnen, Swedish Gymnastics and English Sport – European Diversity in Physical Activities from a Historical Perspective." *Culture, Sport, Society* 6 (1): 61–91.

Pfister, G. 2012. "Warum ist Fussball Männersache? – Fussballspielerinnen sind, 'Trouble Makers' [Why Is Women's Football a Male Thing? - Women Football Players are 'Trouble Makers']." In *Auf den Spuren des Frauen- und Mädchenfussballs*, edited by S. Sinning, 48–50. Weinheim/Basel: Beltz.

Pfister, G., and S. Radtke. 2005. "Sport, Women and Leadership: Selected Results of the German Project 'Women Taking the Lead'." www.idrottsforum.org.

Pike, E. 2012. "Growing Old (Sis)Gracefully?: The Gender/Ageing/Exercise Nexus." In *Women and Exercise: The Body, Health and Consumerism*, edited by E. Kennedy and P. Markula, 180–196. London: Roudledge.

Pronger, B. 1998. "Post-Sport: Transgressing Boundaries in Physical Culture." In *Sport and Postmodern Times*, edited by G. Rail, 277–300. Albany: State University of New York Press.

Quin, G. 2015. "History of Swiss Feminine Gymnastics between Competition and Feminization (1950–1990)." *Sport in Society*.

Ravel, and G. Rail. 2006. "The Lightness of Being 'Gaie': Discursive Constructions of Gender and Sexuality in Quebec Women's Sport." *International Review for the Sociology of Sport* 41 (3–4): 395–412.

Ross, S. R., and K. J. Shinew. 2008. "Perspectives of Women College Athletes on Sport and Gender." *Sex Roles* 58: 40–57.

Schubring, A., and A. Thiel. 2015. "Health-Related Gender Boundary Crossing in Youth Elite Sport." *Sport in Society*.

Schultz, J. 2011. "Caster Semenya and the 'Question of Too': Sex Testing in Elite Women's Sport and the Issue of Advantage." *Quest* 63 (2): 228–243.

Shaw, S., and D. Penney. 2003. "Gender Equity Policies in National Governing Bodies: An Oxymoron or a Vehicle for Change?" *European Sport Management Quarterly* 3: 78–102.

Shaw, S., and T. Slack. 2002. "'It's Been Like that for Donkey's Years': The Construction of Gender Relations and the Cultures of Sports Organizations." *Culture, Sport, Society* 5 (1): 86–106.

Silk, M., and D. L. Andrews. 2001. "Beyond a Boundary?: Sport, Transnational Advertising, and the Reimagining of National Culture." *Journal of Sport and Social Issues* 25 (2): 180–201.

Skenderovic, D. 2003. "Constructing Boundaries in a Multicultural Nation: The Discourse of 'Overforeignization' in Switzerland." In *European Encounters: Migrants, Migration, and European Societies Since 1945*, edited by K. Schönwälder, R. Ohliger, and T. Triadafilopoulos, 186–209. Aldershot: Ashgate.

Star, S. L., and J. R. Griesemer. 1989. "Institutional Ecology, 'Translations' and Boundary Objects: Amateurs and Professionals in Berkeley's Museum of Vertebrate Zoology, 1907–39." *Social Studies of Science* 19 (3): 387–420.

Theberge, N. 2003. "'No Fear Comes': Adolescent Girls, Ice Hockey, and the Embodiment of Gender." *Youth and Society* 34 (4): 497–516.

Thorne, B. 1986. "Girls and Boys Together ... But Mostly Apart: Gender Arrangements in Elementary Schools." In *Relationships and Development*, edited by W. W. Hartup and Z. Rubin, 167–184. London: L. Erlbaum Associates.

Thorpe, H. 2005. "Jibbing the Gender Order: Females in the Snowboarding Culture." *Sport in Society* 8 (1): 76–100.

Thorpe, H. 2009. "Bourdieu, Feminism and Female Physical Culture: Gender Reflexivity and the Habitus-Field Complex." *Sociology of Sport Journal* 26: 491–516.

Thorpe, H. 2010. "Bourdieu, Gender Reflexivity, and Physical Culture: A Case of Masculinities in the Snowboarding Field." *Journal of Sport and Social Issues* 34 (2): 176–214.

Tischler, A., and N. McCaughtry. 2011. "PE is Not for Me." *Research Quarterly for Exercise and Sport* 82 (1): 37–48.

Trangbæk, E. 2000. "One System, Several Cultures: A Comparative Study of Swedish Gymnastics for Women." *International Sports Studies* 22 (2): 42–56.

Travers, A., and J. Deri. 2010. "Transgender Inclusion and the Changing Face of Lesbian Softball Leagues." *International Review for the Sociology of Sport* 46 (4): 488–507.

Vertinsky, P. A. 1990. *The Eternally Wounded Woman: Women, Doctors, and Exercise in the Late Nineteenth Century*. Manchester: Manchester University Press.

Vertinsky, P. 1992. "Reclaiming Space, Revisioning the Body: The Quest for Gender-sensitive Physical Education." *Quest* 44: 373–396.

Wachs, F. L. 2005. "The Boundaries of Difference: Negotiating Gender in Recreational Sport." *Sociological Inquiry* 75 (4): 527–547.

Wade, L. 2011. "The Emancipatory Promise of the Habitus: Lindy Hop, the Body, and Social Change." *Ethnography* 12 (2): 224–246.

Waitt, G. 2008. "'Killing Waves': Surfing, Space and Gender." *Social and Cultural Geography* 9 (1): 75–94.

Wellard, I. 2007. *Rethinking Gender and Youth Sport*. London: Routledge.

Werthner, P. 2005. "Making the Case: Coaching as a Viable Career Path for Women." *Canadian Journal for Women in Coaching – Online* 5 (3).

Wimmer, A. 2008. "The Making and Unmaking of Ethnic Boundaries: A Multilevel Process Theory." *American Journal of Sociology* 113 (4): 970–1022.

Wimmer, A. 2011. "A Swiss Anomaly? A Relational Account of National Boundary-making." *Nations and Nationalism* 17 (4): 718–737.

Woodward, K. 2007. "On and Off the Pitch." *Cultural Studies* 21: 758–778.

The illegal transgression: discourse analysis of the media perception of the transgressive aesthetic of performance and display in top-level sports

Sandra Günter

Department of Sociology and Political Science, Norwegian University of Science and Technology, Trondheim, Norway

ABSTRACT
The debate over Caster Semenya's female sex began shortly after the South African runner won gold in the women's 800 m final at the 2009 Athletic World Championships in Berlin. Her victory was disputed by questioning her right to compete as a woman. Using the theoretical framework of gender and postcolonial theories and the methodology of discourse and dispositive analysis, the paper explores the contextualization of a perceived transgressive, aesthetic, performance and display in the field of top-level sports. The case study analyses the discourses surrounding a non-white, non-male South African runner in eight mainstream Swiss German language print media. The paper argues that the media response to Semenya exemplifies Butler's claim that the discursive framework of gender constructs and naturalizes sex. A key question is, therefore, whether the assignation of deviant bodies to a 'field of deformation' works to pluralize and cross set gender boundaries, or rather, as Butler suggests, calls those bodies into question.

1. Introduction

Gender verification tests at international sport competitions were instituted in 1966 because of the suspicion that a number of Soviet and East German female athletes were not real women. The issue became especially critical during the Cold War, when the relationship between the nations of the West and those of the Eastern Bloc was characterized by mutual distrust (Horne et al. 2013; Wiederkehr 2012). The International Olympic Committee (IOC) and the International Association of Athletics Federations (IAAF) instituted a mandatory test for all non-male athletes to confirm their 'femininity' and disqualify those with a supposed unfair 'male advantage'. The first tests, introduced at the European Track and Field Championships, were 'nude parades', where women were required to walk naked before a panel of judges and undergo a gynaecological examination in order to prove their 'femininity'. The physical exams were replaced by sex chromatin testing, a test that looked for the inactive second X chromosome found in female cells. In 1967, the IOC and other sports organizations adopted a chromosome test that involved taking cells from female athletes and analysing them to identify 'Barr bodies'[1] associated with the XX chromosomes that identify a female (Horne et al. 2013, 115–116).

In the two years that followed, gender verification became integral to the pre-competition protocol for non-male athletes. The IOC even made all non-male athletes produce proof of their gender before permitting them to compete in the 1968 Summer Olympic Games in Mexico City. Beginning with the 1992 Albertville Winter Olympics, gender verification was performed by determining the absence or presence of certain DNA sequences (Wiederkehr 2009).

By the 1990s, there was clear consensus among scientists that human bodies did not fit neatly into the two distinct sex categories around which sports were and continue to be organized; choosing one or more traits to determine if a woman is female would always be arbitrary, subjective and unfair to some people (Schultz 2011). Human bodies are divided in terms of sex chromosome characteristics as well as genetic, cellular, hormonal and anatomical characteristics (Fausto-Sterling 2000). But even though these tests were clearly invalid and unreliable, they were used for over 30 years and led to the mistaken disqualification of many women who had no unfair biological advantage in their sports (Karkazis et al. 2012). After three decades of intense debate among scientists and physicians, the IOC abolished the routine gender verification testing just before the 2000 Olympics in Sydney. Intervention and evaluation of individual athletes could be initiated if there was any question about their female gender identity. However, the organizers of the 2008 Olympic Games in Beijing set up an 'unofficial' gender test lab where they drew blood samples from non-male athletes whose appearance was considered 'suspicious'. This received little attention and failed to identify anyone as a gender fraud (Schultz 2011).

Caster Semenya, at the Athletic World Championships held in Berlin in August 2009, became a case for intervention. Her victory was disputed by questioning her right to compete as a woman, with the IAAF announcing that she would be required to undergo a gender verification test before her victory could be confirmed.

2. Research questions

The paper explores how the 'transgressive aesthetic of performance and display' (Davis 1997, 13) by a non-white non-male South African runner was contextualized in mainstream Swiss German language print publications. The analysis considers the extent to which a globalized media discourse not only constructs and naturalizes but also undercuts and deconstructs the dichotomy of gender stereotypes and ethnic physical hierarchy.

The aim of the case study is to explore and discuss the contextualization of a perceived transgressive aesthetic, performance and display in the field of top-level sports. The case study analyses the discourses surrounding the non-white, non-male South African runner Caster Semenya and how Semenya's body was perceived as deviant or as crossing gender boundaries.

This discourse analysis also explores discourse interceptions that could have implied plural and diverse gender constructs. The ways the media deals with transgression, and the reconstruction or questioning of traditional gender systems are explored in this case study.

The central concern is how transgressively perceived non-white and non-male body works to pluralize and cut across established gender boundaries. By calling those deviant bodies substantially into question, can this perceived deviant body be used, as Butler claims (1990, 17), to reconstruct gender and racial categories? How is 'intersexuality' in top-level sports negotiated as an instance of gender crossing in German-speaking Swiss print publications? What conclusions can be drawn about how (re)constituting processes of dominant values and norms in the field of top-level sports? In the context of values and norms of hegemonic Western top-level sports, how are hierarchies of race, ethnicity, sex, gender and desire revealed in the discussion about the supposedly deviant body of Caster Semenya?

Discourse analysis methods are used to expose the logic and the fractures of a discourse on gender and to reveal the potential for change in gender categories. For this reason, both re- and deconstructive processes need to be analysed. To understand and discuss these processes, gender and postcolonial theories are used to ask the question: What are the recurring themes and underlying discursive structures of this complex discourse?

The focus is on the alleged gender fraud, analysing how, in top-level sports, the female sex is confirmed or questioned using body or movement codes while taking into account the forces in play to maintain body and gender hierarchies. In keeping with Davis' 'transgressive aesthetic of performance and display' (1997, 13), it is important to ask if Semenya's body is resistant and subversive.

Findings on the intersecting assumptions in the categories gender, sex, desire and ethnicity are introduced empirically in the context of the questions.

3. Theoretical approach

Butler criticizes the dual sex/gender differentiation based on the fact that both biological sex and social gender are constituted by performative practices. According to Butler, disregarding this has led to the assumption that female social gender depends on a female biological sex and that gender is understood as an expression of the biological sex.

> [G]ender is not to culture as sex is to nature; gender is also the discursive/cultural means by which 'sexed nature' or 'a natural sex' is produced and established as 'prediscursive', prior to culture, a politically neutral surface on which culture acts. (Butler 1999, 7)

Butler continues this idea by suggesting that the sex/gender differentiation of feminist theory relies on a naturalized materiality of the body. Butler, however, asks which body codes produce sex and gender and make them visible. For her, the gender category intersects with the categories of race, class, ethnicity and sexuality and cannot, therefore, be separated from these intersections (Butler 1999).

Butler's argument that the discursive framework of social gender is constituted in the same way as biological sex is analysed in detail using the media reception of the South African runner Caster Semenya. Taking into account the fact that the athlete whose gender is in question is a non-white[2] non-male South African, the discourses are examined in relation to (post)colonial, racist and sexist patterns of reasoning. It is impossible to analyse the media perception of a non-white, non-male South African athlete without acknowledging the significance of a postcolonial lens. Discussed by Coleman-Bell (2006) and Hall (1997), the non-normative perceived gender performance of 'black sporting bodies' refers to the colonizing gaze. The Swiss, and especially the South African, newspapers drew attention to the link between Sartjie Baartmann (known as the 'Hottentot Venus'), a central figure in gender and postcolonial theory, and Caster Semenya (Brady 2011).

The body-centred gender discourse in the media is, therefore, analysed as one that intersects with biological, racist and sexist discourses (e.g. Birell and McDonald 2000; Lutz et al. 2010; Walgenbach et al. 2007; Winker and Degele 2009). From this perspective, gender and ethnicity are understood as performative embodiment processes, as the body, according to Butler, is genderized and ethnicized according to what is considered typical in the relevant social context (Butler 1999, 5–10).

This paper problematizes the body under the three aspects of feminist theory, the formation of 'difference, domination, and subversion'. From a (post)feminist and postcolonial point of view, the body is negotiated as a subjugated and resisting subversive entity. In the words of Davis (1997, 7), 'the female body [is] the object of processes of domination and control as well the site of women's subversive practices and struggles for self-determination and empowerment'. The analysis also follows the fundamental postcolonial assumption that imperial power relationships which have for centuries influenced the world, continue to do so today (e.g. Bhabha 2009; Hall 1997; Said 1994; Spivak 1985, 1988, 2012).

Said (1994) describes 'modern orientalism' as establishing an asymmetrical dichotomy of a superior occidental self against an inferior oriental other. The enlightened, white, Christian subject is constructed through the multifaceted denigration of the objectified *other* (Hall 1997). This discursive constitution of the colonialized subject takes place in performative practices of attribution, which are referred to as 'othering' processes (e.g. Hall; Spivak). In this context, Spivak was first to develop the central concept of alterity, demonstrating that the construction of the subject, i.e. the self, stands in an interdependent relationship to the construction of the other (Spivak 1985, 1988). The power of definition in the discursive attribution processes lies with the West and, from a postcolonial point of view, refers to current continuities of colonial reasoning and thought patterns (Bhabha 2009).

From this point of view, the postcolonial position can be seen as meaningful in a complex and multidimensional field of research, which can be understood as an interface of the discourses of ethnicity, race, gender, identity and nationality within the discourse of globalization (Ashcroft, Griffiths, and Tiffin 2000).

In globalized top-level sport, continuities of colonial reasoning and thought or organizational patterns in the sense of Bhabha (2009) can be seen in the white male domain of sport leadership. Non-white men and women, as well as white women, remain underrepresented in coaching, leadership and administration in sport organizations and high performance sport (e.g. IAAF, IOC, FIFA, NFL or NBA). These patterns become obvious when considering the success of white athletes, viewed as normal and the success of 'black athletes', perceived as an invasion or a takeover. This has, for example, led sport scientists to search for 'Jumping Genes' in 'black bodies' (e.g. Azzarito and Harrison 2008; Bale and Christensen 2003; Hylton 2009).

4. Method and empirical material

The qualitative method follows the concepts of 'critical discourse analysis' (CDA) and dispositive analysis, using the methodological sequences of Jäger (2001, 2009), Jäger and Maier (2009), Link (1999), Bührmann and Schneider (2008) and Wodak and Meyer (2009). The sources were identified with the help of the Swiss Media Service (SMD) news archives. This analysis was limited to two years, starting 19 August 2009, when Semenya won the gold medal and the media storm began, and ending in November 2011, when rules were set down for intersex athletes. Using the search term 'Caster Semenya', a total of 126 articles based on a 'structural analysis of the strand' were found. Eight paid daily German language Swiss newspapers were included in the structural analysis and were the source of the 126 articles.[3] In the initial evaluation of the material, discourse strands were revealed and typical articles were selected. Nine articles from four daily newspapers[4], representing a wide range of political orientations, were categorized as typical for each ideological orientation based on similar statement events, formation rules and recurrences. The number of nine typical articles was determined through theoretical saturation effects of the analysis.

The discourse and dispositive analysis allowed the identification of central intellectual figures, primary and secondary issues, discourse strands and discourse strand interceptions as well as depth structures (Jäger 2001). To reconstruct general thought patterns that can be typified, the structural analysis used, among other things, methodical sequencing steps, keyword collections (e.g. hermaphrodite, it, boy, etc …), categorizations (e.g. deviant/transgressive) and cluster formation (e.g. scientific–medical discourse) to identify six priority theme complexes on different discourse levels which served as a structural basis for extended detailed analysis. The six detected dominant discourse themes are value discourse,[5] scientific–medical discourse,[6] (sport-)political discourse,[7] sexuality discourse,[8] human rights discourse[9] and cultural studies discourse.[10] The detailed analysis used these as typical selected articles (discourse fragments) and attempted to determine underlying structures that were allocated to the overarching theme of Caster Semenya. The analysis identified various discourse interceptions that along with initial interpretations of the structural analyses became the basis of discussion between the researcher and two research assistants as a part of an intersubjective verification.

Due to the constraint of length, this paper discusses in detail only two of the discourse strands that are related to the topic of this special issue. The discourse strand of the transgressive sporting body focuses, firstly, on the transgressive aesthetic of performance and display, and, secondly, on the (re)construction of the validity of sports values and gender norms. The second discourse strand can be evaluated as a *counter discourse* to normalize and push back any crossing or broadening of boundaries or changes of ethnocentric worth and stereotypical gender norms.

Dispositive analysis is mainly viewed as part of discourse analysis (Jäger 2001). For this paper, the dispositive analysis is used to analyse images as non-discursive practices and so-called materializations. Foucault calls the interplay between discursive and non-discursive practices dispositive (1982). More precise explanation of the interplay and methodological steps associated is beyond the remit of this article, and I would recommend the useful introductory literature by Jäger (2001).

4.1. Ethical aspects of the research

In (de)constructive research, researchers often reconstruct the problem to be analysed and resolved. In research on gender and gender deconstruction processes, we also unfortunately and inevitably reconstruct (for example, gender categories, norms and/or stereotypes). In analysing the media discourses on the gender verification of Caster Semenya, the research reconstructs and restages processes of 'othering', violation and discrimination, and this causes an ethical dilemma.

However, if we want to reveal through research that media discourses are, e.g., sexist or racist or both, we must literally quote the discourses or describe or show the images. This research aims to prevent the rewriting and repetition of sexist and racist discourses and to make readers conscious of media constructions, so creating the potential for future change.

5. Empirical results

5.1. Transgressive aesthetic of performance and display

On 20 August 2009, one day after Caster Semenya's victory, the focus in newspaper articles was on the legality of her victory. On the basis of her physical appearance and performance, fundamental doubts were articulated about her female sex. The headlines of the day proclaimed, 'Is the winner a boy?' (*Bli* 20/8/09, 11), 'A victory with a question mark' (*NZZ* 20/8/09, 51) and 'Waiting for the sex test' (*BaZ* 20/8/09, 35). All newspaper articles consistently raised doubts about her female gender through references such as 'hermaphrodite', 'boy', 'it', etc.

The newspaper *Der Blick* used word play such as 'gold hermaphrodite' (*Bli Online* 25/8/09), and the local paper *Die Berner Zeitung* published late in 2011 an advertisement with the slogan 'Monk and virgin' (3/11/11) in reference to the Bernese Alpine massif *Eiger, Mönch* (monk) and *Jungfrau* (virgin). Both illustrated their labelling with the most frequently published photograph of Semenya, showing her biceps and balled fists after her victory. This picture was caricatured many times (see *Berner Zeitung*, 3 November 2011, http://www.werbewoche.ch/neue-lgk-folgekampagne-fuer-berner-zeitung-realisiert).

At the same time, Semenya's masculine-like movement habitus, facial hair (in particular the upper lip area), low voice, muscular body, sinewy arms, washboard stomach and flat chest were clearly received as supremely unfeminine. Yet, no publication seriously considered that Caster Semenya might be a man. The predominant question, rather, was whether she could be a 'real' woman, with ovaries and a uterus.

As some form of evidence, many people from her home town in South Africa were quoted as saying that as a child she had preferred to play football with the boys rather than skip rope with the girls, wore trousers instead of dresses and that her sex was checked in the toilets by other trainers at sports competitions. Also, she had shown no interest in boys (*Bu* 31/8/09, 2). Public discourse very quickly focused on the idea that Caster Semenya could not be a real or 'true' woman. Her habitus and physique were seen and categorized as masculine.

In response to this, on 10 September 2009, the Athletics South Africa (ASA) federation launched a 'glamour offensive' in *YOU* magazine, publicly displaying Semenya's femininity.[11] The images displayed her in full conformity with globalized Western stereotypes of hetero-normative femininity: straightened hair (no Afro), eye make-up, red lipstick, polished fingernails and jewellery, wearing a dress and tilting her wrists (see *YOU* magazine article on Caster Semenya, reprinted by Swiss daily *Blick*, 10 September 2009, 11.).

The article was received in varying ways by the global media and was also reprinted in the Swiss newspaper Der *Blick* (10/9/09, 11). The article's headline read, 'Wow – look at Caster now!' and 'We turn SA's power girl into a glamour girl – and she loves it!' (*YOU* 10/9/09, cover).

But in the media commentaries, Semenya's body seemed resistant and transgressive in the eyes of the recipients, who were not very convinced by the staging. Even affirming statements such as 'Caster enjoys going girly' and quotes from an interview that she would like to learn how to dress in a feminine way and to wear make-up did not seem entirely convincing. The text and image discourse on four more pages of *YOU* magazine, including a photo series and an interview with Semenya, indicated implicit infantilization and a more deeply underlying racism, sexism and homophobia (*YOU* 10/9/09), similar to what Coleman-Bell (2006) and Hall (1997) identified in relation to non-white women and female athletes. 'The foreign element' is crucially constituted as a deviant, exotic other through the body and the intersecting linking of sex, gender, desire, race and ethnicity (Gilman 1995).

Occasionally, the racist and sexist discourse carried out in the South African press paralleled the story of Sartjie Baartmann (known as the 'Hottentot Venus'), the central figure in gender and postcolonial studies, who was exhibited in the nineteenth-century colonial Europe as a physical example of inferior non-white femininity and exotic sexuality (Nyang'o 2010). In the Swiss daily newspaper *Tages-Anzeiger*, Winnie Madikizela Mandela (identified as 'an ANC politician') was quoted as saying that she regarded this staging as a 'disgusting caricature' and considered it 'the most cruel prank any human could inflict on another' (*TA* 12/9/09, 41).

From the Western, Swiss media perspective, Semenya became stylized as an innocent victim of corrupt and dishonest South African sports politics, which had knowingly used the 'racism card' (*TA* 21/9/09, 7) out of a desire for fame and money (*BaZ* 22/9/09, 29; *Bli* 21/8/09, 2). Semenya's gender ambiguity was put into the context of cheating and moral transgression. In these narratives, Semenya's body became the target of organized deception and corruption.

5.2. (Re)Construction of the validity of sports values and gender norms

The disjunctive two-gender concept of the sports system was questioned only during the first weeks of September 2009, while international top-level sports based on the gender binary was, at the same time, primarily (re)constituted as fair and just. In this respect, the *Die Basler Zeitung* quoted Helmut Digel[12] as an expert. He told the Swiss daily press, 'This is a problem of all sports, how to deal with the third sex [...]. In my opinion, neither the medal nor the achievement can be taken away from her [Semenya].' (*BaZ* 12/9/09, 38). What is remarkable about this statement is that Digel used the term 'third sex',[13] thus already conceptually undermining the construct of the two-gender system.

On the other hand, a frequently printed quote from Arne Ljungqvist, the 'head of the IOC's medical commission', in early April 2011 appears to strongly reconstruct the dual body and gender hierarchy. Under the heading 'The sex test is about to have a comeback', the *Aargauer Zeitung* reported on 7 April 2011 (15):

> According to Ljungqvist, in future a woman shall be allowed to participate in the Olympic Games only if her androgen level is below that of the men or within a range that does not provide her with a competitive advantage [...]. 'If a woman has an excessively high level of male hormones, she will be advised to undergo measures to lower that level to enable her to compete in the women's class. If she does not consent, she loses her eligibility to enter the competition'.

Helmut Digel also picked up the hegemonic gender discourse on 24 April 2011, almost 20 months after his remarkable statements about the 'third sex'. This time, he contradicted his earlier statement by stressing that a clear determination of male or female gender was scientifically possible and also that there is fairness and equality in top-level sports (Digel 24/4/11). In this context, he presented the principles of equality and fair play attributed to the sports system as being in an 'irresolvable dilemma', a 'relationship conflict between fair play and privacy' (Digel 24/4/11) because the public interest and the interest of organized sports 'in maintaining the principle of fair play [has to be] given a higher priority than the protection of privacy' (Digel 24/4/11). He concluded, 'The interest of the community trumps the interest of the individual. From a sports viewpoint, the proposed solution seems to be fair' (Digel 24/4/11). The solution, which primarily aimed at setting a level for the sex hormone testosterone in women, was postulated as a 'milestone' by Digel (24/4/11):

> Setting this rule is a milestone for organized sports. It has given the system the protection it desperately needs [...] [because] the associations have been striving for decades [...] to work with medical, legal, and ethics experts to find mutually acceptable rules which secure the system and protect the principle of fair play.

Sports organizations, who differentiate between two genders, are trying to reconsolidate not only the two-gender system but also the superiority of the male sex. This example is evidence that the discourse, marked as an ethics discourse, is used to assert postulated values of naturalness, fairness and equal opportunity as well as the two-gender hierarchy of top-level sports (Wiederkehr 2012). The public's attention was diverted from an almost unintended medical scheme to confirm the athlete's 'true gender' to a global level where Western values and norms were rearticulated as unambiguous and setting precedence rather than questionable.

6. Discussion

The body of Caster Semenya presented in the media illustrates the discursive, performative effect of the cultural terminology practice described by Butler. As soon as the observer becomes unable to unambiguously read the sociocultural gender codes and thus interprets them as transgressions, the biological sex of the athlete is also called into question (Butler 2009; Nyong'o 2010). Caster Semenya's performance was perceived as transgressive and border crossing (Tolvhed 2013). The quasi-scientific hegemonic view of a Western-dominated power and knowledge hierarchy determines the biological, and therefore also the cultural, categorization of a body that deviates from the hetero-normative unequal two-gender norm (Donnelly 1996). The so-called sex test was not undertaken to identify male exogenous sexual characteristics but because her gender performance was at odds with a sex that was verified and registered at birth.

Butler uses the term 'heterosexual matrix' to describe the components of a recognized and coherent gender existence. First – anatomic sex; second – social gender; and third – sexual desire. According to Butler, it is only this seemingly natural causality of the three components that makes a female subject perceivable as a woman. Semenya's alleged unfeminine appearance, her habitus and physique perceived as masculine, her preference for trousers and football, her excellent athletic performance and her indifference towards sexual relationships with boys are emphasized as obvious indicators in the discourse of deviance. This is exactly when the heterosexual 'sex, gender, and desire' matrix has a reconstituting effect.

The sex test, seen as performative in line with Butler, and the resulting treatment practices were used to define and produce Semenya's gender allocation through academically legitimized methods (Wiederkehr 2012). This management of normalization with the aim of integrating the athlete's 'deviant' body into relatively rigid boundaries and restrictively defended value and norm structures of (top-level) sports is justified by invoking the postulates of fairness and equality of top-level sports (Digel 24/4/11).

The example of Caster Semenya illustrates how the media reconstruct, naturalize and normalize not only dichotomic gender stereotypes but also ethnic and racist body hierarchies. The opportunity to change and expand the Western, white and hetero-normative gender concept was not taken in the discourse about a body of the 'third sex' that went beyond the binary gender limits. The binary sex and gender constructs and the 'heterosexual matrix' were not productively destabilized or transformed to suit Semenya's body, but rather rearticulated throughout these Swiss German print publications.

The racism and sexism accusations articulated in some South African publications were picked up only sporadically by the Swiss newspapers (Gunkel 2012). The counter-discourse primarily conducted in South African media, which drew parallels between the 'Hottentot Venus' and Caster Semenya, can be found in the sports pages of the Swiss papers outside those that were analysed in detail (*BaZ* 04/9/09, 3; TA 24/8/09, 7). In the media discourse, Caster Semenya was fully and publicly exposed, including intimate details about her body. In this process of media colonization of a supposedly deviant body, basic and personal rights were fundamentally disregarded. Her 'exotic' and 'foreign' body and her genitals in particular attracted global interest.

But Caster Semenya is not an isolated case. Other non-white athletes, such as Serena Williams or Florence Griffith-Joyner, have had their femininity questioned. There is a reason why they make use of strongly Western feminine attributes such as jewellery, make-up, long painted fingernails and straightened and/or blond hair to portray themselves (Birell and McDonald 2000). Coleman-Bell (2006) draws a similar conclusion in her discussion of the ways in which the body of tennis player Serena Williams is mediated. She contends that, as a consequence, 'the black female body became a signifier of deviant sexuality' and highlights in particular the attention paid to the size of Serena Williams' buttocks.

Hall draws attention to the ways in which 'black sexuality' has been presented as a marker of the primitivism of the black body throughout colonial history. And he discusses how gender, sexuality and race combine to constitute the female black sporting body as a spectacle of otherness. Hall's examples are evidence that this otherness is made manifest through the function of those bodies as a site of transgression, as the boundary between male and female and, consequently, as a boundary between culture and nature, human and ape (Hall 1997).

This requires an ideal image, a notion of 'real femininity'. The unambiguously clear and striking definition of 'real femininity' happens through negative differentiation, e.g. on a billboard for the Johannesburg nightclub 'Teazers', which drew immense media attention in South Africa in connection with the sex test demanded by the IAAF. The billboard, with the slogan 'No need for gender testing', shows a naked, hyper-sexualized feminine stereotype of a white, busty woman with long, blond hair (Bhula 2012, 127) (*The Telegraph*, 'Pictures of the day', 30 September 2009, http://i.telegraph.co.uk/multimedia/archive/01492/gender-testing_1492031i.jpg).

This example clarifies the intersection of gender, sexuality, ethnicity, race and hetero-normativity and how the body of a non-white and non-male athlete is reconstructed as a supposedly deviant other. The analysis reveals the extent to which a globalized media discourse not only constructs but also naturalizes a dichotomy of gender stereotypes and ethnic physical hierarchy (Lenskyj 2013).

From a postcolonial perspective, the hegemonic view of a Western-dominated power and knowledge hierarchy determines the categorization of a non-white body that deviates from the hetero-normative two-gender norm. This is materialized through a Western-oriented, hetero-normative gender system that builds on dominant gender performances and biological substances such as hormone levels and chromosome sets (Fausto-Sterling 2002). The dual sex/gender differentiation criticized by Butler is highlighted by the assumption that the female social gender depends on a female biological sex and that gender is understood as an expression of the biological sex and not as a performative staging (Butler 1999). Butler (1993) seizes on the challenges as providing the subversive potential of uncertainty and suggests that it is only through transgression that the heterosexual matrix can be subverted. Gender is reproduced through iterative acts and is not fixed in the anatomic body.

7. Conclusion

Using the example of Caster Semenya, this paper demonstrates how the postcolonial female body is reproduced by Western gender norms. International top-level sport is reconstructed as fair, equitable and unambiguous, and the dichotomic gender sports system is considered as an incontrovertible boundary. The media discourse on Caster Semenya and her transgressive body did create the opportunity to broaden and change ethnocentric worth and stereotypical gender norms or the gender bias of the sports system (Tolvhed 2013). But instead, this transgressive female sporting body, as Butler suggested, was called into question and, worse, excluded and normalized.

This happened through varied body technologies, adapted to the hetero-normative, Western-dominated notions of femininity and the binary gender model and subjected to the inherent body hierarchy. Globalized performativity media discourses reconstruct gender boundaries and imperial dominance relationships in the form of power and hegemonic knowledge (Birell and McDonald 2000). Cases of gender ambiguity also demonstrate a (re)constituting of culture and power relations and gender boundaries. These issues present the classification of femininity and how regulatory bodies like the IAAF or IOC set boundaries. The absurdity and dubious ethical stance of the medical definition or the normalization of Semenya on the basis of a two-gender system of top-level sports was not problematized (Schultz 2012; Tolvhed 2013).[14]

The case of Caster Semenya is of interest to gender and queer studies, as Semenya is constructed as a less-than-authentic woman, much less an authentic man and is denied a fundamental structural category of the human classification system (Butler 2009). On the basis of the inability to classify, this physical mode of existence is excluded from the social field of top-level sports. For Butler, this calling into question of one's reality connects gender normality to the limits of being human and the consequent possibility of a 'liveable life' (Butler 1990, 2009).

According to Butler, the two-sex/gender difference overlooks the fact that 'biological gender' (sex) is also constituted by the discursive, regulatory practices that affect social gender. In this process, the body is genderized according to the assumed gender types of the social and cultural contexts.[15]

The power of definition of the discursive attribution process lies with the West and is referenced by a postcolonial viewpoint through current local and global continuities of colonial thought and hegemonic argumentation patterns. The exceeding and crossing of gender boundaries are limited by power relations and this process of 'othering' emphasizes Western humanitarian values of truth, justice and equal opportunity.

Notes

1. Barr body testing (named after discoverer Murray Barr) is a test to determine the presence of an inactive X chromosome in a female's somatic cell.
2. The author has consciously decided to use the term 'non-white' (quotes excluded) as it is difficult to find a not-discriminating, politically correct term without a suggestion of racism, particularly in the context of European and German-speaking recipients with racist and anti-Semitic heritage. The alternative term 'coloured people' is perceived as lightly euphemistic and unnecessarily exoticized. 'Coloured people' only suggests the person is perceived as not white and that this is the substantial reason for discrimination. The purpose of this article to analyse the dominant discourse of a dominant Western, white population meant it was unnecessary to differentiate and negotiate skin colours, even if it has meaning in other contexts.
3. (A) *Aargauer Zeitung* (AZ) 7 articles; (B) *Basler Zeitung* (BaZ) 29 articles; (C) *Der Bund* (Bu) 13 articles; (D) *St. Galler Tagblatt* (Sgt) 19 articles; (E) *Neue Zürcher Zeitung* (NZZ) 7 articles; (F) *Tages-Anzeiger* (TA) 24 articles; and (G) *Blick* (Bli) 27 articles.
4. *Basler Zeitung* (BaZ), *Blick* (Bli), *St. Galler Tagblatt* (Sgt) and *Tages-Anzeiger* (TA).
5. (I) Value and norm structures of (professional) competitive sports, honesty and fairness vs. fraud.
6. (II) Biological, 'natural' femininity and transgressive female physicality through top-level sports, but also intersexuality and transsexuality as supposed effects of doping practices.
7. (III) Apartheid and anti-apartheid, South Africa and the rest of the world. Historical an aktuell discrimination and racism.
8. (IV) Intersexuality, transsexuality and homosexuality.
9. (V) Discrimination and participation, inclusion and exclusion.
10. (VI) (Post)colonial and critical whiteness theories as well as gender studies discourse.
11. It was reprinted by Swiss daily *Der Blick*, 10 September 2009, 11, and thus became part of the sample.
12. Helmut Digel was the former president and honorary president of the German Athletic Association (DLV), an emeritus professor for sport sociology (Tübingen University) as well as the former vice president of the IAAF and the current German council member of the IOC.
13. The 'third sex' is a term used to designate people who cannot clearly be categorized in terms of the binary gender model. In the 1980s and 1990s, the term was increasingly used in *gender and queer theory* as well as in the transgender movement.
14. The Indian professional sprinter Dudee Chand, for example, was the first who in 2014 publicly refused to alter her body to conform with the IAAF rules. She has appealed to the Court of Arbitration for Sport to give her back her sport.
15. But there are some small changes visible in sports policies because sporting practices shape bodies in sport, and these practices form categories and policies. Bodies are gendered and female-categorized athletes have to express racialized and heterosexist stereotypes. Yet, human bodies are extremely difficult to fix by such socioculturally determined criteria and the criteria deployed by governing bodies of top-level sports interconnect with practices of social, cultural, medical and political forces.
    In 1990, the IAAF, as major international sport organization, allowed transsexual athletes to compete with restrictions agreed upon in 2004. This is one example of transgression that proves that bodies can change and cross well-established boundaries (Tolvhed 2013).

Disclosure statement

No potential conflict of interest was reported by the author.

References

Ashcroft, B., G. Griffiths, and H. Tiffin. 2000. *Post-colonial Studies. The Key Concepts*. London: Routledge.
Azzarito, L., and L. Harrison. 2008. "'White Men Can't Jump': Race, Gender and Natural Athleticism." *International Review for the Sociology of Sport* 43: 347–364.
Bale, J., and M. Christensen, eds. 2003. *Sport and Postcolonialism*. New York: Berg.
Bhabha, H. K. 2009. *The Location of Culture*. London: Routledge.
Bhula, V. 2012. "Questioning Gender: The Representation of Race and Gender in Global and Local Print Media Responses Oft He Caster Semenya Saga." Dissertation, University of Witwatersrand, Department of Media Studies. Accessed November 9, 2014. http://wiredspace.wits.ac.za/bitstream/handle/10539/10742/FINAL%20PROJECT%20CHAPTERS.pdf?sequence=2
Birell, S., and M. G. McDonald, eds. 2000. *Reading Sport. Critical Essays on Power and Representation*. Boston, MA: Northeastern University Press.
Brady, A. 2011. "'Could This Women's World Champ be a Man?': Caster Semenya and the Limits of Being Human." *Ante Podium: Online Journal of World Affairs*. Victoria University Wellington. Accessed April 9, 2015. http://www.victoria.ac.nz/atp/articles/pdf/Brady-2011.pdf
Bührmann, A., and W. Schneider. 2008. *Vom Diskurs zum Dispositiv. Eine Einführung in die Dispositivanalyse* [From Discourse to Dispositive. An Introduction into Dispositive Analysis]. Bielefeld: Transcript Verlag.
Butler, J. 1990. *Gender Trouble: Feminism and the Subversion of Identity*. New York: Routledge.
Butler, J. 1993. *Bodies That Matter: On the Discursive Limits of "Sex"*. New York: Routledge.
Butler, J. 1999. *Gender Trouble: Feminism and the Subversion of Identity*. 10th anniversary ed. New York: Routledge.
Butler, J. 2009. *Die Macht der geschlechter und die Grenzen des Menschlichen* [Undoing Gender]. Frankfurt am Main: Suhrkamp.
Coleman-Bell, R. 2006. "'Droppin' It like It's Hot': The Sporting Body of Serena Williams." In *Framing Celebrity: New Directions in Celebrity Culture*, edited by Su Holmes and Sean Redmond, 195–205. New York: Routledge.
Davis, K. 1997. "Embody-ing Theory: Beyond Modernist and Postmodernist Reading of the Body." In: *Embodied Practices. Feminist Perspectives on the Body*, edited by K. Davis, 1–27. London: Sage.
Donnelly, P. 1996. "Approaches to Social Inequality in the Sociology of Sport." *Quest* 48 (2): 221–242.
Fausto-Sterling, A. 2000. *Sexing the Body. Gender Politics and the Construction of Sexuality*. New York: Basic Books.
Fausto-Sterling, A. 2002. "Sich im Dualismus duellieren [Duel of Dualism]." In *Wie natürlich ist Geschlecht? Gender und die Konstruktion von Technik* [Sexing the Body: Gender Politics and the Construction of Sexuality], edited by U. Pasero and A. Gottburgsen, 17–64. Wiesbaden: Westdeutscher Verlag.
Foucault, M. 1982. *The Archaeology of Knowledge*. New York: Pantheon.
Gilman, Sander L. 1995. "Black Bodies, White Bodies: Toward an Iconography of Female Sexuality in Late Nineteenth-century Art." *Medicine and Literature. Critical Inquiry* 12 (1): 204–242.
Gunkel, H. 2012. "Queer Times Indeed? Südafrikas Reaktionen auf die mediale Inszenierung der 800-Meter-Läuferin Caster Semenya [South Africa's Response to the Media Presentation of 800-Meter Runner Caster Semenya]." In *Feministische studien*, edited by Anne Fleig and Kirsten Heinsohn, 44–52. Stuttgart: Lucius & Lucius.
Hall, St. 1997. "The Spectacle of the Other." In *Representation. Cultural Representations and Signifying Practices*, edited by St. Hall, S. 223–290. London: Sage.
Horne, J., A. Tomlinson, G. Whannel, and K. Woodward. 2013. *Understanding Sport. A Socio-cultural Analysis*. 2nd ed. London: Routledge.
Hylton, K. 2009. "Whiteness and Sport." In *'Race' and Sport. Critical Race Theory*, edited by K. Hyton, S. 64–79. London: Routledge.
Jäger, S., and F. Maier. 2009. "Theoretical and Methodological Aspects of Foucauldian Critical Discourse Analysis and Dispositive Analysis." In *Methods of Critical Discourse Analysis*. 3rd ed., edited by R. Wodak and M. Meyer, 34–61. London: Sage.

Jäger, S. 2001. "Discourse and Knowledge: Theoretical and Methodological Aspects of a Critical Discourse and Dispositive Analysis." In *Methods of Critical Discourse Analysis*, edited by Ruth Wodak and Michael Meyer, 32–61. London: Sage.

Jäger, S. 2009. *Kritische Diskursanalyse. Eine Einführung* [Critical Discourse Analysis. An introduction]. Münster: UNRAST Verlag.

Karkazis, K., R. Jordan-Young, G. Davis, and S. Camporesi. 2012. "Out of Bounds? A Critique of the New Policies on Hyperandrogenism in Elite Female Athletes." *The American Journal of Bioethics* 12 (7): 3–16.

Lenskyj, H. J. 2013. *Gender Politics and the Olympic Industry*. New York: Palgrave Macmillan.

Link, J. 1999. "Diskursive Ereignisse, Diskurse, Interdiskurse: Sieben Thesen zur Operativität der Diskursanalyse, am Beispiel es Normalismus [Discursive Events, Discourses, Interdiscourses: Seven Theses on an Operativity Discourse Analysis, Using the Example of Normalism]." In *Das Wuchern der Diskurse. Perspektiven der Diskursanalyse Foucaults*, edited by H. Bublitz, A. Bührmann, C. Hanke, and A. Seier, S. 149–161. Frankfurt: Campus.

Lutz, H., ed. 2010. *Fokus Intersektionalität Bewegungen und Verortungen eines vielschichtigen Konzeptes*. Wiesbaden: VS Verlag für Sozialwissenschaften.

Nyong'o, T. 2010. "The Unforgivable Transgression of Being Caster Semenya." *Women & Performance: A Journal of Feminist Theory* 20 (1): 95–100. doi:10.1080/07407701003589501. Accessed November 10, 2014.

Said, Edward W. 1994. *Orientalism*. New York: Vintage Books.

Schultz, J. 2011. "Caster Semenya and the 'Question of Too': Sex Testing in Elite Women's Sport and the Issue of Advantage." *Quest* 63 (2): 228–243.

Schultz, J. 2012. "New Standards, Same Refrain: The IAAF's Regulations on Hyperandrogenism." *The American Journal of Bioethics* 12 (7): 32–33.

Spivak, Gayatri Ch. 1985. "The Rani of Simur." In *Europe and Its Others*. Vol. 1, edited by F. Barker, P. Hulme, M. Iversen, and D. Loxley, 128–151. Colchester: University of Sussex.

Spivak, Gayatri Ch. 1988. "Can the Subaltern Speak?" In *Marxism and the Interpretation of Culture*, edited by C. Nelson and L. Grossberg, 271–313. Urbana: University of Illinois Press.

Spivak, Gayatri Ch. 2012. *An Aesthetic Education in the Era of Globalization*. Cambridge, MA: Harvard University Press.

Tolvhed, H. 2013. "Sex Dilemmas, Amazons and Cyborgs: Feminist Cultural Studies and Sport." *Culture Unbound: Journal of Current Cultural Research* 5: 273–289. Accessed April 19, 2015. http://www.cultureunbound.ep.liu.se/v5/a18/cu13v5a18.pdf

Walgenbach, K., G. Dietze, A. Hornscheidt, and K. Palm 2007. *Gender als interdependente kategorie. Neue perspektiven auf intersektionalität, diversität und heterogenität* [Gender as an Interdependent Category. New Perspectives on Intersectionality, Diversity and Heterogeneity]. Opladen: Verlag Barbara Budrich.

Wiederkehr, S. 2009. "'We Shall Never Know the Exact Number of Men Who Have Competed in the Olympics Posing as Women': Sport, Gender Verification and the Cold War." *The International Journal of the History of Sport* 559–572.

Wiederkehr, S. 2012. "Jenseits der Geschlechtergrenzen. Intersexuelle und transsexuelle Menschen im Spitzensport [Transgendered. Intersexed and Transsexual People in Professional Sports]." In *Feministische studien*, edited by Anne Fleig and Kirsten Heinsohn. With assistance of Rita Casale, Claudia Gather, Sabine Hark, Kuster, Friederike, Regine Othmer, Ulla Wischermann. Stuttgart: Lucius & Lucius.

Winker, G., and N. Degele. 2009. *Intersektionalität* [Intersectionality]. Bielefeld: Transcript.

Wodak, R., and M. Meyer. 2009. "Critical Discourse Analysis: History, Agenda, Theory & Methodology." In *Methods of Critical Discourse Analysis*. 3rd ed., edited by R. Wodak and M. Meyer, 1–33. London: Sage.

Sources (cited)

AZ 07/04/11, 15 (Aargauer Zeitung 07.04.11). "Der Sextest steht vor einem Comeback [The Sex Test is Facing a Comeback]." Aargau, 15.

BaZ 20/08/09, 35 (Basler Zeitung 20.08.09). "Warten auf den Sex-Test [Waiting for the Sex Test]. Caster Semenya gewinnt – doch ist sie wirklich eine Frau?". Basel, 35.

BaZ 04/09/09, 3 (Basler Zeitung 04.09.09). "Mit Gewalt, ohne Würde. Die beklemmende Ausstellung [By Force Without Dignity. The Oppressive Exhibition] «What We See» in Basel." Von Sigfried Schibli. Basel, 3.

BaZ 12/09/09, 38 (Basler Zeitung 12.09.09). "Caster Semenya Offenbar ein Zwitter. Laut Presse-Berichten soll die 800-Meter-Weltmeisterin definitiv keine Frau sein [Caster Semenya Obviously a Hermaphrodite. According to Press Reports, the 800-Meter World Champion Should not be a Woman Definitely]." Basel, 38.

BaZ 22/09/09 (Basler Zeitung 22.09.09). "Im Fall von Caster Semenya wurde gelogen, dass sich die Balken biegen – nun sind dringend Konsequenzen nötig. [In the Case of Caster Semenya was Lied too much – Now the Consequences are Urgently Required]." Von Andreas W. Schmid Basel, 29.

Bli 20/08/09, 11(Der Blick 20.08.09). "Hosen runter. Ist die Siegerin ein Bub? [Pants Down. Is the Winner of a Boy?] Von Carl Schönenberger." Zürich, 11.

Bli 21/08/09, 2 (Der Blick 21.08.09). "Caster Semenya – Opfer krimineller Funktionäre. Es ist der grosse WM-Skandal. Südafrika und sein Head Coach aus der ehemaligen DDR führen die Welt an der Nase herum. Das Opfer: 800-Meter-Weltmeisterin Caster Semenya [Caster Semenya – Victims of Criminal Officials. It is the Great World Cup Scandal. South Africa and its Head Coach of the Former East Germany Mess Around the World. The Victims: 800-Meter World Champion Caster Semenya]." Zürich, 2.

Bli Online, 25/08/12 (Der Blick Online 25.08.12). "Gold-Zwitter wird frenetisch empfangen [Gold Hermaphrodite is Received Frenetically]." Updated: 14.08.2012. Accessed January 15, 2013. http://www.blick.ch/sport/gold-zwitter-wird-frenetisch-empfangen-id519467.html

Bli 10/09/09, 11 (Der Blick 10.09.09). "Semenya ganz Frau [Semenya Entirely Woman]." Zürich, 11.

Bu 31/08/09, 2 (Der Bund 31.08.09). "Rätsel um das schnelle Goldmädchen [Mystery Surrounding Gold Girl]," von Johannes Dietrich. Bern, 2.

BZ 3/11/11 (Die Berner Zeitung 03.11.11). "Mönch und Jungfrau [Monk and Virgin]. Bei der BZ kommt immer Bern zuerst." Bern. Accessed November 10, 2014. http://www.werbewoche.ch/neue-lgk-folgekampagne-fuer-berner-zeitung-realisiert

Digel, H. (24.04.2011). "Fairplay und Privatheit [Fairplay and Privacy] – Prof. Dr. Helmut Digel in der DOSB Presse." Accessed November 10, 2014. http://www.germanroadraces.de/24-0-22565-fairplay-und-privatheit-prof-dr-helmut.html

Digel, Helmut. (22.09.2009). "Intersexualität und Hochleistungssport – Was ist, wenn ein drittes Geschlecht an die Tür des internationalen Sports klopft? Eine kritische Betrachtung [Intersexuality and High-performance Sports – What if a Third Sex Knocks on the Door of International Sports? A Critical Examination] von Prof Dr. Helmut Digel." In GERMAN ROAD RACES e.V. Medizin. Accessed November 11, 2014. http://www.germanroadraces.de/245-0-12298-intersexualitaet-und-hochleistungssport-was-ist-wenn.html

NZZ Online 20/08/09. (Neue Züricher Zeitung Online: Sport 20.08.09). "Ein Sieg mit Fragezeichen Castor Semenya gewinnt die 800 m, aber noch ist ihr Geschlecht unklar [A Victory with Question Marks. Castor [sic] Semenya Won the 800 Meters Run, But Her Gender is Still Unclear]." Accessed January 15, 2013. http://facts.ch/articles/2788434-ein-sieg-mit-fragezeichen

"'Pictures of the day', No Need for Gender – Testing." 2009. *The Telegraph*, September 30. Accessed November 12, 2014. http://www.telegraph.co.uk/news/picturegalleries/picturesoftheday/6246227/Pictures-of-the-day-30-September-2009.html?image=4

TA 24/08/09, 7 (Tages Anzeiger 21.08.09). "Eine Frau in Männergestalt [A Woman in a Male Body], Von Christian Brüngger und Johannes Dieterich." Zürich, 7.

TA 12/09/09, 41 (Tages Anzeiger 12.09.09). "Semenya ein Zwitter: Angeblicher Beweis – und wütende Reaktionen in Südafrika [Semenya a Hermaphrodite: Alleged Evidence – and Angry Responses in South Africa], von Johannes Dieterich." Zürich, 41.

YOU Magazine (10/9/09, cover). "We turn SA's Power Girl into a Glamour Girl – and She Loves It. Wow, Look at Caster Now." Media24. Cape Town, no 144. http://you.co.za

Approaching a gender neutral PE-culture? An exploration of the phase of a divergent PE-culture

Suzanne Lundvall

The Swedish School of Sport and Health Sciences, GIH, Stockholm, Sweden

ABSTRACT
The aim of this study is to explore the phase of the divergent physical education (PE) culture in Sweden through the enactment of gender and how boundaries are formed and defended by symbolic mediating status and monopolization of resources. The study departures from a literature review with an inductive approach. Inspired by the method of critical incidents technique specific events have been studied to explore the longitudinal phase and the enactment of gender. Five critical incidents demonstrates how difference and similarity were created, maintained and contested, but also how the dismantling of gender differences came to be enacted and socially configured in space and time. The findings of the study point to a slow-but-still ongoing phase of dissolving symbolic and social boundaries. Going for a gender-neutral PE culture in the future seems to require our ability to both be gender sensitive and gender bend in order to transgress traditional gender order.

Introduction

A gender-divergent physical education (PE) culture was gradually established in Sweden during the early 1900s and lasted for almost 100 years. It was built on Swedish Ling gymnastics and a division of gender with separate physical education teaching education (PETE) programmes for male and female students. PE as part of the field of physical culture has had, since its inception at the beginning of the nineteenth century in several European countries, an ongoing battle concerning how to gain the greatest and longest benefits for mind and body (Pfister 2003). These conflicts have represented different points of view about the legitimate agenda of norms and values in PE, leading to the social constructions of specific bodies and movement traditions, not only in Europe, but also in other parts of the world (Kirk 2010; Korsgaard 1989; Lundvall and Schantz 2013; Morgan 2006; Pfister 2003). In her book *Women First*, Fletcher (1984) points to the inscribed banner for women where the calling out for a 'me too', 'to become a part of' (1984, 1), has guided the fight for equality and equity. In line with that, early 'feminism' had, in time, to be dismissed by newer feminisms in order to uncover the complexity of discrimination and segregation. This paper will explore the phase of the divergent PE culture in Sweden through the enactment of gender and how boundaries are formed and defended by symbolic mediating status and the monopolization of resources. A special focus is put on specific events challenging the longitudinal nature of gender-divergent PE culture. The conclusions are discussed in the light of the present day and the field of sport and physical culture.

Theoretical frame of reference and method

The study is based on an explorative literature review of scholar works, including dissertations, representing findings from archive material such as curricula document, annual reports, newspaper articles, films and biographic notes. The review has had an inductive approach were identifiers for the chosen literature have been literature of scholarly significance regarding PE teacher training, physical culture, bodily movement practices and gender. The sample of scholarly works reflects a Swedish PE culture context, but international comparisons are made.

The theoretical frame of reference draws on Foucault's productive concept of power. In a Foucauldian sense, power is omnipresent, positions different subjects and determines their relation to one another (Foucault 1980). To understand contemporary discursive practices within the field of PE, some contours of different periods of time or events need to be given attention. Inspired by the method of critical incidents technique (Cope and Watts 2000; Flanagan 1954), more specific events have been studied to explore the phase of gender-divergent PE culture and the enactment of gender. Events or situations consisting of cultural clashes, challenging the existing norms, have been noted in the literature review and analysed in order to interpret and understand indicative underlying structures, trends and motives. The concepts of symbolic and social boundaries (Lamont and Molnár 2002) have helped to structure the analysis of the events, the configuration of social relations and the role symbolic resources play in creating, maintaining and contesting institutionalized social difference. By exploring particular spaces at a certain time offers possibilities to examine what separates people and whose knowledge is seen as legitimate. A distinction is made, as advocated by Lamont and Molnár (2002), between symbolic boundaries, represented by social actors, categorizing objects, practices, time and space and social boundaries manifested in social difference. What is given space and time in, for example, bodily movement practices, steering documents and career development courses leads to certain contemporary normative, regulatory ideals in terms of attitudes, behaviours and embodied practices. Hence, space is seen as actively constructed, and space-time a configuration of social relations. In other words, as Vertinsky (1999, 20) writes, '[---] the spatial organization of physical culture and body education is integral to the production of the social, and not merely its result'.

The outlining of a gender-divergent PE culture

The Royal Gymnastics Central Institute [GCI] in Sweden (now called the Swedish School of Sport and Health Sciences [GIH]) was the first institute in the world focusing on PETE. The institute was established in 1813 by Per Henrik Ling. The principles of Ling gymnastics were founded on philanthropic ideas of exercising body and mind, and were seen as holistic (Ling [1840] 1979). Ling stated from the very beginning that the male as well as the female body were in need of a PE, a schooling of the body, in a specific systematized and disciplined way. The inclusion of the female body was a quite unique statement for his time, and it is seen by many researchers as a contributing factor to the longevity of Swedish Ling gymnastics in school PE in countries worldwide (See, for example, Carli 2004; Fletcher 1984; Kirk 2010; Pfister 2003). The branches of the Ling gymnastics system that were developed at the institute from the beginning were military, pedagogical and medical gymnastics (Drakenberg et al. 1913). Ling gymnastics' fourth branch, aesthetic gymnastics, was not developed until the beginning of the 1900s (which will be described further on in the text). The military gymnastics courses were never part of the female students' education.

Female students were first admitted to the institute in 1864, 51 years after their male counterparts. They, like the male students, studied courses in both pedagogical and medical gymnastics. This latter form of courses was designed for working with remedial gymnastics (today called physiotherapy). The organization of pedagogical gymnastics and remedial medical gymnastics could not be separated as it was a prerequisite for each other (Ottosson 2005). Being a male physiotherapist was for most of the nineteenth century connected to high status, synonymous with being a nobleman or a man from the upper bourgeoisie, often an officer in the Swedish Army (Ottosson 2005). The unity of pedagogical and remedial gymnastics also created a sound basis for the prospective female practitioner, as she initially was unable to get a position at schools or permission to open a medical (remedial) gymnastics institute on her own.

The women's liberation movement fighting for women's suffrage, access to education and labour market participation, inspired and supported the early examined female gymnasts, and several of them seem to have been abreast of and engaged in women's rights (Lundvall and Meckbach 2013; Ottosson 2005; Trangbæck 1999).[1] At the end of the nineteenth century, the discourse of the modern society made new demands on its citizens and these did not correspond with the traditional ideas and constructions of femininity as passive and emotional. For women, these demands could be interpreted as including new tasks for them and also new and equal rights. A professionalization process could be introduced. The education of the body fitted well in this social engineering project (Ljunggren 2013; Pfister 1999; Trangbæck 1999). Bodily energy was an important resource in women's efforts for emancipation, but also the right to express and perform bodily exercise (Trangbæck 1999). The gradual spread of the health and hygiene discourse also stressed the need for female physical educators to participate in this educational mission (Carli 2004; Fletcher 1984).

A manifestation of a professional platform

In 1902, a group of female physical educators left the *Swedish Association of Gymnastics Teachers* (SGS), and actively sought alternative ways 'to be admitted' to the institutionalized field of PE. Instead of a continued negotiation as female members in a male-dominated organization they created a platform of their own and founded the *Association of the Gymnastics Central Institute* (in Swedish Föreningen GCI). This association was meant for female graduate gymnasts from the institute. The initiative was strongly supported by the first Swedish female physician, Carolina Widerström, also a graduate from the GCI institute. An explicit goal of this association was to avoid the establishment of a female gymnastics proletariat. Hence, the establishment dealt with the question of equal rights and to take command and responsibility over the development of the female physical educator profession in Sweden (Carli 2004; Föreningen GCI 1902). Other goals were to secure competence and expertise and to foster the feeling of companionship and sisterhood, but also to create a labour market with positions to apply for and further training opportunities (Föreningen GCI 1902). Besides an employment bureau and a library, the association organized theoretical and practical courses in gymnastics and remedial gymnastics. It came to act as a trade union for female physical educators until the early 1940s, when the state decided to have only one counterpart (the SGS).

This way of strategically organizing a professional female association created a certain cultural membership contributing to symbolic resources and a symbolic and social boundary drawing, both by the formal education and the practices shared and the moral implications of how to act and behave. These boundaries were also shaped by the institutionalized definitions of who could be allowed membership, which created exclusivity in terms of self-worth, self-appraisal and dynamic dimensions of social relations. The protection of autonomy maintained both a symbolic and social drawing of boundaries between trained and non-trained physical educators, and between male and female physical educators. Male physical educators could not become members, thus the autonomy was strongly protected by this single-gender membership.

The professional development courses held by the association was during the first decade dominated by medical courses concerning functional aspects of what and how to exercise (Hugosson 2002). The role of medical doctors, supporting a physically active female body (within certain frames) in the early phase of the development of the female PE culture is well described by, for example, Trangbæck (1999). The courses upheld the network and exchange of proven competences, but also boundaries of 'normality' in terms of what the body should be, do, and look like. The professional platform challenged the norm of women as passive without taking responsibility and helped to expand the notions and perceptions of femininity. The network represented, what Lamont and Molnár (2002, 187) call, the notion of 'top-notch', supporting the members' self-identity as professionals with a special mandate and responsibility. One example of the mandate that several of the female graduate physical educators perceived was to go abroad to spread the theory and practice of Ling gymnastics (Halldén 1996). This added to the feeling of being a selected and committed social group (see, for example, Carli 2004; Fletcher 1984; Trangbæck 1999).

The broken monopoly of male knowledge

The early 1900s was also a time when new ideas and conceptions of what constituted a child were spread. This discourse of childhood was built on ideas of modernity representing citizenship, science and education (Heywood 2001; Lundquist Wanneberg 2013). In relation to children, these new ideas promoted an acknowledgement of children as active and developing subjects. But what forms of bodily exercise were then appropriate for children?

In 1910, one of the founders of the Association of the GCI, Elin Falk, was appointed as a school inspector for PE in Stockholm. Holding this position, she immediately started to work for a reformation of school gymnastics in elementary schools. Falk had, through her visits in Europe and the USA (she practised in Baltimore for two years), encountered new perspectives on the body and physicality, and with that motives for developing the formal Ling gymnastics (Falk 1908). Her arguments for change came from what she called 'scientific studies'. The praxis of the training of a 'good' posture could be related to new knowledge of orthopaedics. And the effort-saving theory, with the balance between tensed and relaxed, could, for example, be related to how movement and exercises should be taught and executed. Falk also got her arguments from Björkstén, a well-respected Finnish-Swedish female gymnastics leader and a graduate of the institute: rhythm and the sensing of the movements were ways to secure an educative practice. Falk frankly declared that children were not soldiers and therefore needed another type of pedagogy and an active engagement in exercise. What Falk advocated was inspiring and joyful movements, movements characterized by lightness, play and imagination. Her reform ideas created a hostile conflict between Falk and the old Lingians represented by the former school inspector, Captain Sellén, who was newly appointed as the vice chancellor of the Institute of GCI. Thereby Falk was challenged by the strongest possible counterpart: the Institute of GCI. The citation below gives an illustration of Falk's accuracy when advocating an acceptance of her reform ideas.

> I will first of all, to clarify this historical event, give an account of the origin and development of the daily practice of school gymnastics at the schools of Stockholm. … I will thereafter answer the question whether my proposals cause such subversive innovations that my critics claim to have found. (Falk 1913, 1 [author translation])

After three years Falk won the battle, again supported by Widerström, who at that time was an executive member of the school board of Stockholm (Falk 1913). Falk stayed as a school inspector for more than 30 years and was appointed as a member of the board of the Institute. Later she wrote in her book *Gymnastik med lek och idrott* (*Gymnastics with Play and Sport*).

> The aim of bodily exercise, as well as other subjects in school, should be to help every child to develop, in mind and body, such an original personality as possible, with a working loving will … courageous, rich with initiatives and a strong and well-educated body. (Falk 1927, 20)

On the one hand, it is possible to understand the hostile conflict and the resistance to the reformation of school gymnastics as a reaction against certain exercises or ways of how to teach them. On the other hand, the conflict can be interpreted as a question of power: who had the mandate to reform school gymnastics, which also included aspects of the forming of citizens. In many ways, the school reformation conflict strengthened the female PE culture. The acceptance of Falk's work meant that female physical educators were trustworthy and their knowledge legitimate. The space for the social configuration of knowledge represented by females within the field of PE was broadened. This social group could take part and contribute to the formation of a modern society.

The breakthrough of a sensual approach to body and physicality

A third parallel process that can be traced early 1900s is what Vertinsky calls, a 'transatlantic traffic' between Europe and North America: an exchange of thoughts and methods aiming at creating space for forms of expressive movement, such as dance and aesthetic gymnastics in PE (Vertinsky 2009). The philosophy behind this new form of bodily practice corresponded well with that of the 'modern' woman in the early 1900s: '… athletic yet graceful, strong but not overly muscled, adventurous while decorous – in short a figure of accommodation to past and present' (Vertinsky 2010, 1114). And as one of the leading American educators in expressive dance, Genevieve Stebbins, concluded: 'Delsartes' … has given the aesthetics and Ling the athletics of a perfect method' (see Vertinsky 2010, 1117). As the thoughts behind the first steps taken could be motivated to be in line with Ling's intentions of an aesthetic branch of his system, it paved the way for this development in Sweden, although it took several years to move towards a more aesthetic and rhythmical approach to the gymnastics performed at the institute.

The educational philosophy that attracted female physical educators in leading circles was how female physicality could be developed and related to the female body. The core point was to combine, in practice, aesthetic dimensions that could refine the value of a body in motion, without challenging the notion of a feminine body. Initially, this departure from the stiff traditional floor gymnastics met with opposition and resistance from the group's own members (Forsman and Moberg 1990; Wickström 1908, 1936). A clash can be identified in Sweden when these notions of rhythm and the sensing body were implemented in career development courses for female physical educators. Questions of what this had to do with gymnastics were asked: Where was the systematic way of training the body and the theories behind it? Could these movements help the bodily schooling of women? (Wikström 1936) But as the aesthetical and rhythmical gymnastics could be put under the umbrella of Ling's aesthetical branch of gymnastics, there was finally an acceptance for the idea that moving rhythmically could release internal forces, act energetically and be disciplining. Elaborated theories of expressiveness and the concept of effort saving through body and rhythm were spread among the female PE community and female gymnastics leaders (Laine 1989; Ljunggren 2000).

The focus on the educational value of skill development and performance in the context of movement provided a cultural, physical and symbolic capital (Lundvall and Meckbach 2003; Vertinsky 2010). This was a body movement culture represented acceptable forms of expressive physical movements, clothing reforms and a gateway to women's physicality in public life. It also stood for a progressive education in and approach to pedagogy that encouraged aesthetic attention to and dimensions of the body (Vertinsky 2010, 1118). Those teaching aesthetic gymnastics believed in its values, not as a competitive performance but as an educational act, an influence. The body could be looked upon as a tool, not only as a carnal, instrumental thing. This female form of gymnastic dance came to be developed under what could be called a gender legacy. Gradually during the first half of the 1900s, rhythmic and aesthetic gymnastics became an important part of the female PE culture. This development of a female body movement culture on its own contributed to a continued gap between the male and female PE culture. This female form of rhythmic gymnastics was institutionalized by definitions of the female body. But it is not clear how far the pioneers drove this feminist agenda; if gymnastics dance could act as a medium for radical negotiations around gender. The institutionalized form of the male free standing gymnastics continued to be well anchored in its military tradition.

The demasculinization of physiotherapy

The 1800s had witnessed a balance of power between predecessors from the medical and gymnastics fields, where both sides had been sanctioned as representatives of science. This balance of power changed in 1934 after several years of conflict when the medical field in the end took charge of the medical gymnastics. The decision to move the teaching of remedial gymnastics (physiotherapy) to the Karolinska Institute (KI) (Ottosson 2005) represents a regulation of a profession by the medical science. Above all, as Ottosson (2005, 384) writes, 'this was done to ensure/sustain the hegemonic position of KI and the orthopedists'. With that a demasculinization of the programme and a regendering process occurred. The male students were, so to speak, cut off because the programme was downgraded, with admission requirements lowered and the possibility of an academic career taken away. From being a male profession with female practitioners, it became a feminized profession, but without the academic muscles (Ottosson 2005). The loss of courses in remedial gymnastics meant that the tradition and organization of the pedagogical and medical courses as a unit were brought to an end. By transferring medical gymnastics to KI, one of the two pillars of the PE culture, with valuable symbolic resources, was lost. The scientific medical connotations to the male and female physical educator profession came to an end. The exporting of Swedish Ling gymnastics, by male and female physical educators, started its decline with the establishment of this new power order.

The dominating health and hygiene discourses ended in the mid-twentieth century (Palmblad and Eriksson 1995). After the Second World War, new discourses around body, physicality and education started to develop. Male Swedish politicians claimed in debates about school PE that there should be less of the listening and the following (Lindroth 2004, 18). The spread of sport in Sweden, organized and run as a popular movement, had also become part of the welfare state with a shift in movement practices (Eichberg and Loland 2010; Norberg 2004). A slow-but-sure sportification process reached the field of PE, affecting both PETE programmes and school PE in Sweden. A new era in the institutionalized field of PE was coming up with a more scientifically grounded physiological-positivistic-based thinking of how the body was to be trained, combined with the moral and ethical teaching of fair play and social values (Lundvall and Schantz 2013; Olofsson 2007). This shift can be seen in the number of studying hours in the PETE programmes. In 1966, the hours devoted to sport courses started to exceed the hours for gymnastics courses (Lundvall and Meckbach 2003).

The academization process and the call for a co-education reform

In 1977, a higher education reform in Sweden was implemented which supported an academization of teacher education in general. This came to influence the existing PETE programs. In parallel came a call for co-education by the surrounding society (Lundvall and Meckbach 2003). The co-education reform was seen as a means to equalize sex roles, and as part of society's duty to work for equality between men and women, boys and girls (Olofsson 2005). Both the academization and the coeducation reform and the scientifically based rationale for the physiological training and exercising discourse led to a questioning of the shape of the divergent PE culture. The mandate for the state-financed PE programmes was to promote the education of gender-neutral bodies.

The merging of the male and female PETE programmes put on end to the structure of a gender divergent PE culture and paved the way for female students to learn new sports like ice hockey, and for male students to learn expressive dance. This indicates a broadening of gender roles. The construction of the symbolic and social boundaries separating the two cultures had taken as its point of departure two different bodies and what was called the nature of the sexes: a male and female nature (for corresponding changes in other countries, see, for example, Kirk 2010; O'Sullivan, Bush, and Gehring 2002; Scraton 1992; Wright 1996). But the question is whether the shift to co-education and the (actual) mixing of female and male students/pupils led to gender enactment, and whether the organization of bodies and practices changed or challenged the boundaries of the male hegemony in the (educational field) of sport (see, for example, Hargreaves 1994; Mangan 2010; Pfister 2010). Co-education itself was the tool for the transformation of gender discourses and subjectivities.

The Australian scholar Richard Tinning argues that the academization of the field of PE and sport science has meant a strong dominance of medical and natural scientific knowledge about human movement and human performance (Tinning 2010). This legitimate, sometimes evidence-based knowledge, also went hand in hand with how bodily exercise was supposed to be performed and educated. As a consequence, physiology, biomechanics and psychology were assumed as important. These academic disciplines also conveyed a certain view of what true knowledge might be a particular view of knowledge, or a specific knowledge ideal. The problem was that several of these academic disciplines embraced a normative and hierarchical order between the genders; woman as a different form of a male body (Larsson and Lundvall 2014). This led to gender injustice in sports practice within the dominant masculine sport model. Furthermore, the scientific measurements of sports practice did not support a former aesthetical movement culture represented by female PETE educators (Lundvall and Meckbach 2003).

The dynamics of how the relational mechanism worked can be seen through how power, in a Foucauldian sense, position different subjects and their relations to one another (Foucault 1980). Within PE departments, the relational acknowledgement of female physical educators' competence and capacity started to change after the reform and with that a loss of positions for female teachers in male-dominated physical cultures like team ball sports, and in the area of outdoor education (Carli 2004). The latter also gradually became more sportified. To educate gender-neutral bodies resulted as well in a simplified course content in expressive dance, adjusted to male students' 'abilities' and skills. According to interviews with former PETE educators, no or few adjustments were made to meet female students' ability to keep up with the sports courses (Lundvall and Meckbach 2003).

The sportification of the body movement culture in the PETE field did not come in conflict with the exercise physiologist's research about the body's receptiveness to different labour/training and limits. Though, the underpinning logics of the aesthetical dimensions led to a questioning of the basis for the female PE culture. The aesthetical and rhythmical part of the female body movement practice did not fit into the discourse of training and the sports education model, and with that a following marginalization of its specific movement culture and pedagogies occurred (Carli 2004; Lundvall and Meckbach 2003). The male PETE students' gymnastics training were easily adjusted to fitness training as it already had a character of fitness and strength training included in its form.

After the co-education reform of Swedish school PE in 1981, and the subject matter content became the same for girls and boys, the proportion of girls with higher grades in PE dropped and remained at a low level for more than 20 years (Carli 1995, 1997; Lundvall and Meckbach 2004). Today, almost halfway through the second decade of the twenty-first century, this uneven balance between male and female pupils has changed on a school basis, but not on a national one (Larsson et al. 2010). PE is the only subject in Swedish schools where boys have higher grades than girls. Ability and grades have become tightly linked to knowledge of sports practice for both male and female pupils (Redelius and Larsson 2010). Another aspect is curriculum changes position health as an important goal of school PE. Here, international and national reports describe problems for physical educators to accomplish this goal (Hardman and Green 2011; Swedish Schools Inspectorate 2010). One interpretation is that this indicates demands of a shifting of boundaries in co-educated school PE.

Discussion – a gender-neutral PE culture?
Exploring the period of gender-divergent PE culture(s) in Sweden by way of the five critical incidents demonstrates how difference and similarity were created, maintained and contested, but also how the dismantling of gender differences came to be enacted and socially

configured in space and time by either firm and closed, or more open and broadened symbolic and social boundaries. The start for the gender-divergent PE culture was the building, not crossing, of boundaries, which the female physical educators prioritized and obviously regarded as the most strategic way to secure 'a me-too' scenario, be admitted, become part of the field of physical culture and avoid a gymnastics proletariat. The first priority was to create a stable and robust platform and the second was to receive recognition from the surrounding society, both were to be achieved by breaking the male knowledge monopoly. By this the feeling of self-identity and self-worth could be defined, accepted and given recognition. It was through this process that the female PE culture took off and gradually broadened aspects of what femininity could embrace. Bodily training helped to extend perceptions of femininity. The developing of a new form of educational movement culture came to include both separate views on pedagogy and different forms of bodily practices based on a separate rationale for the physical training of body and mind. There was a shifting of symbolic boundaries even though the social boundary was kept, with a continued gender-divergent PE culture.

With the loss of the strong medical connotations represented by remedial gymnastics and the effects of the Second World War, new scientific truths for the education and training of the body were sought and the boundaries of the gender-divergent PE culture started to change. The academization process of the PETE programme enforced this change. This new landscape required a new boundary drawing in terms of what the shared gender-neutral symbolic resources should, or could, be to support gender enactment and a gender-neutral PE culture. The above-described consequences of the social construction of a gender-neutral PE culture and the merging of cultures point to a slow-but-still ongoing phase of dissolving symbolic and social boundaries. But the crossing and shifting of boundaries also suggest that after the merging male supremacy had been reinforced in terms of the underpinning rationales for physical cultures linked to what and how to teach and assess in PE, and why.

Concluding thoughts

This explorative literature overview has its limitations. Although the inductive approach taken has highlighted important events, interpreted as critical incidents, each may need more investigation for further areas of inquiry to examine the complexity of the crossing of boundaries and the sharing of a gender-neutral PE culture. To take the next step towards a more capacious home for different dimensions and spaces within physical cultures seems to have to encompass a broadening view of how the 'doing of gender' can be enacted and constructed. To avoid a future persistent PE culture where certain normative regulations and practices continue to create gender differences, there are reasons to explore the society–body–school nexus (Shilling 2010), and to shift focus to the properties and content of boundary drawings, to the actions and events that constitute bodies, embodiment and inequality. One could also claim, as Pfister (2010) suggests, that the gender enactment in the sports field is presently more subtle, and that this is the case too in PETE and school PE (Larsson et al. 2010; Redelius and Larsson 2010). We need to focus more on what we perform and how the body can be used and less on who we are or what we have. This is a challenging departure point and requires a 'critically gender-sensitive' approach, regardless of gender, and at the same time an awareness of the social and cultural conditions that have an impact on PE practice – and to *challenge* such prejudice. To be 'critically gender sensitive' would also entail adopting a critical approach to scientific research that is often systematically grounded in epistemological starting points where men, or the category 'male', are the norm, or the 'independent variable', to speak the language of statistics. It must be emphasized that scientific research might be a double-edged sword in the pursuit of a gender-equitable PE culture, should it not consciously embrace a critical gender-sensitive perspective. Going for a gender-neutral physical education culture in the future seems to require our ability to both be gender sensitive and gender bend in order to transgress traditional gender order. To recall and learn from the history of a gender-divergent PE culture opens up for ways of thinking of how the field of PETE and PE draws its boundaries and by what properties and symbolic resources gender enactment is signified.

Note

1. The female PE pioneers donated money and/or property to women's liberation organizations to be used for the education and preparation of women for working life. Two of several examples are Madame Bergman Österberg, the founder of Dartford College in England, and Elin Falk, one of the founders of the Association of GCI (Föreningen GCI).

Disclosure statement

No potential conflict of interest was reported by the author.

References

Carli, Barbro. 1995. "Myt och verklighet: Könsperspektiv på ämnet Idrott och Hälsa [Myth and Reality: A Gender Perspective on the Subject Physical Education and Health]." *Tidskrift i Gymnastik och Idrott* 7: 26–37.

Carli, Barbro. 1997. "The Female PE-culture: Is there Anything Worth Rebirth for Tomorrow?" *Föreningen GCI årsskrift* [The Annual Book of the Association GCI 1997], 8–16.

Carli, Barbro. 2004. "The Making and Breaking of the Female Culture. The History of Swedish Physical Education 'in a Different Voice'." PhD diss., Gothenburg University, Gothenburg.

Cope, Jason, and Gerald Watts. 2000. "Learning by Doing – An Exploration of Experience, Critical Incidents and Reflection in Entrepreneurial Learning." *International Journal of Entrepreneurial Behaviour & Research* 6 (3): 104–124. doi:10.1108/13552550010346208.

Drakenberg, Sten, Carl Hjort, Einar Nerman, Astley Levin, and Esther Svalling. 1913. *Kungliga Gymnastiska Centralinstitutets historia 1813–1913* [The History of the Royal Gymnastics Central Institute 1813–1913]. Stockholm: Kungliga Gymnastiska Centralinstitutet.

Eichberg, Henrich and Sigmund Loland. 2010. "Nordic Sports – From Social Movements via Emotional Bodily Movement – And Back Again." *Sport in Society: Culture, Commerce, Media, Politics* 13 (4): 679–690. doi:10.1080/17430431003616431.

Falk, Elin. 1908. *Reseminnen och reformtankar* [Travelling Memories and Reform Thoughts]. The Annual Book of the Association GCI 1907. Stockholm: P. Palmquists aktiebolag.

Falk, Elin. 1913. *Gymnastikfrågan vid Stockholms folkskolor* [The Question of Pedagogical Gymnastics in Stockholm's Elementary Schools]. Stockholm: Palmquists AB.

Falk, E. 1927. *Gymnastik med lek och idrott* [Gymnastics with Play and Sport]. Stockholm: PA. Norstedts & Söners Förlag.

Flanagan, John C. 1954. "The Critical Incident Technique." *Psychological Bulletin* 51 (4): 327–358. doi:10.1037/h0061470.

Fletcher, Sheila. 1984. *Women First: The Female Tradition in English Physical Education 1880–1980*. London: Athlone Press.

Forsman, Cecilia, and Kerstin Moberg. 1990. *Rytmikens inträde i den svenska gymnastiken* [The Introduction of Rhythmics in Swedish Gymnastics]. Idrottslärarlinjen 1990:6. Stockholm: Gymnastik- och idrottshögskolan.

Foucault, Michel. 1980. *Power/Knowledge: Selected Interviews and Other Writings 1972–1977*. New York: Pantheon.

Halldén, Olle. 1996. *Vandringsboken: En femtioårig brevväxling mellan kvinnor* [A Wanders Book: A Fifty Year Exchange of Letters Between Women]. Stockholm: HLS Förlag.

Hardman, Ken, and Ken Green. 2011. *Contemporary Issues in Physical Education*. Maidenhead: Meyer & Meyer Sport.

Hargreaves, Jennifer. 1994. *Sporting Females: Critical Issues in the History and Sociology of Women's Sports*. London: Routledge.

Heywood, Colin. 2001. *A History of Childhood: Children and Childhood in the West from Medieval Time to Modern times*. Cambridge: Polity.

Hugosson, Pernilla. 2002. *Hundra år med Föreningen GCI-GIH: en studie om Föreningen GCI-GIH:s kurs- och föredragsverksamhet under fyra olika tidspe rioder* [A Century with the Association of GCI: A Study of Conducted Courses and Lectures during Four Different Time Periods]. Examensarbete 2002:15. Stockholm: Idrottshögskolan.

Kirk, David. 2010. *Physical Education Futures*. London: Routledge.

Korsgaard, Ove. 1989. "Fighting for Life: From Ling and Grundtvig to Nordic Visions of Body Culture." *Scandinavian Journal of Sports Sciences* 11 (1): 3–7.

Laine, Leena. 1989. "In Search of a Physical Culture for Women – Women's Movement and Culture in Everyday Life; Elli Björstén's Heritage Today." *Scandinavian Journal of Sports Sciences* 11 (1): 15–27.

Lamont, Michèle, and Viràg Molnár. 2002. "The Study of Boundaries in the Social Sciences." *Annual Review of Sociology* 28: 167–195. doi:10.1146/annurev.soc.28.110601.141107.

Larsson, Håkan, Birgitta Fagrell, Susanne Johansson, Suzanne Lundvall, Jane Meckbach, and Karin Redelius. 2010. *På pojkarnas planhalva? – ämnet idrott och hälsa ur ett jämställdhets- och likvärdighetsperspektiv* [On the Boys' Half of the Pitch? Physical Education from an Equity -and Equivalent Perspective]. Rapport 2010: 355. Skolverket [The Swedish National Agency of Education].

Larsson, Håkan, and Suzanne Lundvall. 2014. "Who Decides How Sportswomen Should Look and Behave? Towards a Gender Sensitive Critical Approach." In *Women and Sports*. Scientific Report Series, No. 1. Stockholm: SISU idrottsböcker. http://www.sisuidrottsbocker.se/Global/Kvinnor%20 och%20idrott/WomenAndSport_1_2.pdf.

Lindroth, Jan. 2004. *Ling – från storhet till upplösning i svensk gymnastikhistoria 1800–1950* [Ling – From Grandness to Decline in Swedish History of Gymnastics]. Eslöv: Brutus Östlings bokförlag Symposion.

Ling, Per Henrik. (1840) 1979. *Gymnastikens allmänna grunder* [The General Foundation of Gymnastics]. Facsimile ed. Stockholm: Svenska Gymnastikförbundet.

Ljunggren, Jens. 2000. "The Masculine Road through Modernity: Ling Gymnastics and Male Socialization in Nineteenth-century Sweden." In *Making European Masculinities: Sport, Europe, Gender*, edited by James Anthony Mangan. Vol. 2, 86–111. European Sports History Review. London: Frank Cass.

Ljunggren, Jens. 2013. "Gymnastik, nation och manlighet – grundandet av Gymnastiska Central institutet 1813 [Gymnastics, Nation and Manliness – The Foundation of the Royal Gymnastics Central Institute 1813]." In *200 år av kroppsbildning: Gymnastiska Centralinstitutet/Gymnastik- och idrottshögskolan 1813–2013* [Two Hundred Years of Bodily Schooling: The Royal Gymnastics Central Institute 1813–2013], edited by Hans Bolling and Leif Yttergren, 59–75. Stockholm: GIH.

Lundquist Wanneberg, Pia. 2013. "Falk, GCI och föreställningar om barnet – en analys av gymnastikstriden vid Stockholms folkskolor 1910–1913." [Falk, GCI and Notions of the Child – An Analysis of the Battle of Gymnastics at Stockholm Elementary Schools.] In *200 år Av Kroppsbildning: Gymnastiska Centralinstitutet/ Gymnastik- Och Idrottshögskolan 1813–2013* [Two Hundred Years of Bodily Schooling: The Royal Gymnastics Central Institute 1813–2013], edited by Hans Bolling and Leif Yttergren, 109–130. Stockholm: GIH.

Lundvall, Suzanne, and Jane Meckbach. 2003. "Ett ämne i rörelse – gymnastik för kvinnor och män i lärarutbildningen vid Gymnastiska Centralinstitutet/Gymnastik- och idrottshögskolan under åren 1944–1992." [A Subject in Motion – Gymnastics in the PETE Program at the Royal Central Institute of Gymnastics/GIH during the Period 1944–1992.] PhD diss., Stockholm University, Stockholm.

Lundvall, Suzanne, and Jane Meckbach. 2004. "Fritt, roligt och omväxlande! Lärares bakgrund och tankar om sitt yrke." [It's Free, Fun and Changing and Varying! Teachers Background and Reflections on the PE-profession.] *Svensk Idrottsforskning* 4: 21-26.

Lundvall, Suzanne, and Jane Meckbach. 2013. "Pionjärer med moraliskt mod – ett sekel med en kvinnlig lärarutbildning i kroppsövning." [Pioneers with Moral Courage – A Century with a Female Teacher Education in Bodily Exercise.] In *200 år av kroppsbildning: Gymnastiska Centralinstitutet/ Gymnastik- och idrottshögskolan 1813-2013* [Two Hundred Years of Bodily Schooling: The Royal Gymnastics Central Institute 1813-2013], edited by Bolling, Hans and Leif Yttergren, 161-185. Stockholm: GIH.

Lundvall, Suzanne, and Peter Schantz. 2013. "Physical Activities and Their Relation to Physical Education: A 200-Year Perspective and Future Challenges." *Global Journal of Health and Physical Education Pedagogy* 2 (1): 1-16.

Mangan, James A. 2010. "Social Darwinism and Upper-class Education in Late Victorian and Edwardian England." *The International Journal of the History of Sport* 27 (1-2): 78-97. doi:10.1080/09523360903339106.

Morgan, William J. 2006. "Philosophy and Physical Education." In *Handbook of Physical Education*, edited by David Kirk, Doune Macdonald, and Mary O'Sullivan, 97-108. London: Sage.

Norberg, J. 2004. *Idrottens väg till folkhemmet. Studier i statlig idrottspolitik 1913-1970* [Sports Way Into the Welfare State. Studies in State Sport Policy]. Stockholm: SISU idrottsböcker.

Olofsson, Eva. 2005. "The Discursive Construction of Gender in Physical Education in Sweden, 1945-2003: Is Meeting the Learner's Needs Tantamount to Meeting the Market's Needs?" *European Physical Education Review* 11 (3): 219-238. doi:10.1177/1356336X05056648.

Olofsson, Eva. 2007. "The Swedish Sports Movement and the PE Teacher 1940-2003: From Supporter to Challenger." *Scandinavian Journal of Educational Research* 51 (2): 163-183. doi:10.1080/00313830701191647.

O'Sullivan, Mary, Kim Bush, and Margaret Gehring. 2002. "Gender Equity and Physical Education: A USA Perspective." In *Gender and Physical Education: Contemporary Issues and Future Directions*, edited by Dawn Penney, 163-189. London: Routledge.

Ottosson, Anders. 2005. "Sjukgymnasten – vart tog han vägen? En undersökning av sjukgymnastyrkets maskulinisering och avmaskulinisering 1813-1934." [The Physiotherapists – What Happened to Him? A Study of the Masculinization and De- Masculinization of the Physiotherapy Profession1813-1934.] PhD diss., Acta Universitatis Gothoburgensis, Gothenburg.

Palmblad, Eva, and Bengt Erik Eriksson. 1995. *Kropp och politik: Hälsoupplysningen som samhällspegel från 30-tal till 90-tal* [Body and Politics: The Health Enlightenment from the 1930s to the 1990s as a Mirror of Society]. Stockholm: Carlssons.

Pfister, Gertrude. 1999. "Physical Education from a Male Domain to a Female Profession. The Controversy over Women as Physical Educators in Germany (1880-1914)." In *Gender & Sport from European Perspectives*, edited by Else Trangbæck and Arnd Krüger, 69-82. Viborg: Olesen Offset.

Pfister, Gertrude. 2003. "Cultural Confrontations: German Turnen, Swedish Gymnastics and English Sport – European Diversity in Physical Activities from a Historical Perspective." *Culture, Sport, Society* 6 (1): 61-91.

Pfister, G. 2010. "Women in Sport – Gender Relations and Future Perspectives." *Sport in Society* 13 (2): 234-248. doi:10.1080/17430430903522954.

Redelius, Karin, and Håkan Larsson. 2010. "Physical Education in Scandinavia: An Overview and Some Educational Challenges." *Sport in Society* 13 (4): 691-703. doi:10.1080/17430431003616464.

Scraton, Sheila. 1992. *Shaping up to Womanhood: Gender and Girls' Physical Education*. Buckingham: Open University Press.

Shilling, Chris. 2010. "Exploring the Society–Body–School Nexus: Theoretical and Methodology Issues in the Study of Body Pedagogics." *Sport, Education and Society* 15 (2): 51-167. doi:10.1080/13573321003683786.

Skolinspektionen [Swedish Schools Inspectorate]. 2010. *Mycket idrott och lite hälsa. Skolinspektionens rapport från den flygande tillsynen i idrott och hälsa* [A Lot of Sports and Little Health. Report from the Flying Inspection of the Swedish Schools Inspectorate]. Rapport 2010:2037. Stockholm.

The Annual Book of the Association GCI. 1902. *Föreningen GCI:s årsbok* [Annual Book]. Stockholm: GIH Library.

Tinning, Richard. 2010. *Pedagogy and Human Movement: Theory, Practice and Research*. London: Routledge.

Trangbæck, Else. 1999. "'Purity of Heart and Strength of Will'. The Role of Female Teachers in Modern Sports Movement." In *Gender & Sport from European Perspectives*, edited by Else Trangbæck and Arnd Krüger, 43–67. Viborg: Olesen Offset.

Vertinsky, Patricia. 1999. "Gender Relations, Physical Education and Sport History: Is It Time for a Collaborative Research Agenda?" In *Gender & Sport from European Perspectives*, edited by Else Trangbæck and Arnd Krüger, 13–27. Viborg: Olesen Offset.

Vertinsky, Patricia. 2009. "Transatlantic Traffic in Expressive Movement: From Delsarte and Dalcroze to Margaret H'Doubler and Rudolf Laban." *The International Journal of the History of Sport* 26 (13): 2031–2051. doi:10.1080/09523360903148879.

Vertinsky, Patricia. 2010. "From Physical Educators to Mothers of the Dance: Margaret H'Doubler and Martha Hill." *The International Journal of the History of Sport* 27 (7): 1113–1132. doi:10.1080/09523361003695785.

Wikström, Louise. 1908. "Professor E. Jaques-Dalcroze's Rytmiska Gymnastik." [Professor E. Jaques-Dalcroze's Rhythmical Gymnastics]. *Föreningen GCI:s årsskrift* [The Annual Book of the Association GCI 1907], 68–74. Stockholm: P. Palmquists aktiebolag.

Wikström, Louise. 1936. "Rytmikens genombrott i gymnastiken." *Föreningen GCI:s årsskrift* [The Annual Book of the Association of GCI 1936], 43–46. Stockholm: Bröderna Siösteens boktryckning.

Wright, Jan. 1996. "Mapping Discourses of Physical Education: Articulating a Female Tradition." *Journal of Curriculum Studies* 28 (3): 331–351. doi:10.1080/0022027980280306.

History of Swiss feminine gymnastics between competition and feminization (1950–1990)

Grégory Quin

International Centre for Sports History and Culture, De Montfort University, Leicester, UK

ABSTRACT
Between 1908 and 1985 in Switzerland, there was a clear division between female and male national gymnastics associations. Beyond some links, the two institutions conducted their own policies and promoted their own practices and forms of gymnastics. They made different choices in the 1960s and 1970s, and on the whole female gymnastics saw greater changes and was more innovative, with the emergence of rhythmic gymnastics as a 'flagship' competitive discipline, early experiences in modern physical culture and fitness, etc. Across these developments, this article analyses successively the conditions of the preservation of control over female gymnastics in the 1950s, how those gymnasts and the female national association's leaders used their institutional autonomy to develop many practical innovations and break technical and institutional boundaries during the 1960s and 1970s, before managing the reunification process with male gymnastics, and facing new symbolic boundaries.

Introduction

> ... I was really disappointed ... by the tendency to make women become men. 'Acting' as a man, wearing the same clothes, smoking as much as him, is surely in better taste for Occidental women.
>
> This tendency to 'masculinity', evoking the desire to struggle, and the appetite for wrestling, calling for power and strength as tool for domination, tends to destroy our own house: gymnastics and sport. (*Education Physique Féminine*, June 15, 1952)

As a proof of the importance of gymnastics in Switzerland, a male-only Société Fédérale de Gymnastique (SFG) has existed since 1832. It was founded before the creation of a modern federal State, which originated with the Constitution of 1848. Since then, the country has never ceased to cultivate its original model of physical culture with a compelling domination of gymnastics (Burgener 1952), as a part of the training of future citizen-soldiers but also as a matrix of an 'imagined community' (Anderson 1991), where people share values, representations and rights without knowing most of their fellow-member, and more especially for Switzerland where boundaries between men and women has remained an effective organizational principle until the second half of the twentieth century.

Originally an entirely masculine sport, gymnastics saw the emergence of feminine practices promoted by physicians and pedagogues at the end of the nineteenth century (Craig 2013),[1] when modern sports were also beginning to be developed and diffused all over the country, and some conflicts occurred between the two models of physical activities (Bussard 2007). If many Helvetic citizens were also soon involved in the spread of modern sports across Europe, especially masculine football (Koller 2010), some were also promoting pedagogical innovations, for example Jaques–Dalcroze's 'eurhythmics' in Geneva.

As in other European countries (Pfister 2013), the feminization of Swiss gymnastics accelerated during the first years of the twentieth century and an Association Suisse de Gymnastique Féminine (ASGF) was created in 1908. In Switzerland an institutional distinction remained between the ASGF and the men's organization, the SFG, until the 1980s both at a national and at a cantonal level. This creates a unique situation for historians interested in gender and sport history, since Swiss feminine and masculine gymnastics slowly developed a kind of internal competition between them. During the twentieth century, female gymnastics developed from within an autonomous institution, which became the main sporting federation in the country by the beginning of the 1980s in terms of the number of active members.

Framework and hypothesis

This paper is written as part of a larger research project exploring history of rhythmic gymnastics in Europe since the middle of the twentieth century, and partially supported by the French Olympic Committee through a research grant (Quin 2014b). Our project, which is firstly an attempt to gather original documents about female gymnastics, is from then on underpinned by a substantial documentary source base covering various levels of the development of female gymnastics in Europe (local, national and international), since the official recognition of the practice by the International Federation of Gymnastics (IFG) in the early 1960s, including documents from Bulgaria, Romania, France, Germany, Portugal, Italy and Switzerland. Thus, our ambition is to reveal how an only women sport can expand and shift gender boundaries (Lamont and Molnár 2002), while using masculine symbol or characteristic like competition and preserving stereotypes about femininity.

In Switzerland more precisely, we draw on printed documents from local clubs, from cantonal federations, but also very broadly from the SFG and the ASGF (minutes, annual reports, official bulletins, correspondence, status, etc.). Besides, we also use sources (all printed documents consulted comprehensively) from the IFG (minutes, technical report, official bulletins, etc.), from the Swiss Ecole Fédérale de Gymnastique et de Sport (EFGS: where individuals and groups are trained since the 1960s), and we have made some 'life stories' interviews with all the national trainers (and their assistants) since 1974 (five interviews), all the technical directors and/or presidents (three interviews for rhythmic gymnastics especially) and all the administrative officers (five interviews) from both federations (male and female), but also more randomly some former gymnasts and local trainers, for a total of 30 interviews conducted in Switzerland (between 2012 and 2014).

Many hypothesises inform our analysis of the rise – and its obstacles – of female gymnastics; the idea that competition is 'essentially' masculine, the supposed greater creativity of feminine gymnastics – for instance around the development of 'rhythmic gymnastics'[2] – but also the idea that women used gymnastics as a social space where they could shape greater autonomy (given that the political vote was granted to Swiss women only in 1971) in a country where a conservative vision of women's role and status will remain more efficient until the end of the twentieth century (Studer 1996). As the archives are numerous in Switzerland some historical works, like those by Burgener (1952) or more recently Bussard (2007), are well documented and integrate some small gender perspectives on physical education at school, while Monica Aceti and Christophe Jaccoud provide a more sociological collective book (2012). However, Bussard and Burgener both stop their analysis around the Second World War, so the whole second half of the twentieth century remains widely unexplored even though it is a crucial period regarding the inclusion of women into the sport system and the transformation of gender norms and practices. Furthermore, Swiss sport history suffers from a lack of interest in archival research, mainly due to the recentness of the emergence of sport science departments – in several universities: Lausanne, Neuchâtel, Zurich or Basel – since the 1990s, and especially around gymnastics, which remained the national sport and the biggest federation in the country. It explains the absence of chapters focused on the Swiss case in many books analysing gender issues in sport (Hartmann–Tews and Pfister 2003; Bruce, Hovden, and Markula 2010). Besides, some 'historical works' about gymnastics are themselves questionable as they sometimes produce nonsense and incomprehension about some practices (Manidi 2002), in spite of initial good intentions. Eva Herzog's work is an exception, but it is focused on one canton (Basel) and thus is less effective for the country overall (Herzog 1995).

Within this framework, this article tries to combine an institutional history of female gymnastics in a country where it is considered as a 'national sport' and an analysis of the processes leading to the recognition of an only women competitive discipline to understand the way it challenges structural and symbolic boundaries in a particular society, both within female activities and also in their relation with male sports. Successively, this article analyses the conditions of the preservation of control over female gymnastics and more broadly over women by banning competition in the 1950s, and further it explores how female gymnasts and the ASGF leaders used their institutional autonomy to develop many practical innovations and break technical and symbolic boundaries during the 1960s and 1970s, even though it leads them to promote a practice that is highly feminine in its visual code. More concretely, our aim is then to use the ASGF as a case study, to demonstrate links between the transformations of mentalities, representations and practices, especially when, as part of the subsequent reunification process within Swiss gymnastics, gender boundaries became no longer 'institutional' but (again) symbolic, without losing any of their effectiveness (Lamont and Molnár 2002).

1950–1966: Barring women from competition

Since the late-nineteenth century, Swiss feminine gymnastics have been based on ideas of moderation and control rather than emancipation (Herzog 1995). They are deeply rooted in an 'imagined community' made of conservative values and representations, which places women in restricted social spaces and roles, but are also linked with larger continental processes (Pfister 2013). Inside all the clubs affiliated to ASGF, competition was forbidden from the creation of the institution in 1908. This was re-emphasized in a text promoted by the general assembly of 1950, which took place in Glaris (ASGF 1983). Actually, this position was also nurtured by a rich iconography showing women in stereotypical poses and practices, performing collective exercises in front of mountain landscapes, which are themselves part of a nationalism forged in the cult of a 'primitive' Switzerland arisen from the Alps (Kriesi and Trechsel 2008).

If some critical voices were already heard in the 1940s and despite some debates in the 1950s – especially when the city of Basel hosted the World Championships for Artistic Gymnastics where no Swiss women participated – the official ASGF position endorsed a vision of the fit, graceful female body as symbolizing the nation and also as indicative of women's place in Helvetic society in the 1950s. Actually, the resolution voted by the general assembly in Glaris clarifies that the:

> ... ASGF wants, chiefly, [to] bring the Swiss woman to have better physical health and also a good moral and spiritual balance through reasoned and reasonable practice of games and physical exercises. On the other hand, it considers that preparing and training girls for big athletic events is a huge mistake. (*Education Physique Féminine*, November 15, 1950)

The ASGF's view was not exceptional in Switzerland, where physical education was not compulsory for girls in every canton in the 1950s and where the hygienic and moral ambition of female exercises influenced literally the whole Swiss sports field, drastically limiting women's access to international competitions in all sports.

Besides, both for men and women, elite (competitive) sport had only limited support from the State in the 1950s, in spite of reforms following the poor results of Swiss athletes at the Berlin Olympics in 1936 (Favre 2004). As a consequence, public interest was only important for some international football matches, and specifically around 'national games' (hornuss, stone throw (traditional shot put) or Swiss wrestling) and gymnastics events, like the Fête Fédérale de Gymnastique organized every four, five or six years, and whose 'feminine section' also forbade competition until the 1960s (Herzog 1995). Nevertheless, thanks to the organization of events like the gymnastics World Championships in Basel (1950) or the football World Cup (1954), public opinion became more engaged with the highest sporting level and came to appreciate that despite ideological speeches about the dangers of sporting excess, those practices could also have certain virtues, including for women.

Nevertheless, at the onset of the 1960s, mentalities within gymnastics societies and organizations were still quite reluctant, not to say resistant, towards the idea of authorizing competition for women and all its potential excesses and endangerments of their bodies. In an interview, published in the ASGF's official bulletin, Charles Moret, who was also a member of the Central Board, recalled that 'the idea which presided over the foundation of the Swiss Association [was to]: "develop women's physical strength and spread physical exercises. Through physical exercise, it look[ed] for the harmonious development of the body, spirit, soul"' (*Education Physique Féminine*, April 15, 1960, 26).

In some ways, the debates around the question of giving women the right to vote presented similar arguments, when mentioning that the 'right place for women is at home', and that 'the disaggregation of the family is due to the emancipation of the women, more occupied outside their house' (Studer 1996, 369). Such very conservative viewpoints were broadly shared within the elite governing physical and gymnastic activities in Switzerland at that period, even across a split between defenders of modern sports and proponents of gymnastics, which had been in contention since the early twentieth century (Bussard 2007).

Lastly, but significantly, until the 1960s the ASGF's Central Board and many committees still consisted of men, whose activities and gendered representations contribute to the preservation of a 'conservative' frame around Swiss female gymnastics. In the mid-1960s, positions and representations started to change very slowly, creating the conditions for the emergence of new possibilities for women in sport. So in 1964, on the occasion of a symposium organized in the Swiss 'College' of Sport in Macolin, participants were requested to address the theme: 'Should young women devote themselves to sport and gymnastics?' It is notable that this was still phrased as a question, demonstrating the trouble caused by this topic in a society that still refused women the right to vote at the federal level (Studer 1996).

The same year, the Olympic Games in Innsbruck are a turning point for the development of the Helvetic 'sports field', as the delegation returned without any medals, a situation that initiated more serious discussions about opportunities to reform the sport system. Early consequences of those debates were the creation of a National Committee for Elite Sport (CNSE), an increase of the federal subvention to national federations and more significantly the constitutional and legislative modifications of the years 1970–1975, which would make physical education compulsory for girls in all the cantons. The ambition was to empower elite athletes in the key disciplines, but at the same time without losing sight of mass sports and gymnastics, including at schools (Quin 2014a).

At the same time, in 1966, the question of letting women participate in gymnastics competitions returned to the forefront during an ASGF cantonal presidents' conference, which recognized the liberty of each member to practice competitive gymnastics (ASGF, Central Committee, May 20, 1966). In the book published on the occasion of the ASGF's seventy-fifth birthday, a few years later, the authors make this position clear, explaining that, 'at the time, the public and the younger gymnasts could no longer understand our attitude, even if it was based on valid ethical and medical considerations' (ASGF 1983). Thus, ethical and medical boundaries stayed firm, but the desires of a younger generation started to weaken them.

Besides this new position, inside the national institution as inside local societies, the situation remained complex, also because of the administrative hierarchy that existed between the ASGF and SFG, where SFG remained the only Swiss institution recognized by the IFG and was thus responsible for the registration of Swiss gymnasts for every international competition. As usual in Switzerland and after the ASGF allowed their better gymnasts to participate in competition (a decision made at the General Assembly of November 1966), a consensus emerged whereby the SFG was recognized by contract as 'responsible for the training of elite female gymnasts' (ASGF, Central Committee, May 15, 1966) and their registration for competitions for artistic gymnastics. While allowing competitive practice, this 'delegation of power' was also an opportunity for the women's institution not to speak too much about its new arrangement on competition, as opponents were still active and numerous.

1966–1974: Between competitions and innovations

While the opposition to women's participation in sporting competitions tells us a lot about the long-term 'conservative' vision of women in Helvetic society, there is also behind this opposition another characteristic of the Swiss sports field, namely a real distrust of elite sport due to a worship of amateurism, which prevailed for a long time during the twentieth century (Vonnard and Quin 2012). In an article published in 1968 in the ASGF's official bulletin, an official regrets the period:

> ... when our competitors were fighting with others from other nations, trained in conditions more or less similar, who did not place training before their jobs and also who did not consider the national prestige as so important. At that time, there were only few 'state' amateurs.
> (*Education Physique Féminine*, October 15, 1968, 98)

During the second half of the 1960s, as discussions about the restructuring of the Swiss sport system continued, authorities were also committed to 'recognize female gymnastics as an advanced requirement' (*Education Physique Féminine*, February 15, 1969, 14) and establish compulsory physical education in primary and secondary schools all over the country.

At the same time, and far from taking the increasing membership as an end in itself, the ASGF encouraged innovation and diversification of its activities, taking advantage of the effervescence of 'youth' in those years (Klimke and Scharloth 2008) and its desire for new activities. If competition was now possible, the subordination to SFG did not completely satisfy the leaders of the women's association, like Anna Grob, technical president from 1965, who argued in favour of the participation of ASGF gymnasts at the 1969 Modern Gymnastics World Championships, in Varna (Bulgaria) (ASGF, Central Committee, July 11, 1968). This form of gymnastics, exclusively feminine, based on music, choreography and work on rhythm (Langlade 1966), could contribute to create a special practice for the institution – hence separate from SFG's guardianship – and was also seen as something that could be positively considered by proponents of a more traditional gymnastics, while promoting an acceptable and traditional vision of femininity.

Thus, regarding those processes, innovation around competition and specialized practices was not the only horizon for the leaders, as they continued actively to promote the mass practices more deeply rooted in the traditional mode of feminine activities. In 1969 they organized a jubilee for the twenty-fifth anniversary of the creation of a special category of young gymnasts ('Pupillettes') and the fifth Gymnastraeda in Basel. If the latter was not an entirely 'feminine' event, it was a sort of incarnation of the changes happening inside female gymnastics, because though the event did not include competitions or rankings, it created some opportunities for demonstrations of the new way of doing gymnastics (Meckbach and Lundquist Wanneberg 2011).

At the beginning of the 1970s, as competition had been recognized and authorized, even if it was under the supervision of the SFG for training and athletes' preparation, the ASGF came to develop its own elite practice. As the SFG presented female gymnasts for the first time at the highest level,[3] the leaders of women's associations made the choice to develop 'modern gymnastics' as their specific form of elite gymnastics. Formal organization began in 1970 when a 'demonstration group from the ASGF' went to Rio de Janeiro to participate in an international festival of modern gymnastics (*Education Physique Féminine*, February 15, 1971, 14). The event was not competitive, just an occasion to discover new practice and 'to experiment [with] continuous movements, precision and gestural elegance, and musical arrangement' (*Education Physique Féminine*, February 15, 1971, 16). A few months later, again outside any formal competition, the committee for mass gymnastics organized two courses in modern gymnastics, the first surprisingly supervised by a man: Fernando Dâmaso. A Portuguese physical education teacher, embodied in a Latin culture, he was about to become the main innovator in a women's institution that though previously very conservative was contending with changing times and was now administered only by women. Thus, it is important to emphasize that the accession of women at all the main ASGF's governing functions leaded to the promotion of an activity presenting all the characteristics of the traditional ways of thinking female bodies.

Having first attended the Swiss Sport College in Magglingen in the late-1950s, Dâmaso obtained his degree at the German Sport College in Cologne between 1954 and 1957, where he learned gymnastic practice from Medau and Bode, before contributing to the diffusion of modern gymnastics in Portugal during the 1960s (Interview with Fernando Dâmaso, former Swiss national coach, October 18, 2012).

From then on, the major turning point in the institutionalization of modern gymnastics in Switzerland, as in many countries, was the 'ASGF's official observation mission' sent to the modern gymnastics World Championships in Rotterdam, in November 1973. Anne–Lyse Fragnière – president of the committee for non-competitive gymnastics – went together with Fernando Dâmaso, to study the highest level of practice and to imagine possibilities to develop it back in Switzerland. After Prague, Budapest, Copenhagen, Varna and La Havana (in 1971), Rotterdam was the first competition to be organized in western Europe, and it was a 'shock' both for the participants and the spectators; Jenny Candeias – sent by the Portuguese federation to study the practice – told us about the tears running down Dâmaso's face during the Bulgarian exercise (Interview with Jenny Candeias, former Portuguese international judge, March 27, 2013), and as Dominique Muller (present on behalf of the French federation) also told us, she felt similar (Interview with Dominique Muller-Lauth, former French Technical president, January 12, 2013).

Returning from Holland, the two Swiss observers were soon able to share this enthusiasm by introducing the practice within local clubs and creating the condition of a national recognition by the ASGF. Not later than 2 February 1974, they showed some movies taken in Rotterdam to demonstrate the specificity of modern gymnastics to cantonal technical presidents, though their first reaction was one of the hesitation, because of 'the possible saturation of the gymnastics scene and more especially about difficulties to find trainers and instructor[s] for this new practice, above all in the smallest clubs' (ASGF, Technical Committee Minutes, February 2, 1974, 5). There were still residues of old ways of thinking and reservations around the 'modernity' of 'modern gymnastics' in particular its competitiveness and its specificity regarding the duration of the trainings. Dâmaso immediately tried to reassure his audience, by proposing they start with an 'experimental group', whose first mission would be to contribute to the diffusion of the practice in the country, after a basic training under his own supervision. He also emphasized that this development should not signify 'the rapid production of an elite group', and that 'each participant will be selected after the end of her mandatory school period' (ASGF, Technical Committee Minutes, February 2, 1974, 6).

At the beginning, between February and August, the idea was to gather in Magglingen, all the young women interested in the new practice and to select an 'experimental group' of women from 18 to 26 years old. This process culminated on 14 and 15 December 1974 with the official selection, during which Dâmaso examined the apparatus and rhythmic work, strength, flexibility and mobility, and also at some specific modern gymnastics exercises.

1974–1985: On the international scene

In spite of Dâmaso's initial promises, the experimental group quickly became involved in international competitions, even participating at IFG's seventh World Championship in Madrid in November 1975. The situation was then quite unique in sports history, with a national team competing before there were any gymnasts in local clubs. It was especially significant for the ASGF, since the international team was organized under its own banner.

It is therefore all the experiences and practices of a traditional 'school of the body' (Interview with Cathy Fanti, former member of Swiss national team, November 5, 2012), promoted in each ASGF club since the inter-war period, that were the basis of the practice more than any special training or courses given during the previous years, even for Dâmaso who was still a neophyte and met some opposition because he was a man.[4] Those technical underpinnings were enough to earn the Swiss team the 10th place in Madrid. Modern gymnastics was still in some ways imprecise in its rules and in the interpretation made by the judges (Interview with Egle Abruzzini, former IFG technical president, September 24, 2014). Incidentally, the 10th place for a first World Championship can also be explained by the absence of almost all the Soviet countries after the death of Franco several days before the beginning of the competition. The ASGF annual report for 1975 emphasizes that the competitive development of the practice was very important during this second year of its existence on Swiss soil, with one course for the cantonal leaders, four weekends for future trainers, one weekend for future judges and already 27 weekends training for the national team (ASGF, Technical Committee, Annual Report 1976, 6). If Dâmaso's selection was based on physical abilities, it was also motivated by the idea of developing the practice all over the country, which explains why half the team was composed of future physical education teachers (*Frauenturnen*, October 15, 1976, 12–13) from all the education centre in the country (Basel, Zurich, Lausanne, etc.). His ambition was to promote modern gymnastics but also to deal with all the governing levels of the sporting field, as cantonal organizations were still powerful, especially regarding financial support.

A few years after women got the right to vote in Switzerland, modern rhythmic gymnastics saw many social and sporting changes, promoting competition for women but in the meantime maintaining them in a very traditional feminine frame. Quoting words, first published in *24 Heures*, the ASGF official bulletin, *Frauenturnen*, points out the great increase of women's involvement in gymnastics, and that:

> … every man with a normal sexual instinct has to admit that, performance set apart, media coverage of the last Olympic Games in Montreal shows us several beautiful faces and silhouettes, by far more interesting than … the 'fat bottom[s]' that our fellow countrywomen show us at the beach or at the swimming pool. (*Frauenturnen*, November 1, 1976, 7)

A vector of contradictory representations, the article praises both some positive attributes of women involved in competition (voluntarism, resistance, etc.), but also presents them as 'eye candy' to attract men, mostly on the basis of their plastic qualities. The 1970s emancipation of women was evident but ambivalent, both in the sphere of gymnastics and society as a whole. Thus, modern gymnastics is ambivalent as its development resulted from a women initiative but which promoted 'traditional' movements and gestures.

More broadly, those changes are also visible in the wider transformations of the sporting field, where military control of physical education weakened, and the institution 'Jeunesse et Sport' replaced the compulsory 'military instruction'. This allowed girls and young women – as well as boys and young men – to become instructors, facilitating the 'development of women's sport' (interview with Gilberte Gianadda, former Swiss technical president, March 15, 2013), but not any form of coeducation at all, as girls and women were trained for female practices (gymnastics, dance, etc.).

Early involved in Jeunesse et Sport, and the first person in charge of the Gymnastic and Dance branch, Fernando Dâmaso was not only involved in the promotion of competitive gymnastics. He also participated in the first introduction of gym-jazz in Switzerland, a form of practice based on a mixture between gymnastics and dance, executed to jazz music. Considered as a means of expression, gym-jazz can be seen as something near rhythmic gymnastics both in its claims to creativity and its aesthetic dimensions. The aim was to get 'a real preparation for dance ... where the gymnasts will be able to feel self-fulfilment, and where youth will find both health and enjoyment' ('Jeunesse et Sport', Official bulletin of the institution, September 1977, 214). A great success in Switzerland in the second half of the 1970s, those practices prefigured aerobics and fitness, which became very popular about 10 years later and were part of a deep change of physical cultures.

In the meantime, in 1977 Switzerland hosted the eighth rhythmic gymnastics World Championships, two years only after its first participation. In the specific context of the development and the promotion of a new sport, the organization of such a great event was very significant for the national federation, following the Netherlands in 1973 and Spain in 1975, and preceding London in 1979, Munich in 1981, Strasbourg in 1983 and others. In Basel, where the competition was organized, the Swiss group confirmed its 10th place, and Suzanne Zimmermann finished in 39th place. Damasco had completely changed the composition of the group since 1975, calling on a younger generation and returning the girls from the 'experimental group' to their original cantons. Seen as a 'transition year for Rhythmic Gymnastics in Switzerland' (ASGF, Annual Report, 1978, 7), 1977 also saw the ASGF organize a first national tournament (*Eco di Locarno*, March 26, 1977, 9) in March in Sion, though this was not a truly 'national' event since only few clubs were in a position to participate. This competition nevertheless promoted modern gymnastics and specifically encouraged clubs to create dedicated sections (interview with Mariella Markmann, former Swiss national assistant coach, February 21, 2013, 203). Nevertheless, two years later, Fernando Dâmaso still reported that:

> ... the organization of national competition remains a concern. It appears that, besides the clarification made during courses, trainers and clubs are too much influenced by what is done by the national team. They fear this high level. The new organization should allow more space and time to explain how the practice can be progressive. (ASGF, Annual Report, 1979, 10)

From then on, the diffusion inside the country progressed more rapidly, and between 1977 and 1980, a growing number of instructors and trainers discover an interest in rhythmic gymnastics. The practice broke down barriers very quickly, moving the boundaries of Swiss feminine gymnastics towards more physical performance, new structures of training – both with very young children and with adult gymnasts – and towards new body representations, disturbing the dominant model(s) of femininity inside the country and urging the central institution to revise its governance even faster.

It becomes clear that innovation had a cost to the ASGF, whose budget grew rapidly during the 1970s. If in 1970, the budget was balanced around CHF 400,000, it exceeded CHF 1,500,000 at the beginning of the next decade, just before ASGF was reunited with the male institution. A more detailed analysis of those budgets shows that the growth was mainly due to the new 'elite sport' and its organization. In 1977, rhythmic gymnastics were the first budgetary item above CHF 100,000, with a total of CHF 700,000.

Those evolutions also concerned the practice itself as Fernando Dâmaso introduced professionalism among his gymnasts and his team of trainers, breaking another totem of the Swiss sporting field. For the gymnasts, though it did not amount to a concrete salary, it meant that assiduity would be rewarded each season, to compensate expenses incurred by the federation and their family. In its four-year plan for 1985–1988, Dâmaso emphasized that 'it is the role of a federation to promote sport at all levels and, in specific cases, to make more resources available for the better gymnasts, in a way that they can realize their desires' (ASGF, Rhythmic Gymnastics Committee, Training Planification 1985–1988, 8). For the

Table 1. Compared statistics from SFG and ASGF (in 1970 and 1984) (Le Gymnaste Suisse, no. 39, 1970; Le Gymnaste Suisse, no. 19, 1984).

1970	SFG (masculine)	ASGF (feminine)	Total
Youth	42274	39760	82034
Total	120753	103683	224436
1984	SFG	ASGF	Total
Youth	45735	75011	120746
Total	141858	177288	319147

gymnasts, where it was necessary to have a full-time training, many reward systems were tested at the end of the 1970s, such as prize money depending on results, but it remained mainly linked to their presence at each training session. It was never possible to make it like a real salary, as the gymnasts were not of full age, but the gymnasts could repurchase their training hours for CHF 8 each (by their attendance), which means CHF 8000 a year approximately (which is also the estimated level of the annual expenses for such an activity ranging from 15 to 20 h weekly).

If results were not immediately as high as expected – and promised by Fernando Dâmaso – rhythmic gymnastics modified the landscape of Swiss feminine gymnastics, giving a real autonomy to the ASGF even if, around 1980, the leaders of both ASGF and SFG started to discuss more seriously a future reunification of their institutions.

1985–1992: Reunification and new boundaries

Some first attempts were made in the mid-1970s, with a first planning commission, whose report was then sent to the central committees of the two institutions. If the project did not succeed at that time for many reasons, the situation with two separate institutions is presented as:

> … on the one hand, not at all balanced regarding the relative importance of feminine and masculine gymnastics in the country; and on the other hand not fair for equality between women and men. An equality that has become more obvious nowadays … (ASGF, Reunification Commission, October 7, 1975, 9)

Nevertheless, the delegates made no clear proposal on how to resolve the situation and due to a lack of will on both sides the situation did not change. The masculine institution in effect refused to pursue the topic, whereas the leaders of the ASGF pointed out the insufficient guarantees given to feminine practices and their specialisms, adding that they did not want to make the refusal too abrupt, in order not to 'damage the relations with the SFG' (ASGF, Annual Report, 1976, 2). In fact at that period the ASGF outstripped the SFG in terms of its membership and the information (see Table 1). It became the biggest sports federation in the country, and continued the innovation in its speciality feminine gymnastics. Both these developments enhanced the credit of its leaders when in discussion with their male counterparts. At the same period, 10 years after getting the right to vote, feminist movements obtained Constitutional equality between women and men.

It seems then significant that women gymnastics leaders claimed to act without using 'feminist militancy' (ASGF, Annual Report, 1981, 1), underlining again their concern about the balance of power in a new united federation, when in May 1980 discussions began again between the two institutions. After five years of discussions behind the scenes, a more official 'planning commission' started work during the spring, with the mandate to focus especially on the balance of power between feminine and masculine practices (Whitson 1994), and more broadly to secure the place of gymnastics in the Swiss sporting field.

In spite of interesting discussions during the first months and some proposals, the balance of power issue pushed women delegates to refuse temporarily any reunification during the General Assembly of 1982 in Luzern: 'In a future unique association, we [women] will have to make efforts at all times in order to protect the interests of our gymnasts and to continue the promotion of a beautiful and genuine gymnastics, while keeping our femininity' (*Frauenturnen*, March 1, 1983, 5).

Gilberte Gianadda, who represented the ASGF on the planning commission as a vice-president of her own association, told us that the women were genuinely afraid of being relegated to the position of only the 'secretary of the new unified federation' (Interview with Gilberte Gianadda, March 15, 2013). At the same period the SFG was experiencing a crisis of vocation amongst its volunteers, especially locally in the clubs and in the cantonal organizations. But the discussions continued and finally succeeded in 1985. Effective on 1 January 1986, the reunification led to the dissolution of the previous feminine and masculine associations, which were then gathered under the new name of *Fédération Suisse de Gymnastique* (FSG).

In the early 1980s, the ASGF – and soon the FSG – were confronted by a new form of practice, which came directly from the United States and which was going to revolutionize the sporting field and its institutions. Its name? Aerobics. Promoted by film star Jane Fonda, it was soon analysed in every newspaper in the continent as:

> … an endless suite of exercises (no muscle, no ligament, no curves are spared), to be repeated three times a week, by increasing the duration if possible ('each exercises needs to be a new challenge'), whose aim is to burn as many calories as possible, to modify the body shape and to soften it while strengthening heart and lungs. (*Journal de Genève*, January 15, 1983)

Heavily promoted in the media and practised to very fashionable 'disco' music arrangements, aerobics created a major upheaval of the image of women throughout the West and in Switzerland especially. Resolutely modern, aerobics represented several characteristics of its period including individualization, a search for health through physical activities, the unveiling of bodies and a quest for an eternal youth. The inclusion of this practice in the programmes of the Swiss gymnastic clubs was not immediate. This was not least for institutional reasons, as aerobics was something that was initially practiced in front of the television and not within a classic gymnastic club. But the presence of advertisements for equipment and clothes dedicated to aerobics in the official bulletin of the ASGF and FSG (since 1983) shows that the practice was of some interest for the institutions.

In the second half of the 1980s, as aerobics was introduced in the gyms, rhythmic gymnastics came to know its first growing pains. Between 1975 and 1985, Swiss gymnasts were always present for international competitions, including when in 1984, rhythmic gymnastics made its first appearance at the Olympic Games in Los Angeles. Nevertheless, as a national team and as individual competitors, they always remained in the second half of the ranking. As he could not manage to qualify his gymnasts for the 1988 Olympic Games in Seoul, Fernando Dâmaso left office at the end of that year, making necessary the restructuring of the practice at all levels.

Newly associated with trampoline and artistic gymnastics (both feminine and masculine) in an 'elite sports' division of the FSG, rhythmic gymnastics seems nevertheless, in a contradictory way, to have been able to become firmly established in sections of local clubs and even in totally new clubs dedicated to this practice. But as there were no further possibilities to participate in international competitions, some tensions seem evident at the beginning of the 1990s and the process of growth slowed. In 1992, the decision of FSG's Central Committee to cut the budget for rhythmic gymnastics by half, due to the lack of international results, created a first conflict inside FSG. Pointing the relative lack of diffusion inside the country, the delegates tended to emphasize that the fate of the elite sport was not mirrored by the mass participation through local clubs.

Conclusion

Four years after the deletion of half the budget, the threat become more direct, when FSG's Central Committee aimed to abolish the 'elite sport' status of rhythmic gymnastics, because of the continuous lack of results. The sport was in some respects a victim of its greater popularity in the French-speaking part of Switzerland, while the FSG was controlled by delegates from the German-speaking side – a specific case of the very pronounced linguistic cleavage in Switzerland (Chollet 2011). However, rhythmic gymnastics saved itself because of a large mobilization of local clubs, proof of its successful implantation.

If rhythmic gymnastics shifted landmarks of a gendered symbolic and institutional order, through the valuation of competition and of an institutional modernity, the ASGF also remained a vector of a more traditional and conservative discourse about feminine gymnastics until the late-1980s, also promoted by rhythmic gymnastics itself. Thus, boundaries were mainly shifted within women gymnastics, and the masculine domination was never really endangered (Aceti and Jaccoud 2012). After the reunification in 1985, the abolition of the institutional border allowed a new greater efficiency of symbolic boundaries (Barker-Ruchti 2009), drawing on new expressions of gender stereotypes and new distrust of feminine gymnastics. For instance, in the official newspaper of the new federation and even after the integration of several women in the editorial team, female gymnastics was then still presented in a very traditional way – and also practised in the same way, putting attention on non-competitive practices more than on competitive aspects like in rhythmic gymnastics. In the meantime, even if competition is now accessible entirely and if women are more numerous than men during the Fête Fédérale de Gymnastique (since 1991), lots of interviews reaffirming the prime importance of gymnastics as a means of empowering girls and women are also celebrating and justifying a traditional vision of their place and role in society (Swiss television documentary, June 15, 1991, http://www.rts.ch/archives/tv/information/tele-journal/4800452-emancipation-feminine.html).

Far from being a new situation, this sounds like a 'classic' in the history of female sports, as had already happened in the inter-war period, when initiatives from Alice Milliat ended with the integration of women's sports in the Olympic programme and in several international sporting institutions, while failing to make women's sports immediately more legitimate (Pfister 2001).

More broadly, our case study highlights the continuous negotiations that accompanied the transformation of feminine sporting practices in the specific context of a Swiss 'imagined community' balanced between extraversion and conservatism. If we give due attention to Swiss women's movements, gymnastics allow us to understand 'political battles' which went alongside those leading to the acquisition of greater political rights, and to discover the existence of social areas where a feminine power existed throughout the twentieth century.

Notes

1. The first feminine gymnastics clubs from Switzerland opened in 1893 in Zurich (Herzog 1995).
2. This 'sport' changed its name many times since its recognition by the international federation in 1961. It was known as 'modern gymnastics' from 1961 to 1971, as 'modern rhythmic gymnastics' from 1971 to 1973, as 'sporting rhythmic gymnastics' from 1975 to 1998 and as 'rhythmic gymnastics' since then. For practical reasons and to be well understood, we will use 'rhythmic gymnastics' in the whole article.
3. Swiss female gymnasts made their first appearance on the Olympic scene in Munich (1972).
4. At that time, it was not possible for him to go with his team near the carpet as the area was forbidden to men by the IFG's rules.

Disclosure statement

No potential conflict of interest was reported by the author.

Funding

This work was supported by the French National Olympic Academy in 2014. Title of the project: Becoming an Olympic Sport. Comparative History of the Rhythmic Gymnastics in France and in Switzerland (1961–2011).

References

Aceti, Monica, and Christophe Jaccoud. 2012. *Sportives dans leur genre? Permanences et variations des constructions genrées dans les engagements corporels et sportifs* [Sportswomen in Their Kind? Permanences and Variations of the Gendered Constructions in the Physical Activities and Sports]. Bern: Peter Lang.

Anderson, B. 1991. *Imagined Communities: Reflections on the Origin and Spread of Nationalism.* London: Verso.

Association Suisse de Gymnastique Féminine. 1983. *75 ans* [75 Years]. 1908–1983. Aarau: ASGF.

Barker-Ruchti, Natalie. 2009. "Ballerinas and Pixies: A Genealogy of the Changing Gymnastics Body." *The International Journal of the History of Sport* 26 (1): 43–61.

Bruce, Toni, Jorid Hovden, and Pirkko Markula. 2010. *Sportswomen at the Olympics. A Global Content Analysis of Newspaper Coverage.* Rotterdam: Sense.

Burgener, Louis. 1952. *La Confédération suisse et l'éducation physique de la jeunesse* [Swiss Confederation and the Physical Education of Its Youth]. La Chaux-de-Fonds.

Bussard, Jean-Claude. 2007. *L'éducation physique suisse en quête d'identité* [Swiss Physical Education Searching for Its Identity] *(1800–1930)*. Paris: L'Harmattan.

Chollet, Antoine. 2011. "Switzerland as a 'Fractured Nation.'" *Nations and Nationalism* 17 (4): 738–755.

Craig, Maxime Leeds. 2013. *Sorry I Don't Dance. Why Men Refuse to Move.* Oxford: Oxford University Press.

Favre, Christian. 2004. *La Suisse face aux Jeux Olympiques de Berlin 1936* [Switzerland Facing the Berlin Olympic Games from 1936]. Fribourg: Aux sources du temps présent.

Hartmann-Tews, Ilse, and Gertrud Pfister. 2003. *Sport and Women. Social Issues in International Perspective.* London: Routledge.

Herzog, Eva. 1995. *Frisch, Frank, Fröhlich, Frau. Frauenturnen im Kanton Basel-Landschaft* [Fresh, Frank, Joyful, Women. Women Gymnastics in the Basel-Land Kanton]. Bâle.

Klimke, Martin, and Joachim Scharloth. 2008. *1968 in Europe: A History of Protest and Activism, 1956–77.* New York: Palgrave Macmillan.

Koller, Christian. 2010. "Football Negotiating the Placement of Switzerland within Europe." *Soccer & Society* 11 (6): 748–760.

Kriesi, Hanspeter, and Alexander Trechsel. 2008. *The Politics of Switzerland: Continuity and Change in a Consensus Democracy.* Cambridge: Cambridge University Press.

Lamont, Michèle, and Virág Molnár. 2002. "The Study of Boundaries in the Social Sciences." *Annual Review of Sociology* 28: 167–195.

Langlade, Alberto. 1966. *Recherches sur les origines, l'intégration et l'actualité de la gymnastique moderne* [Research on the Origins, the Integration and the Current Events of Modern Gymnastics]. Paris: FFGEGV.

Manidi, Marie-José. 2002. *Nos mères et nos grands-mères allaient à la gym: mais qu'y faisaient-elles donc?* [Our Mothers and Grand-Mothers went to the Gymnastics: But What did they do There?] Lausanne: Réalités sociales.

Meckbach, Jane, and Pia Lundquist Wanneberg. 2011. "The World Gymnaestrada – A Non-Competitive Event: The Concept 'Gymnastics for All' from the Perspective of Ling Gymnastics." *Scandinavian Sport Studies Forum* 2: 99–118.

Pfister, Gertrud. 2001. "Die grossen Frauen in der FSFI Alice Milliat und Eliott Lynn – zwei aussergewöhnliche Sportlerinnen-Biographien" [Famous Ladies from the FSFI Alice Milliat and Eliott Lynn - Two Amazing Sporting Biographies]. In *Olympisches Spiele. Bilanz und Perspektiven im 21. Jahrhundert* [Olympic Games. Records and Perspectives for the 21st Century], edited by Michael Krüger, 138–145. Münster: Lit Verlag.

Pfister, Gertrud. 2013. "Developments and Current Issues in Gender and Sport from a European Perspective." In *Gender Relations in Sport*, edited by Emily A. Roper, 163–180. Rotterdam: Sense.

Quin, Grégory. 2014a. "Constitution et développement du sport scolaire dans le canton de Vaud" [Constitution and Development of School Sport in the Kanton Waadt] (1970–2010). In *Pensées sur le sport scolaire – Penser le sport scolaire* [Thoughts on School Sport - Thinking School Sport], edited by Jean-Nicolas Renaud, Julie Grall, and Yann Delas, 125–131. Paris: AFRAPS.

Quin, Grégory. 2014b. *Devenir un sport olympique. « Jalons pour une » Histoire comparée des développements de la gymnastique rythmique en France et en Suisse* [Becoming an Olympic Sport. First steps for a Comparative History of the Rhythmic Gymnastics in France and in Switzerland] *(1961–2011)*. (Research Report), Académie Nationale Olympique Française (ANOF).

Studer, Brigitte. 1996. "'L'Etat c'est l'homme'. Politique, citoyenneté et genre dans le débat autour du suffrage féminin après 1945 ['The State is Masculine'. Politics, Citizenship and Gender in the Debates surrounding Women's suffrage after 1945]." *Revue Suisse d'Histoire* 46 (3): 356–382.

Vonnard, Philippe, and Grégory Quin. 2012. "Eléments pour une histoire de la mise en place du professionnalisme dans le football suisse dans l'entre-deux-guerres: processus, resistances et ambiguïtés [First Steps for an History of the Introduction of Professional Football in Switzerland during the Interwar Period: Process, Resistances and Ambiguities]." *Revue Suisse d'Histoire* 62 (1): 70–85.

Whitson, David. 1994. "The Embodiment of Gender: Discipline, Domination and Empowerment." In *Women, Sport and Culture*, edited by Susan Birrell and Cheryl L. Cole, 353–371. Champaign: Human Kinetics.

'It has really amazed me what my body can now do': boundary work and the construction of a body-positive dance community

Joanne Hill[a], Rachel Sandford[b] and Eimear Enright[c]

[a]Institute of Sport and Physical Activity Research, University of Bedfordshire, Bedford, UK; [b]School of Sport, Exercise and Health Sciences, Loughborough University, Loughborough, UK; [c]School of Human Movement and Nutrition Sciences, The University of Queensland, Brisbane, Australia

ABSTRACT
Boundaries around normative embodiments in physical cultures can be exclusionary if one's embodied identity does not 'fit'. Normative boundaries are particularly marked in codified forms of dance such as ballet. Moves towards body positivity aim to challenge these normative boundaries by redefining what dancers' bodies can look like and how they should move. This paper stems from an appreciative inquiry undertaken with one such project, a gender-neutral, LGBTQ-friendly adult ballet school in the UK; a subcultural context that marks itself as distinct from broader cultures of dance. Interviews with learners are analysed through a Bourdieuian lens to explore the construction and maintenance of a body-positive subculture. Findings suggest that boundaries of ability were crossed, with celebration of all bodies' capabilities, and boundaries of normative gender expression were transformed through a commitment to gender-neutrality and LGBTQ-friendly behaviours. However, boundaries around technical and aesthetic norms, while shifted or challenged, ultimately remained in place.

Introduction

Kirk (1999, 65–66) defined the notion of physical culture as 'a range of practices concerned with the maintenance, representation and regulation of the body', which are centred on 'highly codified, institutionalized forms of physical activity'. Physical culture, manifested in texts, resources and spaces, provides discourses of the body with which people narrate or make sense of their movement (Hargreaves and Vertinsky 2007). Individuals produce 'appropriate' bodies through a series of repeated practices, which are relevant to the context, established over time and always in process. One focus in the construction and regulation of bodies is gender. The oppositional construction of the archetypal masculine body as strong and muscular, and the feminine body as slender and submissive (Bordo 1993; Connell 1995), can be noted as a gender-normative and heterosexual boundary that regulates behaviour, movement and embodied identity. The construction of ability in physical cultural spaces is also related to gender, with what counts as a highly able body being mediated by the gender performance of that body (Butler 1998). Some research in physical culture has focused on the challenges faced by individuals as they negotiate boundaries of gender, sexuality and ability, providing a rich understanding of bodily dissatisfaction and disengagement from physical activity (Berg and Lahelma 2010; Wellard 2006).

Recently, there has been a growth in body-positive approaches, which purport to be about creating safe spaces for inclusivity and bodily acceptance (Sastre 2014). While physical cultures can be seen as bounded by regulatory body practices, Kretchmar's (2000) use of the generative concept of 'movement subcultures' to talk about meaning-intensive places, where participants construct personal and shared meanings within a commitment to mastering movement, offers a constructive way to examine the creation and maintenance of body-positive spaces. Responding to Kretchmar's (2000) call for more research on movement subcultures, and to the relative dearth of literature on body-positive physical activity, this paper represents an effort to understand how one positive subculture has formed and flourished. Before discussing our case, we briefly outline the context within which this body-positive, gender-neutral and lesbian, gay, bisexual, trans and queer (LGBTQ)-friendly adult ballet school became necessary.

Codified forms of dance such as ballet have been a popular research space for understanding the construction of embodied (gendered) identities, conformity and body image (Langdon and Petracca 2010; Radell et al. 2014). The evidence suggests that dance can promote both positive and negative body images (Ravaldi et al. 2006; Wellard, Pickard, and Bailey 2007). The 'traditional' perception that dance is intended for lean, graceful women has undoubtedly contributed to the norm that ballet dancers need to be thin and lithe to dance well (Aalten 2004; Langdon and Petraca 2010). Indeed, the ballet environment has been found to encourage dancers to lose weight to meet this body norm (Ravaldi et al. 2006). Social stereotypes concerning bodily norms can also be applied to thinking about the construction of gendered ballet bodies. Risner (2002) points out that dance education is both heterosexist and silent on homophobia. The female ballet body is already feminized and heterosexualized within constructions of sex-gender-sexuality (Youdell 2005), or what Butler (1993) calls the heterosexual matrix: the ideal female body in ballet is slender to reify feminine weakness, and dances with men to reify heterosexuality. The non-normative (non-heterosexual, non-cissexual, gender queer and fat) is thus marginalized by ballet's dominant gendered body boundaries (Aalten 2004). Ballet has been defended as a site of agency where physical challenge achieves technical prowess, 'where physical excellence is valuated' (Aalten 2004, 274); yet the aesthetic still reproduces cultural norms of passivity in women that contrast with the valuing of strength in men. As a physical culture, ballet can be argued to support the creation of boundaries between physically excellent bodies and other (read inferior) bodies.

In contrast, research on community dance programmes (Burgess, Grogan, and Burwitz 2006; Erfer and Ziv 2006; Houston 2005) suggests that dance may contribute to building a sense of body empowerment. At their heart, many of these community dance programmes aim for social inclusion and they provide rich data on how dance has been used and received in projects targeted at transforming and empowering disenfranchised communities and individuals (Bartlett 1996; Houston 2005). As community dance commentator Anthony Peppiatt (1996, 8–9) remarks:

> The most central place of radical value and meaning within community dance at this time [...] lies in the body as site. The powerful and transforming experience of discovering pleasure through movement and through the body, of developing physical abilities, of expanding the physical imagination, and of a new liberation of the physical, mental, emotional, and spiritual self.

While any declarations of transformation and empowerment should be interpreted with a degree of caution, dance scholars at least seem confident that dance can provide a context where body positivity is a realizable pursuit (Houston 2005). Dance can, therefore, be a space in which participants can challenge and rewrite the boundaries and meanings of their physical culture through the co-construction of shared localized values (Kretchmar 2000). Considering this, we draw on the following theoretical framework to explore how body positivity was created and maintained within the context of dance community at the heart of this research.

Boundary shifting, crossing and transforming in Bourdieu's concept of habitus

Within this paper, our thinking is informed by theoretical approaches that help us consider the links between the body, physical cultures and the construction and embodiment of gender, sexuality, and ability norms noted above (Bordo 1993; Butler 1993; Kirk 1999). In order to illuminate the regulation of the (gendered) body, yet also the possibilities for the shifting, crossing and transforming of boundaries (Barker Ruchti et al. 2015; Lamont and Molnár 2002), we draw notably from French social theorist Pierre Bourdieu's (1985, 1993) tools of habitus, field and capital. Habitus, as the means by which society is 'written into' the body (Bourdieu 1990a), offers a way of understanding how social structures, norms and ideals can come to influence an individual's corporeal practice at an unconscious level. Habitus can be understood as a set of socially constituted dispositions or tastes: subconscious schemes of perception and appreciation that collectively orchestrate practice (Bourdieu 1990b). These dispositions are afforded differing values (levels of capital) depending on the context, and serve to position individuals within a given field. Bourdieu highlighted three forms of capital: cultural, social and economic, to which Shilling (1991) added a fourth, physical. Applying Bourdieuian theories to sport and physical activity contexts, Shilling (1993) argued that the body becomes a reflexive 'project', with individuals working on the body in order to maximize the accumulation of physical capital and attain exchange value within relevant fields. In this way, the body comes to represent a site of both practice and power (Shilling 1991) and the constant reproduction of gendered practice can lead to embedding of discourses (including those of physical culture) through the habitus.

As lisahunter, Smith and Emerald (2014, 3) argue, Bourdieu's work can be particularly useful in researching physical culture, as it helps to 'articulate the dialogue between structures that shape a society and their interaction with the individual person'. Physical culture can be understood as a complex, multi-dimensional site, comprising a number of key fields and sub-fields that interact and intersect in various ways (Bourdieu 1985). Bourdieu (1993) argued that the boundary of a field could be understood as being where the 'effects' of that field are felt. However, the boundaries between fields and sub-fields are often blurred and can represent points of disjuncture (Reay 2008). Although habitus can seem deeply embedded (Bourdieu 1990a), others have called for a more fluid approach (e.g. Robbins 2000), seeing habitus not as constraining an individual but as something they are able to manage in a more conscious way. If habitus can be reworked over time, then it is likely to reflect key differences within an individual's experiences, such as crossing the boundary between one field and another, where they have engaged in self-reflexivity (Emerald and Barbour 2014; Reay 2004). This possibility for transformation resonates strongly with the context at the heart of this research and provides a valuable framework for understanding, in part, how the body-positive focus of an alternative dance community helps to facilitate and support individuals' construction of embodied identities. It is also very much in line with the strengths-based approach underpinning this research (Enright et al. 2014), which, in turn is driven by a desire to uncover 'what works' as the starting point for positive change and ongoing development.

Methods

Within this project, we selected a qualitative case study approach to explore how body positivity was created and sustained within a dance community, using methodologies informed by appreciative inquiry (AI). AI can be perceived as an orientation to research and to change, underpinned by the belief that every culture, and every person in that culture, has strengths that should be the starting point for positive change (Cooperrider and Whitney 2001). It is based on the assumption that our research agendas determine what we discover. AI always begins with a positive question or an affirmative topic (Whitney and Trosten-Bloom 2010). Various typologies of the AI process have been outlined with the most popular model being Cooperrider and Whitney's (2001) 4D cycle: *discover* the best of what is, in order to then *dream* the best of what can be, *design* proposals for change based on common dreams and realize a *destiny* by creating sustainable transformation. Following our identification of AI as an alternative approach to researching what works in physical education (Enright et al. 2014), we sought a case study with which we could work to investigate the best elements of a physical education-related positive movement subculture. The case presented here is a London-based dance school called Irreverent Dance (ID), which identifies as a body-positive space. It is a context in which teachers and learners have created their own meanings surrounding dance and dance education.

The research question guiding this project was: *How do learners and teachers in Irreverent Dance create and maintain body positivity?* Prior to commencing the research fieldwork, full ethical clearance was obtained by the researchers and relevant processes relating to informing participants, obtaining consent and ensuring participant anonymity were followed. Participants agreed for the real name of the school to be used. While AI is not a technique or method, there are methods and questions which are more aligned with the approach. Positive comments are sought deliberately within applications of AI, but the aim is not to avoid being critical but to approach critique constructively, focusing on the positive elements already in practice. The specific methods used within this project are outlined below.

Data sources

Within the programme of research activities, five visits were made to ID so that the researchers could inform individuals about the project, ascertain their interest in being involved and arrange interviews. In addition, these visits allowed the researchers to observe a number of dance classes in action. In total, 12 participants (nine learners and three teachers) were interviewed using a semi-structured interview schedule inspired by AI, with positively framed questions. In this respect, the 4D approach proved valuable for guiding the writing of interview questions: for instance, it was structured around *discovering* the positives of engagement in dance classes (e.g. *How/Why do you think this dance school is successful in engaging individuals in dance? What are your favourite aspects of the dance class?*) and *dreaming* about developments in the dance school (e.g. *What can you envisage other dance classes/movement classes learning from this one? What would you like to see yourself doing/ achieving in terms of your movement experiences in the next few years?*).

Each interview lasted between 30 and 60 min in length. The interviews were audio recorded and transcribed verbatim. It should be noted that only learners' interviews, not teachers', are quoted in the sections below and pseudonyms are used to ensure anonymity. Additional data sources (observation notes, the school's website, blog posts and magazine articles created by members of ID) were also collated, in order to provide additional context. Analyses of the verbal and visual data were undertaken to help construct narratives of the participants' experiences and highlight elements of practice and culture that were felt to contribute to a positive environment for movement. More specifically, the qualitative interview data were analysed using a thematic approach akin to constructivist grounded theory as described by Charmaz (2000). In this way, the individual interview transcripts were first reviewed and then analysed systematically by coding in stages (Strauss and Corbin 1998) until themes (drawn from common responses and areas of interest) were generated and verified. Moreover, in order to enhance validity and ensure inter-coder reliability (Miles and Huberman 1994) the initial coding of transcripts was done independently by two researchers before these analyses were shared and a consensus reached on the coding structure. The researchers then worked together to build up the core themes that emerged from the analysis. Following this, the core themes identified through the analysis were shared with learners and teachers (distributed in a report provided for the ID AGM) by way of a member check (Creswell and Miller 2000); helping to ensure the interpretation was meaningful to the participants.

Crossing, shifting and transforming boundaries in ID

Looking at 'what works' in ID provides us with a way to investigate and appreciate what people enjoy and achieve from their engagement in this movement subculture. Within this section, we highlight how this particular movement subculture created and maintained body positivity by considering how and to what extent boundaries around ballet, dance and gender/sexuality were shifted, crossed or transformed. Throughout these narratives, we note some powerful epiphanies (Emerald and Barbour 2014) related to dance cultures, physical movement and identity.

Crossing boundaries in dance: from unable to able, from non-dancer to dancer

Celebrating body capability was an important element of ID participants' ('IDers') achievements in dance and an element of body-positive pedagogy that can be seen as a marker of crossing boundaries – and in some cases, transforming boundaries – in dance. There was a high level of celebration of what bodies *can* do, no matter their size, appearance or gender. This sense of achievement was expressed both in relation to specific ballet technique and in terms of general physical ability. Some of the achievement that Greg felt in this respect was highlighted in his reflections on the previous term's classes:

> A lot of emphasis is put on how far you've come and in how much time and often what a short amount of time that is […] they've had eight hours of formal training, look, now they're doing a dance.

Greg also commented on the physical sensation of dancing, suggesting that there is a sense of an improved awareness of the body through feeling or seeing limbs move, stretch and ache:

> When you first watch it, it looks completely ungainly but then all of a sudden – something clicks into place. It fits and it feels like a natural movement to make.

At first, as Greg suggests here, dancers can feel as though they were putting the body on display and experience initial discomfort (Stahl 2013). Considering how far they have come is also an element of a reflexive process that assists in (re)developing a dance habitus (Emerald and Barbour 2014). IDers were able to develop their dancing ability at a pace they were comfortable with, progressing gradually through ballet grades and repeating terms if they wished. Calling it 'a bit of reverse psychology really', Sal said:

> Because [...] you can do it at your own pace, it makes me more likely to actually push myself and to make sure I go to classes. To make sure that I do my best.

According to the ID website, body positive means a space in which people can learn without feeling like they are being judged, implying a place that is freer from socially constituted corporeal norms and expectations. Members of ID certainly reflected this philosophy, although there were also often individual interpretations. Greg, for example, considered body positivity to be simply about 'the joy in human movement'. Cath felt that 'it's sort of quite soothing, learning to do these things with your body', suggesting that physical learning is facilitated in a safe space. Similarly, Greg noted:

> The thing that really draws people and engages them is when they're being shown that they can do a thing that they didn't even think was possible.

Muscularity and strength as examples of physical developments resulting from ballet training were celebrated as tangible or visible measures of the dancers' achievements. For example, Guy noted that 'my body is more useful than it was and it's something I did through dance'. Furthermore, celebrating her body's capability, Cath exclaimed:

> It has really amazed me what my body can now do. I didn't know I could stand on my tip toes on one foot and swing my other leg round with my arm and, like, do it in a really controlled manner.

Others also expressed that they could forget everything else and concentrate by getting 'in touch' with their bodies. These connections were conscious attempts to think through the body and suggest that ID also offers a mental space in which to focus attention on the 'whole me', as Cassie expressed it:

> And it really helps you focus, because you just – everything else falls away, you're just thinking, where do my feet go for this exercise?

The learners' reflections suggest that understandings of the body as 'not capable' of doing something might have arisen in previous dance or movement experiences. Sal, for example, noted that in previous activity experiences, she had felt 'your worth to the group depends on how well you do it', with a lack of ability (or physical capital) resulting in a perception of failure or feelings of 'I can't'. In ID, however, learners were actively encouraged to think 'I can' – reflecting the realization that they were physically capable and would not be barred from dancing or performing. To borrow Emerald and Barbour's (2014) language, when learners crossed into the ballet subfield of ID (a crossover of dance and LGBTQ fields), it was possible for positive elements (such as technical aspects) to be kept and more negative corporeal aspects (the valorizing of slender, gender-normative or highly able bodies) to be left aside. A key element of body-positivity, then, was encouraging revised perceptions of capability.

Physical changes to the body (and associated changes in perceptions of self) were celebrated and the gaining of a powerful physicality reconnected many dancers to their bodies. Some learners' relationship with themselves changed as a result of 're-finding' an identity as a dancer. For Greg, performing this identity as a dancer included dressing the part:

> When I first started coming I started wearing like running gear and football shorts and stuff like that and I made a point of buying myself tights and shoes and a dance vest. Just to go, look, I'm a dancer, this is what you can wear [...] you know, dressing up as a dancer doesn't make you a dancer, but also it does legitimate – your interpretation of what you want to look like is part of legitimising yourself, there's that identity.

Sal explained that claiming an identity as a dancer was especially powerful for her:

> So having a chance to take it back for myself and say no, this is who I am, this is how I am, this is how I want to be, is I mean, I can't even begin to explain how important it's been for me.

Sophy claimed that dancing enabled her to be 'comfortable and re-acquainted myself with my own body'. She expressed powerful feelings in accepting and celebrating a body that might previously have been 'something that let me down'. It suggests a disjuncture between habitus and field in other contexts (Reay 2008). Stahl (2013) argues that it is important to recognize that disjunctures can foster transformations and suggests that habitus only truly becomes transformative when the 'unthinking habitus' is jolted into consciousness (Reay 2004).

Owning an identity as a dancer was an important element of embodiment that could be gained by crossing into the ID space. Celebrating bodily capabilities appeared especially possible when dancers said that they were able to just 'be' in the ID space, where they have found the potential to become (re-)embodied. Sophy and Cassie explained what feeling disembodied felt like: '[not] feeling comfortable in my own skin' or 'see[ing] a stranger in the mirror'. Laura noted that this 'freeing' feeling was a part of the social environment created in ID, with a commitment to inclusion, respect and not judging others. As she stated, physically crossing into the subculture space, entering the ID studio,

> leaves you free to focus on so many other things like actually learning the dance [...], it is like packaging up society's nonsense in a suitcase and leaving it by the door as you go in and then, okay, you might have to pick it up when you go out again, but hopefully not.

The physical act of crossing into the ID dance studio was the entering into a designated dance studio; however, there were some physical and pedagogical adaptations made to the space that marked some differences with other dance spaces and with non-dance spaces. A typical dance studio includes a mirrored wall that, as an instrument of surveillance, might encourage self-criticism and discipline (Radell et al. 2014). In response, the ID teachers gave dancers a choice and a curtain was pulled halfway across the mirrored wall to assist. However, watching in the mirror might be a subversive act when physical strength rather than normative appearance is celebrated. Mirrors gave a strong visual feedback on body capability: 'you can look in the mirror and sort of think, god yes when I first started going to this I couldn't lift my leg that high' (Laura). Self-surveillance could contribute to reflexivity and the jolting into consciousness of the habitus (Reay 2004). By adapting the dance environment, the boundary from body negativity to body positivity could be crossed, and potentially be a transformative experience.

Transforming body negativity into body positivity

Some participants identified that becoming an IDer had been a transforming experience in their relationship with their embodied self:

> I actually quite like my body now, I don't think it's disgusting. That's quite a massive, massive turnaround. (Cath)

> That's something that's been a really steep learning curve over the last few months, I've just started looking at myself completely differently and thinking – there is nothing to feel ashamed of, this is my body. (Cassie)

Learners noted how they were much more accepting of their bodies within ID, a key element of body positivity. In one instance, Sal highlighted feelings that it was she herself who could be in control of her body and identity, through dance:

> It allows me to feel in control of my body and not let other people's thoughts and ideals that are put onto me from them affect me. […] I can have control of my body as a person rather than thinking about how other people view me.

Cassie expressed that 'with the first five minutes of the first class, I just felt completely welcome and settled and like, this is where I want to be'. The teachers requested that everyone respect themselves as well as others. This was an epiphany for Cassie: realizing that if you wouldn't judge someone else then you shouldn't judge yourself either. The values of supportiveness and respect for self and others were something explicitly created by the teacher at the start of the first class. This ensured that the boundaries of this specific context were recognized and understood.

The epiphanies experienced in crossing the non-dancer to dancer boundary have corporeal effects but, as the learners' language here suggests, these effects are transformative in terms of their relationships to themselves and their embodied identities. As noted earlier, feelings of physical incapability or aesthetic dislike of the body had been common body-negative experiences that some IDers had felt in other dance or physical cultures. This was often grounded in perceptions that their bodies were too far removed from the 'ideal' within those contexts and therefore lacked physical capital. They framed their experiences in ID specifically in contrast to this. Offering a body-positive space may attract learners who have previously experienced a disconnection with their physical selves. The creation of a positive movement subculture seems then an act of resistance, in response to negative experiences influenced by rigid boundaries and adherence to heteronormative values in other contexts. Emerald and Barbour (2014, 56) discuss the process of 'dance training as habitus' and make the point that 'the habitus of the contemporary dancer offers a reflexivity about self in relation to the world through training sensory awareness, embodied expression and presence – ultimately embodied ways of knowing'. The ballet training in ID encouraged reflexivity about the self and critique of the norms that had shaped learners' perceptions of their embodied selves within other dance contexts. In this way, it perhaps fostered a sense of disjuncture (Reay 2008) from the broader field of dance and opened up the possibility of transforming or interrupting the habitus (Gorely, Holroyd, and Kirk 2003; Stahl 2013) through encouraging more conscious reflection on the norms and ideals that are used to shape practice.

Transforming gender/sexuality boundaries through gender-neutrality

Levels of awareness of the body were particularly articulated concerning dancer identities, as noted above, but also with gender identities and expressions. All learners valued the relationships they developed within and beyond classes, suggesting that the sharing of values (particularly the redefining of corporeal norms) promoted inclusivity and safety. Diversity was a key element of the community. As Laura articulated:

> [We] might feel like a bit of a misfit for one reason or another but get all of us in a room together and we're not misfits anymore because we all fit because we don't if you see what I mean.

By promoting difference, difference mattered less. However, neither were learners and teachers who were white, cis-sexual, heterosexual and/or male made to feel excluded due to their privilege, as Greg pointed out:

> Nobody is excluded [...] Which is not a trivial concern, because I'm a straight male, and I am the scary person for most people who have any kind of lack of privileges, I am the threat [but] I am expressly welcome. [...] It is something that's seen as a safe space [...] and that's really a welcome thing – that it's not a space for everyone *but* me. (emphasis in original)

Gender boundaries within and around sports cultures can be particularly durable (Berg and Lahelma 2010; Wellard 2006). Challenges to these boundaries can be especially transformative. Against ballet's typically gendered spaces and structures, ID outlined a commitment to personal choice in gender presentation, so that each dancer could decide what was comfortable for them. Sophy explained:

> People [are] doing it because they want to and doing the things that they feel comfortable doing, regardless of who's supposed to be doing them, you know no one's just doing the boy steps because they're boys, people are doing the men's steps because they like jumping and they enjoy the strength and the freedom that you can get from that.

Elements of dance that have typically gendered boundaries were resignified; for example, men were invited to learn to dance *en pointe* if they wished. Dancers commented that their perception of what their bodies *could do* developed positively, when heteronormative and cisnormative boundaries (in dance movement and performance) were eliminated. This is a powerful element in reflecting that it may be gender normativity in other fields that restricts positive movement experiences, as Lizzie's explanation of gender-neutrality and LGBTQ-friendly indicates:

> Nobody's going to be sort of, assuming anything about anybody, or guessing anybody's gender or assuming that somebody doesn't want to be the size they are and would rather be a different size.

On the other hand, Sal noted that she was able to feel feminine in ID classes, something that she had not been able to achieve before. Similarly, for Laura:

> I'd always just thought, well I'm not graceful so ballet's not for me, it never occurred to me, of course ballet teaches you to be graceful, so that I think sold it to quite a lot of us that [the teacher] could teach us to be the graceful coordinated creatures we never thought we were.

Sal and Laura's comments appear to be reifying gender by re-centring feminine and graceful aesthetics in their performance of ballet bodies. However, they were empowered within ID to embody identities that they had not previously perceived as being open to them; their physical capital lacking exchange value (Shilling 1993) within the broader field of dance. Physical capital in femininity has been fundamentally linked to body size as well as aesthetics – not only conventionally attractive but slender (Bordo 1993). Far from prohibiting any gender identity, gender neutrality in the dance space signified transgression by valorizing fat or non-gender-normative bodies as graceful. Sal and Laura actively seek to experience an embodiment not accessible to them before. Drawing from Sykes' (2011) discussion of fat bodies as queer adds a further dimension to the normalized body in the sex-gender-sexuality constellation (Youdell 2005). Fat female bodies have been objectified as not feminine (or heterofeminine), partly because fat, like butch, appears to contest desirability only being possible in slender and heterofeminine women. By identifying non-normative bodies as capable and valued (redefining their physical capital), these participants rewrote what could be read as a ballet body in their eyes. As Sykes and McPhail (2008) argue, fat subjectivities can be validated with inclusive curricula and pedagogies. Nevertheless, drawing from Butler (1993), they note that because those subjectivities were formed in resistance to dominant slender norms, they remained limited by the dominant discourses that produce their agency. While boundaries might be transformed or even erased within the ID space, learners could not help but be aware of how gender and other body norms affect their lives beyond the studio.

Shifting the boundaries of a codified dance: challenging ballet norms

A central element in the learning and community of ID was deconstructing ballet's gender boundaries; challenging dominant notions about what gendered ballet bodies look like, what they should do and what progress must be made. Some learners reflected on how they had been looking for a dance class that would suit their 'uncoordinated', 'geeky back of the class loner' or 'fat' bodies. These were feelings they claimed to have experienced in other dance classes at both novice and elite levels, which is indicative of a physical culture of restrictive embodied and gendered boundaries in mainstream ballet. The learners' perceptions were that their own bodies did not 'fit' inside these traditional boundaries because of both ability and aesthetic norms. Technical aspects were taught but Emma noted that the ID teachers adapted them for different bodies and capabilities:

> Obviously a lot of ballet schools would [say this is] not good enough because you're not doing the exercise in the official proper way, but [ID says] as long as you're doing it and you're making the effort to do it as well as you can, that's what matters.

Emma's perceptions of the technical progress that ballet dancers *should* make are affected by the social construction of dancing as requiring years of discipline and sacrifice (Aalten 2007). Laura's views of ballet, even beginners' classes, had also been that it was 'really intimidating for people that weren't natural dancers or that weren't natural exercisers'. ID aimed to deconstruct 'natural' ability with learners encouraged to see themselves as capable of moving and stretching as ballet requires. What constitutes dancing or a dancer, at least in the eyes of the learners, was challenged by ID. Ballet norms in the sense of technical requirements, language, music and dress styles were recognized (those boundaries only shifting) but with gender boundaries transformed this meant that learners who would previously have not had access to ballet (been 'in' ballet) could find a space that was safe and positive for them. Although risking a critique of the broader physical culture of ballet, by centring the IDers' narratives we recognize that their habitus was developed in part as a reaction to other ballet spaces. While dancer and gender identity boundaries were crossed or transformed respectively, ballet boundaries were only shaken or shifted somewhat, remaining largely in place.

Conclusion

Individuals in ID were encouraged to challenge dance and gender norms by experiencing and becoming a part of a community that focused learning around creating body positivity. This led to many IDers redefining their perceptions of body capability and worth, empowering them to transform gender boundaries and enabling them to claim an identity as a dancer. In this way, ID represented a point of disjuncture (Reay 2008) for many and offered the opportunity to begin a transformation of habitus through revising the schemes of perception and appreciation that shaped their practice (Stahl 2013). Crossing into the ID space allowed individuals to shift into a landscape with redefined boundaries, in which alternative perspectives on bodily appearance, capability and worth (physical capital) were possible.

ID, then, could be considered a 'border space' (Sastre 2014) within the fields from which it and its participants draw, a space that is in flux in different ways for different participants (Bourdieu 1985; lisahunter 2014), as it is constructed and bounded by its relations to other fields, including ballet, dance, LGBTQ and fat activism. ID redefined traditional boundaries (e.g. relating to gender roles, body norms and ability) to facilitate access, but maintained some observance of the values of style and technique in ballet. Non-gender-conforming dancing bodies could be able, strong and graceful, deconstructing the traditional habitus of a dancer. As such, traditional symbolic boundaries of ballet are retained, but social boundaries are dismantled (Lamont and Molnár 2002). The focus on individual worth is significant here because it allows for physical capital to have an 'exchange value' (Shilling 1993) that is specific to each dancer, which helps to underpin the concept of a body-positive approach. Adjusting their thinking to fit these redefined boundaries allowed many learners in ID to find a reconnection with their own body and begin a process of 'interrupting' their habitus, challenging accepted norms regarding gendered bodily ideals and practices and opening their eyes to new possibilities. Arguing for a gender-relevant physical education, Gorely et al. (2003) contend that de-stabilizing of stereotypical femininities and masculinities is necessary in order to facilitate the empowerment of all. Similarly, the challenging and redefining of boundaries around ballet, dance and gender/sexuality within ID can be seen to empower individuals through facilitating their access to and achievement within a physical culture that would otherwise marginalize them.

While ID was successful in creating and maintaining body positivity, however, it is worth noting that in other movement subcultures, the possibilities may look different because of alternative field configurations. Nonetheless, it would seem that a body-positive approach is important as a means of transforming boundaries around dance movement, gender expression and the body, legitimizing individuals' practice within the shared understanding of a meaning-intensive movement subculture (Kretchmar 2000). This is integral to how ID supports learning and might go some way to redefining the gender boundaries and body work that have been necessary in physical cultures.

Acknowledgements

The authors gratefully acknowledge the financial support of the School of Sport, Exercise and Health Sciences, Loughborough University, and would also like to recognize the invaluable contribution made by the Irreverent Dance community, in particular those individuals who were active participants in the research process.

Disclosure statement

No potential conflict of interest was reported by the authors.

Funding

This work was supported by the School of Sport, Exercise and Health Sciences at Loughborough University.

References

Aalten, A. 2004. "'The Moment When it All Comes Together': Embodied Experiences in Ballet." *The European Journal of Women's Studies* 11 (3): 263–276.
Aalten, A. 2007. "Listening to the Dancer's Body." *The Sociological Review* 55: 109–125.
Barker-Ruchti, N., K. Grahn, and E.-C. Lindgren. 2015. "Shifting, crossing and transforming gender boundaries in physical cultures." *Sport in Society*. doi:10.1080/17430437.2015.1073942.
Bartlett, K. 1996. "Community Dance and Politics." In *Thinking Aloud: In Search of a Framework for Community Dance*, edited by C. Jones, 15–16. Leicester: Foundation for Community Dance.
Berg, P., and E. Lahelma. 2010. "Gendering Processes in the Field of Physical Education." *Gender and Education* 22 (1): 31–46.
Bordo, S. 1993. *Unbearable Weight: Feminism, Western Culture and the Body*. London: University of California Press.
Bourdieu, P. 1985. "The Social Space and the Genesis of Groups." *Theory and Society* 14 (6): 723–744.
Bourdieu, P. 1990a. *In Other Words: Essays towards a Reflexive Sociology*. Cambridge: Polity Press.
Bourdieu, P. 1990b. *The Logic of Practice*. Stanford: Stanford University Press.
Bourdieu, P. 1993. *Sociology in Question*. London: Sage.
Burgess, G., S. Grogan, and L. Burwitz. 2006. "Effects of a 6-week Aerobic Dance Intervention on Body Image and Physical Self-perceptions in Adolescent Girls." *Body Image* 3: 57–66.
Butler, J. 1993. *Bodies that Matter*. London: Routledge.
Butler, J. 1998. "Athletic Genders: Hyperbolic Instance and/or the Overcoming of Sexual Binarism." *Stanford Humanities Review* 6 (2): 103–111.
Charmaz, K. 2000. "Grounded Theory: Objectivist and Constructionist Methods." In *Handbook of Qualitative Research*. 2nd ed., edited by N. K. Denzin and Y. S. Lincoln, 509–536. London: Sage.
Connell, R. W. 1995. *Masculinities*. London: Polity Press.
Cooperrider, D., and D. Whitney. 2001. "A Positive Revolution in Change: Appreciative Inquiry." In *Appreciative Inquiry: Rethinking Human Organization towards a Positive Theory of Change*, edited by D. Cooperrider, P. F. J. Sorensen, D. Whitney, and T. F. Yaeger, 3–26. Champaign, IL: Stipes.
Creswell, J. W., and D. L. Miller. 2000. "Determining Validity in Qualitative Inquiry." *Theory into Practice* 39 (3): 124–130.
Emerald, E. and K. Barbour. 2014. "'I'll Go Back Next Week – It's Complicated'. Returning to Dance with the Help of Bourdieu." In *Pierre Bourdieu and Physical Culture*, edited by lisahunter, W. Smith, and E. Emerald, 27–36. London: Routledge.
Enright, E., J. Hill, R. Sandford, and M. Gard. 2014. "Looking Beyond What's Broken: Towards an Appreciative Research Agenda for Physical Education and Sport Pedagogy." *Sport, Education and Society* 19 (7): 912–926.
Erfer, T., and A. Ziv. 2006. "Moving toward Cohesion: Group Dance/Movement Therapy with Children in Psychiatry." *The Arts in Psychotherapy* 33: 238–246.
Gorely, T., R. Holroyd, and D. Kirk. 2003. "Muscularity, the Habitus and the Social Construction of Gender: Towards a Gender-relevant Physical Education." *British Journal of Sociology of Education* 24: 429–448.
Hargreaves, J., and P. Vertinsky. 2007. *Physical Culture, Power and the Body*. London: Routledge.
Houston, S. 2005. "Participation in Community Dance: A Road to Empowerment and Transformation?" *New Theatre Quarterly* 21 (2): 166–177.
Kirk, D. 1999. "Physical Culture, Physical Education and Relational Analysis." *Sport, Education and Society* 4 (1): 63–73.
Kretchmar, R. S. 2000. "Movement Subcultures: Sites for Meaning." *Journal of Physical Education, Recreation and Dance* 71 (5): 19–25.
Lamont, M., and V. Molnár. 2002. "The Study of Boundaries in the Social Sciences." *Annual Review of Sociology* 28: 167–195.
Langdon, S. W., and G. Petracca. 2010. "Tiny Dancer: Body Image and Dancer Identity in Female Modern Dancers." *Body Image* 7 (4): 360–363.
lisahunter, W. Smith, and E. Emerald. 2014. *Pierre Bourdieu and Physical Culture*. London: Routledge.
Miles, M. B., and A. M. Huberman. 1994. *Qualitative Data Analysis: An Expanded Sourcebook*. 2nd ed. Thousand Oaks, CA: Sage.

Peppiatt, A. 1996. "The Voice of Lost and Drifting Generations: An Enquiry into the Meaning and Value of Community Dance." *Research Papers on Community Dance* 2: 8–9.

Radell, S. A., M. L. Keneman, D. D. Adame, and S. P. Cole. 2014. "My Body and its Reflection: A Case Study of Eight Dance Students and the Mirror in the Ballet Classroom." *Research in Dance Education* 15 (2): 161–178.

Ravaldi, C., Alfredo Vannacci, E. Bolognesi, S. Mancini, C. Faravelli, and V. Ricca. 2006. "Gender Role, Eating Disorder Symptoms and Body Image Concern in Ballet Dancers." *Journal of Psychosomatic Research* 61: 529–535.

Reay, D. 2004. "'It's all Becoming a Habitus': Beyond the Habitual use of Habitus in Educational Research." *British Journal of Sociology of Education* 25 (4): 431–444.

Reay, D. 2008. "Class Out of Place: The White Middles Classes and Intersectionalities of Class and "Race" in Urban State Schooling in England." In *The Way Class Works*, edited by L. Weis, 87–100. New York: Routledge.

Risner, D. 2002. "Re-educating Dance Education to its Homosexuality: An invitation for Critical Analysis and Professional Unification." *Research in Dance Education* 3 (2): 181–187.

Robbins, D. 2000. *Bourdieu and Culture*. London: Sage.

Sastre, A. 2014. "Towards a Radical Body Positive: Reading the Online 'Body Positive Movement.'" *Feminist Media Studies* 20 (3): 929–943.

Shilling, C. 1991. "Educating the Body: Physical Capital and the Production of Social Inequalities." *Sociology* 25 (4): 653–672.

Shilling, C. 1993. *The Body and Social Theory*. London: Sage.

Stahl, G. 2013. "Habitus Disjunctures, Reflexivity and White Working-class Boys' Conceptions of Status in Learner and Social Identities." *Sociological Research Online* 18 (3): 2.

Strauss, A. L., and J. Corbin. 1998. *Basics of Qualitative Research: Techniques and Procedures for Developing Grounded Theory*. 2nd ed. Thousand Oaks, CA: Sage.

Sykes, H. 2011. *Queer Bodies*. New York: Peter Lang.

Sykes, H., and D. McPhail. 2008. "Unbearable Lessons: Contesting Fat Phobia in Physical Education." *Sociology of Sport Journal* 25: 66–96.

Wellard, I. 2006. "Able Bodies and Sport Participation: Social Constructions of Physical Ability for Gendered and Sexually Identified Bodies." *Sport, Education and Society* 11 (2): 105–119.

Wellard, I., A. Pickard, and R. Bailey. 2007. "'A Shock of Electricity just Sort of Goes Through my Body': Physical Activity and Embodied Reflexive Practices in Young Female Ballet Dancers." *Gender and Education* 19 (1): 79–91.

Whitney, D., and A. Trosten-Bloom. 2010. *The Power of Appreciative Inquiry*. San Francisco, CA: Berrett-Koehler.

Youdell, D. 2005. "Sex-Gender-Sexuality: How Sex, Gender and Sexuality Constellations are Constituted in Secondary Schools." *Gender and Education* 17 (3): 247–270.

Gendered body ideals in Swedish competitive youth swimming: negotiating and shifting symbolic boundaries

Karin Grahn

Department of Food and Nutrition, and Sport Science, University of Gothenburg, Gothenburg, Sweden

ABSTRACT
This article explores how gendered body ideals are constructed and negotiated among 12 competitive youth swimmers in three Swedish clubs. Of particular interest are the ways boys and girls negotiate body ideals inside and outside of swimming contexts and how they shift gendered symbolic boundaries. The paper is framed by gender theory, and it draws on concepts of sport culture and social culture as well as symbolic boundaries. Interpretative repertoires were analysed to explore the language use in swimmers' conversations related to the body and body ideals. Data were produced through interviews with competitive youth swimmers. My findings show that both girls and boys negotiate body ideals. The functional body was an interpretative repertoire important in the negotiations and shifting of gendered boundaries between the athletic body in sports and the aesthetic body in society. Swimmers also used an interpretative repertoire of similarity to negotiate symbolic gender boundaries. Furthermore, both identifying with a group and being accepted in that group are suggested to be important factors involved in shifting symbolic boundaries.

High-performance swimming has been portrayed as promoting an instrumental view of the body (Jones, Glintmeyer, and McKenzie 2005; Lang 2010; McMahon and Dinan-Thompson 2011; McMahon, Penney, and Dinan-Thompson 2012). According to research into Australian swimming by McMahon and Dinan-Thompson (2011) and McMahon, Penney, and Dinan-Thompson (2012), for instance, it is argued that the swim culture reproduces a 'slim to win' ideal and emphasizes a lean body as a fast body. A slim but muscular ideal was also found in research on body image among adolescent swimmers in the United States (Porter, Morrow, and Reel 2013) and Scotland (Howells and Grogan 2012). The 'slim to win' ideal, however, can lead athletes to use extreme measures to keep their bodies slim (Jones, Glintmeyer, and McKenzie 2005; McMahon and Dinan-Thompson 2011; McMahon, Penney, and Dinan-Thompson 2012). This existing body of research provides important knowledge on the negative effects of conforming to body practices with the aim of constructing performing bodies. The majority of previous research, however, was conducted on female swimmers and does not include gender analysis (an exception is McMahon and Barker-Ruchti 2015). In this paper, thus, focus is placed on how male and female adolescent swimmers in co-educated training groups challenge body ideals.

To analyse challenges of gendered body ideals, I draw on previous research on body ideals in sport and society and employ a gender lens. Howells and Grogan's (2012) research on swimming suggests that some adolescent female athletes experience tensions between feminine body ideals and developing an athletic and muscular body (for similar findings, see Larsson 2003; Krane et al. 2004; George 2005. As described by Krane et al. (2004), this paradox between traditional feminine ideals (i.e. thin bodies) and athletic ideals (i.e. muscular bodies) leads women to experience divergent cultural ideals. While much attention has been placed on female body ideals, fewer research studies have explored male body ideals (Muren and Don 2012) and only a few studies have shown that athletic and aesthetic body ideals are similar among boys (Larsson 2003; Ricciardelli, McCabe, and Ridge 2006; Andreasson 2007).

Thus, there exists a lack of knowledge on how athletes (both girls and boys) challenge traditional body ideals, or, specific to the theme of this special issue, shift or transform gender boundaries relating to corporeal ideals.

The aim of this study is to examine how gendered body ideals are constructed and negotiated among 12 competitive youth swimmers who are members of three clubs in the Southern part of Sweden. Of particular interest are the ways through which boys and girls in this specific context come to negotiate social- and sport-specific body ideals and how this may be seen to shift gendered symbolic boundaries. The paper will explore (a) how competitive youth swimmers describe gendered body ideals, (b) the linguistic resources that swimmers draw on to describe, negotiate and/or shift boundaries between gendered body ideas in and outside of sport and (c) what aspects of the sporting culture influence the negotiation and/or shifting of boundaries between athletic bodies and traditional feminine and masculine body ideals. Potter and Wetherell's (1987) and Edley's (2001) concept 'interpretative repertoires' (which they describe to mean linguistic resources drawn upon to talk about aspects of the world), were employed to analyse data. The results present interpretative repertoires identified in the process of shaping and negotiating boundaries.

Research on body ideals

It has widely been argued that athletes strive for athletic bodies and take part in body practices that shape both their body appearances and their lived experiences of their bodies (George 2005; Harris 2005; Ross and Shinew 2008; McMahon and Dinan Thompson 2011; Porter, Morrow, and Reel 2013). Research has shown that female athletes encounter body ideals that on the one hand prescribe a thin body without defined muscles; and on the other hand, a body that reflects traditionally masculine ideals (i.e. strength and muscularity) (Larsson 2003; George 2005; Andreasson 2007). A high-performance body is desirable for both male and female athletes. However, physical strength and muscles are viewed as masculine (George 2005). This understanding shapes gendered boundaries to separate masculine and feminine bodies and construct different ideals for girls than boys.

However, sports participation also enables empowerment (Garrett 2004; Krane et al. 2004; Strandbu and Hegna 2006; Porter, Morrow, and Reel 2013) and positive self-identification (Garrett 2004). By participating in sports, some women negotiate and contest traditional feminine body ideals. As an example, Ross and Shinew's (2008) research showed that college athletes displayed 'selective femininity' by choosing when to be portrayed as traditionally feminine. Research by Andreasson (2007), Azzarito (2010), Harris (2005) and Krane (2001) suggest that the athletic body is central in constructing alternative femininities. Research on ideals among Swedish girls doing sports revealed that just as many girls were unsatisfied with lacking muscles than with lacking thinness (Lunde and Frisén 2011). This research suggest that boundaries between feminine and masculine body ideals may be shifted, however, more research is needed to understand more specifically how these boundaries are moved.

In contrast to research on body ideals among female athletes, studies on male athletes have shown that social cultural ideals and sport ideals were similar rather than contradictive (Larsson 2003; Ricciardelli et al. 2006; Andreasson 2007). According to Larsson's (2003) research on track and field athletes and Andreasson's (2007) research on handball players, a desirable, attractive body for men is intertwined with a functional, performing body. Furthermore, Ricciardelli et al. (2006) showed that adolescent boys perceived an aesthetic male body to be a functional body. However, boys/men may encounter pressure to live up to body ideals, which is shown in a study by Coffey (2013), in which 18- to 33-year old men felt that they had to live up to certain body ideals. Further, Lunde and Frisén (2011) found that Swedish boys doing sports worried about being too thin and unmuscular.

Theoretical framework

Gendered body ideals in sport and social culture

There are cultural expectations of femininity and masculinity that influence gender constructions in diverse contexts. These expectations are shaped in social practices (Krane et al. 2004), or as Ambjörnsson and Ganetz (2013) put it, social meanings are shaped both in 'practices of everyday life and in texts of different kinds' (127). Specific meanings are shaped within specific cultures; as an example, Krane et al. (2004) described athletic women as part of a sport culture and a social culture that both shape contradictive body ideals. The idea that social meaning is constructed in diverse cultures is part of the theoretical stance of feminist cultural studies, and this idea has previously been applied in studies of athletic women and their bodily experiences (e.g. Krane et al. 2001, 2004). Even though feminist cultural studies are foremost used in studies of female athletes, I consider the theoretical concept of cultures useful for the purpose of this research. In this paper, I thus build on the concepts of sport culture (i.e. youth competitive swimming in elite/youth elite groups in three Swedish clubs) and social culture (i.e. society, and more specifically school) (Krane et al. 2004). Different cultures construct diverse, although not totally different, meanings for the body and body ideals, as well as diverse meanings for the gendered body and gendered body ideals.

Symbolic and social boundaries

This paper draws upon Lamont and Molnár's (2002) concept of boundaries. Boundaries are shaped between girls and boys and between body ideals in the sport and in social culture. Symbolic boundaries are used to categorize people, objects or practices, and they therefore define group membership and shape feelings of community; conversely, they can also separate people from a group. When these categorizations become more stable and are manifested in structural differences, they construct social boundaries (Lamont and Molnár 2002). In sports, such symbolic and social boundaries divide men and women and femininity and masculinity (Coakley and Pike 2014). There is a boundary between the muscular body that is perceived as masculine and the thin body that is perceived as feminine. Contesting these ideals means crossing gender boundaries. Boundaries 'establish the differences and commonalities between women and men, among women and among men, shaping and constraining the behavior and attitudes of each gender group' (Gerson and Peiss 1985 in Lamont and Molnár 2002). In other words, gendered boundaries are both used to divide men and women, and they are also used to highlight differences between, for example, women based on different femininities. Such symbolic boundaries are resources that people use to differentiate between women conforming to preferred femininities or non-preferred femininities in a social context.

The study

This paper is written as a part of a larger research project that explores gender construction in two sports. The results in the article stem from one interview study with six athletes from three Swedish swim clubs, as well as two group interviews from an ethnographic study of competitive youth swimmers in one club. Four themes were explored in the main study: performance, training, the body and gender. For the purpose of this paper, data on the body and body ideals were included.

Swimming was chosen based on the result of a previous study (Grahn 2008) that showed that swimming was one of few sports that portrayed girls and boys equally in textbooks used in Swedish Sports Coaching education. This generated interest for additional research. Further, Swedish swimming has an even distribution of female and male athletes (RF 2013), and co-training of girls and boys is common in Swedish clubs. Both female and male Swedish elite swimmers have had international successes and receive media attention by national media. Female swimmers are highly valued in Sweden as evidenced by Sara Sjöström receiving the prestigious 'Jerring- prize' by votes of the Swedish people (SR 2015).[1] These are some of the reasons that make swimming important and interesting to analyse from a gender perspective.

Participants

Youth swimmers and coaches were chosen for the research since the main study aims to explore discourses in competitive youth sports. Three swim clubs were included based on having groups of adolescent competitive swimmers at national level, and being located in a specific geographical area in Southern Sweden. With the help of a person in the local swim confederation, I first approached a couple of clubs in a larger town, but they did not show interest for the study. At this stage, I decided to make contact directly with coaches in three clubs. These coaches were willing to participate, and I found them open and willing to share their views on swimming. Prior to the interviews with the coaches, they helped to choose swimmers for the interviews. Swimmers (both boys and girls) were selected based on age (13–16 years of age), level of competition (competitive youth swimmers on national level), being part of the youth elite or elite group in the club, and being swimmers in their investment years (Durand-Bush and Salmela 2002). Since coaches helped to choose athletes for the interviews, there was a risk of the coaches selecting athletes that would express opinions similar to those of the coaches. To limit this risk, I explained the inclusion criteria (described above) to the coaches and talked to them about potential swimmers for the interview. In the included clubs, and in each swimming group, a limited number of swimmers with the right age, gender and competitive level were available, which limited the chance that the coach could choose an athlete that best suited the coach's interest. However, since I did not know the group of swimmers, I depended on the coach to help me in the process of selecting swimmers.

Data production

In-depth interviews were conducted individually with three girls and three boys. Every swimmer was interviewed twice to enable a deeper understanding of their comments and viewpoints. As an example, the second interview included more questions on body ideals and gender since interviewees may feel more at ease to talk about such questions when being more familiar with the interviewer. Interviews resembled a conversation; however, a semi-structured interview guide was used on both occasions. Interviews included similar questions, but they were asked with flexibility and related to what the interviewees were talking about. This meant that the order of the questions differed, and subsequent questions varied. Questions were asked to enable the interviewees to talk and describe in order to obtain in-depth knowledge about their ideas of the themes of the study (Brinkman and Kvale 2015).

After the interview study, one of the clubs was selected for an ethnographic study. A mixed-sex training group consisting of competitive swimmers between the ages of 15 and their early twenties was observed. As part of this study, group interviews (Madriz 2000; Krane et al. 2004; Brinkman and Kvale 2015) were conducted with all of the 15- to 16-year olds in the group, focusing on performance, training and the swimmers' body. The swimmers were divided into two interview groups. The groups discussed the themes of the main study, and no focus was specifically placed on body ideals. The interview started with a discussion on what type of sport swimming is, which was then followed by a discussion on performance in swimming. I then asked for the interviewees' views on the performing body in swimming. This led to a discussion of the body and body ideals inside and outside of swimming. Data from this discussion were both interesting and important, and therefore included in this article.

I decided to do the group interviews in mixed-sex groups. This felt most natural since the girls and boys trained together. However, since each group consisted of only three swimmers (one girl was absent), this meant an uneven number of girls and boys. One group consisted of two girls and one boy and the other group consisted of two boys and one girl. If the group interview was designed to specifically explore gender ideals, I would have considered dividing girls in one group and boys in another, but since a discussion on body ideals was not the main aim of the interviews, I did not make such a decision. It can be viewed as problematic to discuss issues of the body in mixed-sex groups; however, the group constellation did not seem to affect the swimmers' willingness to discuss these issues. Even so, group interviews may create uneven power dynamics (Madriz 2000). Indeed, this was observed: In the first interview, the two girls were more predominant, and in the second interview, a boy and a girl were more active in answering and discussing. This means that some voices were heard more than others. Even so, I felt that the swimmers who all knew each other well seemed at ease to talk about these issues in the group. To further make sure that the swimmers could talk freely about the topics of the interview, I requested that the participants respected that things said in the group interview remained in the group and that it was not discussed with others outside of the interview context. I made the decision to do the interviews in the end of the ethnographical study. In this way, the swimmers were familiar with me since I had observed them during their training for a couple of sessions per week in a period of about two months. It also enabled me to ask questions on what I had observed.

The research project was given consent by the ethical advisory committee of the University of Gothenburg. All swimmers and their parents gave their consent in writing. In the results below, individual interviewees are represented with pseudonyms: Eric, Julia, Jenny, Tim, Susanne and Thomas. The first group of interviewees includes Ebba, Sara and Linus, and the second group includes Linn, Peter and Simon. Small adjustments were made to the quotes for clarity.

Analysis

To make meaning of the world, people draw on interpretative repertoires (i.e. linguistic resources such as words, metaphors, grammar) (Potter and Wetherell 1987; Edly 2001). Interpretative repertoires can be equated to local discourses that are produced or reproduced in social interaction, such as a conversation or an interview (Edly 2001). Since language is important in shaping reality, it is also an important source for analyses. Interpretative repertoires were analysed by reoccurring patterns in text and talk (Potter and Wetherell 1987; Edly 2001). In other words, interview transcripts were analysed with the goal of finding repetitive patterns but also variations in language use.

All of the interviews were recorded and transcribed verbatim. The initial transcripts were read and coded after the themes of the main study. Key words were noted, and interesting aspects were commented upon (Potter and Wetherell 1987). Every theme was sorted into subthemes, and the contents of these subthemes were analysed to see what linguistic resources they included. Patterns that started to emerge were labelled as potential interpretative repertoires. These were then put in a document together with quotes to support each repertoire. This enabled detailed analyses of the text such as exploring specific expressions, recurring words, metaphors and/or grammar (Potter and Wetherell 1987; Edly 2001), as well as how these fitted in to larger patterns of the text. In other words, transcripts were read by going back and forward between larger patterns and details. Finally, each repertoire received a label and was explored in relation to gender (i.e. how the diverse repertoires positioned girls and boys) (Edly 2001) as well as culture (i.e. interpretative repertoire included in speech regarding swimming, respectively, social culture) (Krane et al. 2004). This made it possible to interpret the speech of swimmers regarding body ideals in sport and social culture, as well as how symbolic boundaries were shaped and shifted in competitive youth swimming.

Result

This section describes symbolic boundaries and linguistic resources in the interviewed swimmers' descriptions of body ideals in a specific sport culture (competitive youth swimming in elite/youth elite groups in three clubs in southern Sweden) and social culture (society and school). Further, I present how gendered symbolic boundaries are shifted by the interviewed swimmers.

Body ideals in sport and social culture

My findings suggest that both girls and boys negotiate body ideals that they experience in sport culture and social culture. Interpretative repertoires on body and body ideals could be divided into *functional body* and *aesthetic body*. The first includes a muscular and a lightweight/slim body that is perceived functional for swimmers. The second includes a muscular body for boys and a thin, non-muscular body for girls. These repertoires shape diverse symbolic boundaries. These will be explored in the next two sections of the text.

Boundaries constructing similarities – the functional body

When swimmers described the body in sport culture, they referred to a functional body. This constructs a boundary that includes male and female swimmers while separating swimmers from people not participating in sports. As athletes, girls and boys share the same type of body. This was shown by recurring words used by both girls and boys in individual and group interviews to describe the swimmer's body. As an example, Ebba and Sara used words like 'big feet', 'broad shoulders' and 'strong arms'. They described that the body looks 'like a V'. In these descriptions, swimmers use an *interpretative repertoire of similarity*. Susanne explains that body ideals for girls and boys in swimming are probably similar: 'well-trained but not too muscular'. There were few associations with gender differences when swimmers talked about what kind of body is functional and competitive in swimming. This can be interpreted as the masculine body being the norm in swimming. However, in relation to research by McMahon and Barker-Ruchti (2015) that suggests that the male body is the norm in swimming, this research showed that both female and male elite swimmers were exemplified as having ideal bodies. As an example, Therese Alshammar, Sara Sjöström and Michael Phelps were common examples of swimmers having an optimal performance body. All of the swimmers emphasized muscles while talking about functional bodies.

A slim and lightweight body was also included in the interpretative repertoire of a functional body. A lightweight body was portrayed as beneficial for both boys and girls. The swimmers expressed the importance of having strong but not heavy muscles, as exemplified by Susanne: 'I want to become as strong as possible, but I don't want to get as much muscles so that they get [lactic] acid or I don't want them to be too heavy'. Even though having a slim body was part of having a swimmer's body, the swimmers did not idealize the 'slim-to-win' body described by McMahon and Dinan-Thompson (2011) and McMahon, Penney, and Dinan-Thompson (2012). None of the swimmers talked about wanting to be slimmer. Rather, they explained that they got slim by all the practice, as Ebba stated, 'You get thin [from training] […] when you train swimming you never have to think about what you eat (Sara agrees), it's great'. Feelings of not being slim were only brought up once by a boy who talked about the frustration he felt when he could not train due to injury. Tim explained thinking: 'Aah, I want to train' and as a result of not training Tim thought 'I feel fat'.

Boundary constructing differences – the aesthetic body

When the aesthetic body was described, boundaries were constructed to separate girls' and boys' ideals. This was done by portraying girls and boys as having disparate bodies. In descriptions of the aesthetic body, muscles were only desirable to boys. As Jenny explained: 'You see a nice male body as muscular, with abdominal muscles, arm muscles, and tall'. In contrast to the aesthetic masculine body, the aesthetic feminine body does not include muscles, or at least it does not include visible muscles. This fact makes the aesthetic body framed by a gendered symbolic boundary that divides girls from boys. Ebba and Sara explained that boys should have muscles, and girls should be thin and not be muscular. When I asked why, Ebba said, laughing: 'It looks good [on boys]' and 'On girls muscles are not that good looking'. In other words, when swimmers talked about the aesthetic body, gender differences were shaped, and boundaries between girls and boys maintained. When swimmers talked about body ideals in society or school, the interpretative repertoire of the functional body was absent.

Negotiating and shifting symbolic boundaries

In this section, the descriptions and negotiations of swimmers regarding two gendered body ideals are exemplified. These have been labelled the 'top model ideal' and the 'beef ideal' and build upon words/metaphors used by some of the swimmers. For girls, the most dominant feminine ideal was described as the thin body of a top model. The most dominant masculine ideal for boys was a muscular body described as 'beef' or to be 'beefy'. These ideals shaped symbolic boundaries between girls that portray traditional femininity (conforming to the top model ideal) and girls that portray an athletic functional body (not conforming to the ideals) as well as boys that exhibit traditional masculinity and boys who do not conform to traditional masculinity.

A top model ideal vs. the athletic body ideal

When describing girls, Linn said that they are supposed to be 'thin, small, and cute'. Recurrent in both the individual and group interviews was the notion of thinness as a key aesthetic ideal for girls. The top model ideal is exemplified by Jenny who described ideals shared by girls in her school: 'I think that most of them think that you should be tiny-tiny, because if you look at models and so on, all of them are really super skinny'.

Similar ideals were present in the discussion of Sara, Linus and Ebba about the athletic body vs. aesthetic ideals in school and society:

Sara: Well, you get thin [practicing swimming]. But at the same time girls are supposed to be quite thin, but we, or athletes in general, don't quiet look like that, they [athletes] develop muscles, and if you look at models they are really tiny.
Ebba: There are no muscles.
Sara: It's not at all as how we look like, but well, that's the difference.
Ebba: Girls are thin, while we are kind of ...
Sara: A little more ...
Ebba: Muscular.
Sara: Giggling
Ebba: More manly kind of (laughing), no but ...
Sara: Yeah, yeah.
Ebba: No but, it's like that.

The conversation shows that muscles on girls are perceived as masculine. This is also expressed in individual interviews. Julia said, 'You look manly if you have too much muscle', and Eric said:

> Girls they don't want to be too beefy, if you know what I mean ... Girls don't want to be as muscular, because it's not good looking ... The girls need muscles, but I don't think it is good looking if a girl has huge muscles.

Eric's statement indicates the paradox between the female athletic body and the traditional feminine ideal. On the one hand, he knows that female swimmers need muscles to perform; on the other hand, muscles are not perceived as good looking on a girl. Just as in previous research (Larsson 2003; Krane et al. 2004; George 2005; Howells and Grogan 2012), being torn between opposing body ideals was expressed by some of the girls in this study. Jenny summarizes this tension by saying, 'In swimming you want to look beefy, but when you are at school, you don't want to look beefy'. This statement exemplifies the experience of different values in sport and social culture, as described by Krane et al. (2004). Susanne further explains, 'In society, it's assumed that girls are not supposed to show that they have muscles, because it is not viewed as normal or as nice looking'.

However, top model ideals were also negotiated and contested by some swimmers. These negotiations shifted symbolic boundaries of femininity, i.e. the aesthetics of a female body. This shift of boundaries foremost consisted of girls aiming to develop more muscles. Jenny said, '... no one that trains is really fat, so you kind of compete for who weighs the most, because then you have the most muscles'. Furthermore, Jenny also explicitly turns against a top model ideal by saying the following:

> I think that girls should have quite a lot of muscles, not like a body builder, but not too thin either... And I think that one should have quite a lot of curves and not be tiny-tiny. I just don't think that [tiny-tiny] is good [...]. Like, starving yourself.

While none of the swimmers talked about wanting to get thinner, most of them talked about training to develop more muscles. In contrast to Krane et al. (2004), who found that college athletes experienced social cultural ideals of femininity to negatively affect their body image, the girls in this study seemed to be quite content with their athletic bodies. In the group interviews, I asked Ebba and Sara if they thought that they gained something positive from swimming. Sara answered, 'Actually, you get the perfect body in swimming'. They mentioned aspects such as core stability, slimness and being strong. These responses are in line with alternative body ideas and new femininities described in previous research (Azzarito 2010; Lunde and Frisén 2011).

A Beef-ideal vs. the athletic body ideal
Boys' ideals were foremost described by the swimmers as muscular and can be summarized as 'beefy'.

Linn:	Guys should be ...
Peter (cuts in):	Beefy.
Linn:	Yes.
Simon:	To be beefy that's nearly everything that guys think about.

Even though this word was sometimes used to describe both girls' and boys' muscularity in swimming, it also symbolized masculinity since muscles were described as masculine. Further, despite the fact that a muscular body was described as desirable for boys, it was not obvious that big muscles were desirable when the swimmers talked about themselves. In the individual interviews, Eric and Thomas said that they tried not to bother about social cultural ideals (i.e. being 'beefy'). Instead, they explained that they desired a functional swimmer's body, which in their view did not equal being 'beefy'. Thomas explained, 'You think about not being too big, but you are not supposed to be weak either, so in this case you have to balance how to train'.

Furthermore, in Eric's view, being too muscular was not in line with his aesthetic ideal. When asked to describe a nice-looking body, Eric said, 'Guys should have a little more muscles, but they should not be too beefy, because that doesn't look good'. The result shows that some of the boys negotiated body ideals in social culture against body ideals in sport culture, shifting the boundaries of masculinity.

Shifting boundaries in co-ed training groups

Differences of body ideals in the culture of the swimming group and social culture were discussed in the second group interview, which consisted of both boys and girls. The interviewees perceived the two cultures as very different, as Linn explains:

> […] it's really two different things [ideals in school and swimming], like different worlds here [at swimming] and in school" (Simon agrees). Well, here you can be yourself, you get accepted almost no matter what.

The swimmers expressed that the swimming milieu put less pressure on how to look:

Linn:	It is a lot of pressure [in school].
Simon:	Yes.
Linn:	It is.
Simon:	In swimming, I don't think it is so much [pressure], you know … you know each other so well here [in swimming], you see each other every day, like a family. So you accept one another for who you are.
Linn:	Yes, I think that the acceptance is much greater.
Simon (cuts in):	In swimming.
Linn:	In the world of swimming […] compared to school.

School is described as a culture where you have to fit in and a culture that puts a lot of pressure on conformity. The swimmers explained that traditional masculine and feminine traits such as acting macho as a boy or being timid as a girl were norms in school but not in the swimming group. In the same manner, they explained that a certain hairstyle, make-up and clothing were normalized in school but not in swimming. As exemplified by the quote above, both Linn and Simon agree that they experience less pressure to conform to ideals in the specific sport culture: 'You do not need to keep up the pretense at swimming' (Linn).

Further, the group interview exemplified how being part of a swimming group was important to escape from pressures to conform to feminine and masculine ideals. Using words like 'being like a family' and 'accept each other', the swimmers emphasized the importance of friendship and familiarity to be able to frame themselves distinctly from traditional feminine and masculine body and beauty ideals.

Judging from the results of this study, swimming culture (as it is experienced by the interviewed swimmers in the second group interview) helps relieve pressure to look or act in certain ways. This experience may not be true of all swimmers since swimming has been described as putting pressure on maintaining a low body weight in research by Jones, Glintmeyer, and McKenzie (2005), Lang (2010), and McMahon and Dinan-Thompson (2011) and McMahon, Penney, and Dinan-Thompson (2012) and to confirm to male body ideals (McMahon and Barker-Ruchti 2015).

The swimmers' shared experiences from the specific sport culture helped to shift gendered symbolic boundaries. Some of the girls explained how acceptance of a muscular body arose from sharing this muscularity with other swimmers or athletes. Jenny describes, 'I think that we girls develop a lot of muscles when doing swimming and we have accepted that we won't be tiny-tiny'. This quote suggests that identifying with each other is important to shift boundaries.

Gendered symbolic boundaries in swimming were also shifted within an interpretative repertoire of similarity. When the swimmers talked about themselves and their friends in the swimming group, they drew less upon differences and more upon similarities. As an example, a lot of experiences were shared by girls and boys in co-ed swimming, such as training in similar ways, having fun together, travelling and living together during camp and competitions. However, similar body experiences did not equate to similar ways that swimmers viewed male and female bodies. For example, boys were described as more muscular; still, the swimmers shared similar body ideals and experiences from training. Linn said, 'In swimming, all of us have similar bodies, to a certain degree. All of us are athletically built'.

Discussion

The research shows that the 12 interviewed swimmers negotiated their views of the body inside and outside of swimming by using linguistic resources and cultural aspects from the swimming context that they were included in. This study suggests four resources that swimmers used to shift boundaries. First, the functional body was an interpretative repertoire included by both girls and boys in their negotiations of body ideals from the social culture. By emphasizing functionality, swimmers could resist the top model and beef ideal. This helped them to shift the symbolic boundaries that frame the female body as traditionally feminine (i.e. thin) and the male body as traditionally masculine (i.e. muscular). Second, within an interpretative repertoire of similarity, swimmers could identify as a group that had similar experiences and similar body ideals. This view shifted symbolic boundaries that differentiate girls from boys. Third, by being part of a co-ed swimming group, swimmers constantly cross gender boundaries that typically exist in sports. Co-training is part of the culture of swimming in the studied clubs. Similar experiences among girls and boys were an important part of shaping the interpretative repertoire of similarity described above. Fourth, a recourse that was especially vivid in the group interview was acceptance. Being part of a group and identifying with other swimmers became resources for swimmers to shift symbolic boundaries between the athletic body ideal and traditional feminine and masculine aesthetic body ideals.

The result adds to previous research by showing that both girls and boys included in the study negotiated body ideals. For some of the boys, the cultural beef ideal was not always equivalent to a functional swimmer's body. Even though muscles were viewed as being important to look good and to perform (Larsson 2003; Andreasson 2007), having huge muscles or too heavy muscles was not seen as functional.

The result confirms previous research that suggests contradictive body ideals for girls (Krane et al. 2001, 2004; Larsson 2003). However, the interviews also reveal negotiations and resistance against traditional feminine body ideals, similar to Ross and Shinew (2008) and Porter, Morrow, and Reel (2013). The girls expressed that muscles were desirable to perform well in sports. As discussed above, the functional body seems to be important to escape traditional gendered body ideals. This finding is in line with research by Howells and Grogan (2012) that showed that within the swimming context, function was emphasized more than the aesthetic look of the body. Just as girls used an interpretative repertoire of the functional body to justify a muscular feminine body, some boys used this repertoire to avoid getting too 'beefy'.

In line with research by Porter, Morrow, and Reel (2013) and Howells and Grogan (2012), the slim and muscular swimmers' body was idealized in this study. However, the 'slim-to-win' body (Jones, Glintmeyer, and McKenzie 2005; McMahon and Dinan-Thompson 2011; McMahon, Penney, and Dinan-Thompson 2012) was not idealized by the swimmers. While research by McMahon and Dinan-Thompson (2011) and McMahon, Penney, and Dinan-Thompson (2012) and Jones, Glintmeyer, and McKenzie (2005) were done with elite athletes, this research was conducted on club level and mainly among youth athletes that had not yet reached the highest international competitive level. It should also be noted that the coach in the club that took part in the ethnographic study worked to sustain well-being, the athletes' learning and a good group climate (Grahn 2014), which may have countered regulative practices such as the ones described elsewhere (Jones, Glintmeyer, and McKenzie 2005; McMahon and Dinan Thompson 2011; McMahon, Penney, and Dinan-Thompson 2012). Additionally, the coaches included in the interviews said that they did not encourage their swimmers to lose weight due to anxiety of eating disorders (Grahn 2015).

The swimmers used body experiences from the specific sport culture to negotiate and in some cases transgress traditional gendered body ideals. Even though the shifting of boundaries was more obvious among girls, the research adds important knowledge about boys' negotiations and shifting of gendered symbolic boundaries. The girls shifted boundaries by using the swimming culture to normalize being or wanting to be muscular. In so doing, some of them shifted traditional views of how to look like a woman by drawing on athletic ideals. However, in contrast to McMahon and Barker-Ruchti's (2015) results, the boyish body was not the only ideal since girls incorporated muscles as being part of the female athletic body. Wanting more muscle has also been shown to be a desire among Swedish girls (Lunde and Frisén 2011). However, judging from McMahon and Barker-Ruchti's (2015) research, idealizing the (male) athletic body may become problematic for girls doing swimming. This research, however, suggests that being part of a group of swimmers that all share a common body appearance seems to be part of accepting and normalizing an athletic build and a muscular body for girls (cf. Porter et al. 2013 and Howells and Grogan 2012).

In the second group interview, the group was viewed as important to be able to feel good about one's self and to relieve pressure from social culture. Research by Steinfeldt et al. (2011) showed that valuing relationships and collaboration with others was vital for women with a high level of body esteem. The authors interpret the social support of friends as being important. Judging from the results of the interviews in the current study, as well as the ethnographical data in the main project, friendship and social relationships were highly valued among the swimmers. This fact is interpreted as an important part of why traditional gendered body ideals can be negotiated and shifted. Friendship as a resource for shifting boundaries needs to be further explored in research, not only as a female norm as in work by Steinfeldt et al. (2011), but also as a possible norm in co-educated training groups. Furthermore, Steinfeldt and colleagues suggest that the sharing of body ideals among girls is an important part of the athletic environment. Similar results were found in this study.

While the sample of this research is restricted to a few youth competitive swimmers in three Swedish swim clubs, the study provides insights in how some swimmers can shift symbolic gendered boundaries by using sociocultural aspects from swimming and specific linguistic resources. The inclusion of these clubs was based on the fact that coaches were willing to let me attend and/or ask questions about their practice. This may have resulted in getting access to clubs and coaches that were more open to being studied than others that would not participate. The club that participated in the ethnographic part of the research is also overrepresented in the study (i.e. it was included in both individual and group interviews). Since the coach of this swimming group was considered to work in a quite sustainable coaching practice (Grahn 2014), this may have affected the positive results in this study.

A limitation of this study is that the data only give an idea of how swimmers in this specific context negotiate body ideals that enable the shifting of symbolic boundaries. The data do not tell us if the swimmers actually cross symbolic and social boundaries in contexts beyond the specific swimming contexts. One could further explore if shifting symbolic boundaries through sports actually enables shifting or crossing social boundaries in the social culture, e.g. in a school context. This could be done by exploring the 'two different worlds' expressed in the second group interview and whether gendered boundaries are shifted or crossed in everyday situations outside of swimming. Additionally, there is a need to explore how the interpretative repertoires of the functional body work for swimmers to shift boundaries in the long run. Does this repertoire continue to work as a positive force against traditional gendered ideals, and how does this repertoire work to shape body images when swimmers cease competitive sports and spend more of their everyday life in social culture?

Conclusion

In this paper, I have argued that youth competitive swimmers in three Swedish clubs employed linguistic resources that were used to negotiate gendered body ideals and to shift symbolic boundaries. These resources were identified as an interpretative repertoire of a functional body and an interpretative repertoire of similarity. Further, being part of and accepted in a group, sharing similar body ideals and corporal experiences, are suggested to be important factors involved in negotiating and shifting symbolic boundaries. The research shows how important it is to include analyses of language to obtain knowledge on how gendered symbolic boundaries are shifted in specific sport contexts and can further be used as a point of departure to explore processes of shifting and crossing gendered boundaries and corporal ideals in sports.

Note

1. The prize is instituted in memory of the reporter Sven Jerring. Every year since 1979, an athlete has been awarded for the best Swedish sport performance.

Disclosure statement

No potential conflict of interest was reported by the author.

Funding

This work was supported by the Swedish National Centre for Research in Sports.

References

Ambjornsson, F., and H. Ganetz. 2013. "Introduction: Feminist Cultural Studies." *Culture Unbound: Journal of Current Cultural Research* 5: 127–131.

Andreasson, J. 2007. Idrottens kön: genus, kropp och sexualitet i lagidrottens vardag [The gender of sports: Gender, body and sexuality in the everyday life of team sports]. PhD diss., Lunds University.

Azzarito, L. 2010. "Future Girls, Transcendent Femininities and New Pedagogies: Toward Girls' Hybrid Bodies?" *Sport, Education and Society* 15: 261–275. doi:10.1080/13573322.2010.493307.

Brinkman, S., and S. Kvale. 2015. *InterViews. Learning the Craft of Qualitative Research Interviewing*. 3rd ed. Thousand Oaks, CA: Sage.

Coffey, J. 2013. "'Body Pressure'. Negotiating Gender through Body Work Practices." *Youth Studies Australia* 32: 39–48.

Coakley, J., and E. Pike. 2014. *Sports in Society: Issues and Controversies*. London: McGraw-Hill Education.

Durand-Bush, N., and J. H. Salmela. 2002. "The Development and Maintenance of Expert Athletic Performance: Perceptions of World and Olympic Champions." *Journal of Applied Sport Psychology* 14: 154–171. doi:10.1080/10413200290103473.

Edley, N. 2001. "Analysing Masculinity: Interpretative Repertoires, Ideological Dilemmas and Subject Positions." In *Discourse as Data: A Guide for Analysis*, edited by M. Wetherell, S. Taylor and S. Yates, 189–228. London: Sage.

Garrett, R. 2004. "Negotiating a Physical Identity: Girls, Bodies and Physical Education." *Sport, Education and Society* 9: 223–237. doi:10.1080/1357332042000233958.

George, M. 2005. "Making Sense of Muscle: The Body Experiences of Collegiate Women Athletes." *Sociological Inquiry* 75: 317–345. doi:10.1111/j.1475-682X.2005.00125.x.

Grahn, K. 2008. Flickor och pojkar i idrottens läromedel: konstruktioner av genus i ungdomstränarutbildningen [Girls and boys in sports textbooks. Constructions of gender in youth coaching education programmes]. PhD Diss., University of Gothenburg: Acta Universitatis Gothoburgensis.

Grahn, K. 2014. "Alternative Discourses in the Coaching of High Performance Youth Sport: Exploring Language of Sustainability." *Reflective Practice* 15: 40–52. doi:10.1080/14623943.2013.868795.

Grahn, K. 2015. "Lång och biffig men lätt Och smal." *Svensk Idrottsforskning*, 3: 1–5, 14, 24–28. http://centrumforidrottsforskning.se/wp-content/uploads/2014/12/SVIF-4-2014-Utseendeideal-unga-elitsimmare.pdf.

Harris, J. 2005. "The Image Problem in Women's Football." *Journal of Sport & Social Issues* 29: 184–197. doi:10.1177/0193723504273120.

Howells, K., and S. Grogan. 2012. "Body Image and the Female Swimmer: Muscularity but in Moderation." *Qualitative Research in Sport, Exercise and Health* 4: 98–116. doi:10.1080/2159676X.2011.653502.

Jones, R. L., N. Glintmeyer, and A. McKenzie. 2005. "Slim Bodies, Eating Disorders and the Coach-Athlete Relationship: A Tale of Identity Creation and Disruption." *International Review for the Sociology of Sport* 40: 377–391. doi:10.1177/1012690205060231.

Krane, V. 2001. "We Can Be Athletic and Feminine, But Do We Want to? Challenging Hegemonic Femininity in Women's Sport." *Quest* 53: 115–133. doi:10.1080/00336297.2001.10491733.

Krane, V., J. J. Waldron, J. Michalenok, and J. Stiles-Shipley. 2001. "Body Image Concerns in Female Exercisers and Athletes: A Feminist Cultural Studies Perspective." *Women in Sport and Physical Activity Journal* 10: 17–54.

Krane, V., P. Choi, S. Baird, C. Aimar, and K. Kauer. 2004. "Living the Paradox: Female Athletes Negotiate Femininity and Muscularity." *Sex Roles* 50: 315–329.

Lamont, M., and V. Molnár. 2002. "The Study of Boundaries in the Social Sciences." *Annual Review of Sociology* 28: 167–195. doi:10.1146/annurev.soc.28.110601.141107.

Lang, M. 2010. "Surveillance and Conformity in Competitive Youth Swimming." *Sport, Education and Society* 15: 19–37. doi:10.1080/13573320903461152.

Larsson, H. 2003. "A History of the Present on the 'Sportsman' and the 'Sportswoman.'" *Qualitative Social Research* 4, Atr. 9. http://www.qualitative-research.net/index.php/fqs/article/view/751.

Lunde, C., and A. Frisén. 2011. Man mår bättre, får mer muskler och ser bättre ut [You feel better, get more muscles and look better]. *Svensk Idrottsforskning* 20: 24–28.

Madriz, E. 2000. "Focus Groups in Feminist Research." In *Handbook of Qualitative Research*. 2nd ed, edited by N. K. Denzin and Y. S. Lincoln, 835–850. Thousand Oaks, CA: Sage.

McMahon, J., and N. Barker-Ruchti. 2015. "Assimilating to a Boy's Body Shape for the Sake of Performance: Three Female Athletes' Body Experiences in a Sporting Culture." *Sport, Education and Society*. Advance online publication. doi:10.1080/13573322.2015.1013463.

McMahon, J., and M. Dinan-Thompson. 2011. "'Body Work—Regulation of a Swimmer Body': An Autoethnography from an Australian Elite Swimmer." *Sport, Education and Society* 16: 35–50. doi:10.1080/13573322.2011.531960.

McMahon, J., D. Penney, and M. Dinan-Thompson. 2012. "'Body Practices – Exposure and Effect of a Sporting Culture?' Stories from Three Australian Swimmers." *Sport, Education and Society* 17: 181–206. doi:10.1080/13573322.2011.607949.

Muren, S. K., and B. P. Don. 2012. "Body Image and Gender Roles." In *Encyclopedia of Body Image and Human Appearance*, edited by T. F. Cash, 128–134. Amsterdam: Academic Press.

Porter, R. R., S. L. Morrow, and J. J. Reel. 2013. "Winning Looks: Body Image among Adolescent Female Competitive Swimmers." *Qualitative Research in Sport, Exercise and Health* 5: 179–195. doi:10.1080/2159676X.2012.712983.

Potter, J., and M. Wetherell. 1987. *Discourse and Social Psychology. Beyond Attitudes and Behavior*. London: Sage.

Ricciardelli, L., M. McCabe, and D. Ridge. 2006. "The Construction of the Adolescent Male Body through Sport." *Journal of Health Psychology* 11: 577–587. doi:10.1177/1359105306065018.

RF (Riksidrottsförbundet/The Swedish Sport Confederation). 2013. Idrotten i siffror [Sports in numbers]. http://www.rf.se/ImageVaultFiles/id_48735/cf_394/2013_-_Idrotten_i_siffror_-_RF.PDF.

Ross, S. R., and K. J. Shinew. 2008. "Perspectives of Women College Athletes on Sport and Gender." *Sex Roles* 58: 40–57. doi:10.1007/s11199-007-9275-4.

SR (Sveriges Radio/Swedish Radio). 2015. Jerringpriset till Sara Sjöström [The Jerring-prize to Sara Sjöström]. http://sverigesradio.se/sida/gruppsida.aspx?programid=3295&grupp=16930&artikel=6071812.

Steinfeldt, J. A., R. Zakrajsek, H. Carter, and M. Clint Steinfeldt. 2011. "Conformity to Gender Norms among Female Student-athletes: Implications for Body Image." *Psychology of Men & Masculinity* 12: 401–416. doi:10.1037/a0023634.

Strandbu, Å., and K. Hegna. 2006. "Experiences of Body and Gender Identity among Young Female Norwegian Basketball Players." *Sport in Society* 9: 108–127. doi:10.1177/0044118X12445177.

Health-related gender boundary crossing in youth elite sport

Astrid Schubring[a] and Ansgar Thiel[b]

[a]Department of Food and Nutrition, and Sport Science, University of Gothenburg, Gothenburg, Sweden; [b]Institute of Sport Science, University of Tübingen, Tübingen, Germany

ABSTRACT
Gender has been found to play an important role in moderating health outcomes and behaviours. However, strong similarities in male and female athletes' handling of pain and injury have been noted. The dominance of health practices associated with 'orthodox masculinity' references elite sport's risky body culture. Drawing on the concept of 'gender boundary crossing', we question how athletes negotiate orthodox masculine health practices and body–self relationships in the process of socialization. Our analysis draws on qualitative interviews with male and female athletes aged 14–19 performing at the national level in German youth elite sport. Our findings indicate that while practices of pain ignorance and instrumental body relations dominate among female and male adolescent athletes, some develop less orthodox practices such as caring for the body and avoiding health risks. Critical events and alternative social networks were found to promote this health-related gender boundary crossing in elite sport.

Introduction

High-performance sport has been characterized as a masculine sphere. This is, for one, rooted in the history of modern sport, as an invention 'by men for men' (Kidd 2013; Pfister 2013). Additionally, high-performance sport celebrates values and behaviours that are widely associated with 'orthodox masculinity' (Anderson 2005; Pronger 1990),[1] such as performance, vigour, stamina, body control and a combative mind-set (McKay 2000; Messner 1990). This nexus of high-performance sport and orthodox masculinity remains a powerful force in shaping athletes' bodies and identity construction (Berg, Migliaccio, and Anzini-Varesio 2013; Drummond 2010; Kidd 2013).

The impact of orthodox masculine ideals is particularly evident in the way injuries, illnesses and bodily flaws are handled in elite sport. Sociological studies state that ignoring pain, suppressing bodily needs, stigmatizing weaknesses and sacrificing long-term health constitute normative health practices in high-performance sport (Safai 2003; Schubring and Thiel 2011; Theberge 2008; Thiel, Mayer, and Digel 2010; Young, White, and McTeer 1994). The adoption of these risky practices has been reconstructed as a socialization effect of the masculine body culture in high-performance sport, and thus applies to both male and female athletes (Charlesworth and Young 2006; Kidd 2013; Messner and Sabo 1990; Nixon 1992). However, micro-level analyses indicate that athletes' health-related practices are not so homogenous and that some athletes do not conform to the orthodox masculine body culture (Anderson and McGuire 2013; Berg, Migliaccio, and Anzini-Varesio 2013; Pike 2005; Schubring and Thiel 2014). Such findings exemplarily refer what Lamont and Molnár (2002) have termed 'boundary crossing and boundary shifting', a process through which social constructions of gender sameness and otherness are challenged either on an individual, an organizational or a symbolic level.

It is the purpose of this special issue to explore the shifting, crossing and transforming of gender boundaries in physical culture[2] (Barker-Ruchti, Grahn, and Lindgren 2015). With our focus on high-performance sport, our first aim is to explore normative health practices and body–self relationships in order to then demonstrate how, through the adoption of unorthodox health practices and more caring body–self relationships, individual athletes negotiate and shift gender boundaries. Our investigation of this intersection focuses on adolescent athletes. This age group is ideal for our purposes for several reasons: adolescence is the central period for the development of one's own identity and for socialization into society (Hurrelmann 2007; Richartz 2000). At the same time, adolescents experience major body changes, which require them to negotiate their own body understanding against the backdrop of socially available gender norms (Azzarito and Katzew 2010; Kolip and Buksch 2012; Lorber 2001). Within this process, health-related practices play a key role (Evans et al. 2011). Finally, within elite sport, the time between 14 and 19 years of age is characterized by both increased inclusion in the high-performance system and critical career transitions (Barker-Ruchti and Schubring 2015; Richartz 2000; Schubring and Thiel 2014).

In the following, we first provide background knowledge on the interrelatedness of gender constructions and health behaviours. We then describe our methodology and present findings from high-performance sport that illustrate how orthodox masculine norms in relation to health are interpreted and challenged. To demonstrate athletes' boundary crossings, we focus on two case studies. Finally, we discuss conditions that may have led the respective athletes to counter the dominant norms.

Health-related practices and gender constructions

Gender has been found to play an important role in moderating health outcomes for adults and youths (Bordo 1990; Currie et al. 2012; Evans et al. 2011; Sointu 2011). For example, the Health Behaviour in School-Aged Children (HBSC)[3] study found the prevalence of severe injuries significantly higher in boys, while girls rated their health systematically lower and reported more psychosomatic problems (Currie et al. 2012). Although these gender differences are intersected by socioeconomic status, place of residence and social networks, significant gender gaps have also been found in the health and risk behaviours of children and continue to increase into adolescence (Currie et al. 2012; Kolip and Bucksch 2012).

Health-related gender differences, however, cannot be reduced to sex-specific biogenetic dispositions and maturation processes. Rather, the interrelation between gender and health reflects the dominant social ideals about masculinity and femininity to which individuals relate in their bodily practices (Bordo 1990; Evans et al. 2011; Drummond 2010). Analysing eating disorders from a cultural feminist perspective, for instance, Bordo (1990) argues that the Western idealization of feminine beauty as slender and fat free contributed significantly to the rise of 'disordered' body–self relationships in women.

Bodily enculturation effects have been theorized by body sociologists such as Bourdieu (1984), who outlined that socialization involves the 'incorporation' of context-specific patterns of perception, thought and action. From this perspective, socialization not only transforms and cultivates the body, but also shapes 'the way of treating it, caring for it, feeding it, maintaining it' (Bourdieu 1984, 190). Hence, socialization involves the embodiment of context-specific body–self relationships and health-related 'somatic practices' (see, Boltanski 1976; Bourdieu 1984; Meuser 2005).

Against this theoretical backdrop, gender ideals can thus be understood as 'symbolic boundaries' (Lamont and Molnár 2002), which orient identity constructions and body–self relationships. Furthermore, gender constructions have the potential to materialize into 'social boundaries' (Lamont and Monlnár 2002), constraining individuals' behaviours and access to social positions or groupings. In the context of health, gender boundaries manifest themselves, for example, when 'the "boys-don't-cry" doctrine' deters boys from reporting health complaints. Such complaints may result in the questioning of their masculinity by peers or even to social exclusion. Persisting health discrepancies in men and women also reflect the boundary function of gender constructions. As 'health-promoting behaviours are linked with femininity and risk-taking health behaviours are linked with masculinity' (Evans et al. 2011, 8), individuals may intentionally (or not) position themselves within these norms. Essentialist and opposing conceptions of risk-taking men and caring women refer to orthodox conceptions of masculinity and femininity, where manliness is associated with physical toughness and emotional stoicism (Anderson 2005; Evans et al. 2011; Messner and Sabo 1990), and femininity with fragility and emotionality (Meuser 2005; O'Brien, Hunt, and Hart 2005; Pfister 2013). These stereotypical gender conceptions are still embedded in many social structures, affecting socialization processes even today.

Gender theories have, however, pointed out that gender identity is neither given nor simply transferred but acquired and communicated through 'doing gender' (West and Zimmerman 1987), or challenged and resisted through 'undoing gender' (Deutsch 2007). Furthermore, an increasing amount of feminist, masculinity and gender studies research outlines how stereotypical constructions of femininity and masculinity are being challenged (Anderson and McGuire 2013; Deutsch 2007; Howson 2006; O'Brien, Hunt, and Hart 2005), as individuals draw on and adopt both masculine and feminine body signifiers and practices in order to construct more 'fluid' (Azzarito and Katzew 2010) or 'inclusive' (Anderson 2005) gender identities. As a result of this, new categories have emerged acknowledging the co-existence of a range of masculinities and femininities,[4] which differ from 'orthodox' (Anderson and McGuire 2013) or 'hegemonic' (Connell and Messerschmidt 2005) forms. As individuals frequently 'cross' binary gender constructions (Azzarito and Katzew 2010), gender boundaries have now become more flexible in many fields. This is precisely the focus of this special issue, as it is assumed that boundaries can be shifted and crossed. Within this process, health-related practices represent powerful symbols through which gender is constituted, challenged or transformed (Evans et al. 2011; Lee and Frayn 2008; Meuser 2005; O'Brien, Hunt, and Hart 2005). This interrelation is of particular interest with regard to elite sport, where orthodox masculine practices and body signifiers have long been highly valued.

Health-related practices in high-performance sport

Elite sport has been characterized as a high-risk activity that entails considerable health costs, including short- and long-term injuries and overuse problems (for overview see Loland, Skirstad, and Waddington 2006). Beyond structural conditions, health problems have been traced back to a powerful 'culture of risk' (Nixon 1992) that values 'making sacrifices for The Game, striving for distinction, accepting risks and playing through pain, and refusing to accept limits' (Hughes and Coakley 1991, 309–310). This value system is further supported by a 'win at all costs' attitude, which encourages 'those who become athletes to treat their bodies as instruments and to submit to physical and psychological injury and to inflict it on others' (Kidd 2013, 559). The elite sport body culture thus has significant consequences for those who are socialized into it, and risky health practices have been reported in both male and female athletes (e.g. Berg, Migliaccio, and Anzini-Varesio 2013; Theberge 2008; Thiel, Mayer, and Digel 2010).

Indeed, athletes are expected to prove their status through the adoption of body strategies that overlap largely with what Courtenay (2000, 1389) lists under 'health-related demonstration of hegemonic masculinity', namely 'the denial of weakness or vulnerability, emotional and physical control, the appearance of being strong and robust, dismissal of any need for help … the display of aggressive behaviour and physical dominance'. These context-specific behavioural norms are found to have a strong impact on adolescent athletes, who strive to establish themselves in the elite sport system (Barker-Ruchti and Schubring 2015; Malcom 2006; Moegling 2006; Schubring and Thiel 2011, 2014). Recent findings reveal, however, that some athletes challenge the orthodox masculine body culture. For example, Berg, Migliaccio, and Anzini-Varesio (2013) report that some female football players did not hide pain but talked openly about it (182), and Anderson and McGuire (2013) observed male rugby players offering emotional support to injured team members instead of stigmatizing them.

Drawing on these findings and the metaphorical concepts of 'gender boundary shifting, crossing, and moving' (Barker-Ruchti, Grahn, and Lindgren 2015), we thus argue, on the one hand, that the construction of an athletic identity constitutes a heavily orthodox masculine practice. On the other hand, we regard the adoption of health-protective and caring behaviours as unorthodox and thus a practice through which athletes shift normative boundaries. Based on this understanding, two questions lead our empirical study: First, how do adolescent athletes construct their body–self relationships within the orthodox masculine body culture of high-performance sport? And second, in which health-related practices do they engage and what are the conditions that allow them to cross dominant gender boundaries in elite sport?

Methodology

The following analysis of gender boundary construction and shifting draws on the qualitative study of a research project on the health situation in German youth Olympic sport. Ethical approval for the study was obtained from the medical faculty of Tübingen ethics committee (222/2009BO1) and a detailed study report is found elsewhere (Thiel et al. 2011).[5]

Sampling and data collection

The qualitative study includes youth athletes from the Olympic disciplines biathlon, artistic gymnastics, handball and wrestling. These disciplines were purposefully selected as each involves different demands, training regimes and health risks. For data collection, a multi-method approach was chosen including biographical interviews with youth athletes, expert interviews with coaching and medical staff as well as several days of participation in each discipline (see Thiel et al. 2011). In this article, we have focused on 24 athletes' biographical narrations (equal numbers of girls and boys in each discipline), and used the other data sources only for contextualization. All participating athletes held national squad status and were between 14 and 19 years old at the time of their interview. Most of the athletes in the study were in the youth level squads. Some, however, had already reached the junior or even senior level (e.g. in women's artistic gymnastics). All interviewed adolescents were guaranteed confidentiality and participation was entirely voluntary, in keeping with ethical standards of interviewing (Amis 2005).

For the interviews, a narrative approach with open-ended questions was chosen (Chase 2011; Denzin 1989) in order to gain insight into the youth athletes' processes of meaning-making. Furthermore, narrative interviews have been valued as 'windows into peoples' lives (Denzin 1989) that give insight into critical life events and display the sociocultural shaping of individual biographies (Chase 2011; Sparkes 1996). In the interviews, the following themes were covered: career development, experiences and handling of health and illness/injury, health-preventive behaviours, eating habits, health care and support systems. During the interviews, athletes were also asked to draw developmental lines for their subjective well-being and the importance of health and nutrition at different moments in their career (see, Schubring 2014, 77). The use of this self-developed graphic tool strengthened the biographical dimension and helped the adolescents to recall critical experiences and changes over time. Interviews were either conducted at training centres or during national training camps; some were also conducted at the athletes' homes. They lasted from 50 to 150 min. All interviews were transcribed verbatim using a simplified conversation analysis transcription system (Selting et al. 1998).

Data analysis

For the data analysis, we first read the transcripts in-depth in order to reconstruct each athlete's biographical development and identify the central themes within each interview. This resulted in a thematic coding of the interviews. In the next step, we focused on the youth athletes' descriptions of handling pain, injury and illness and use of health-preventive strategies. We used a hermeneutic approach (Denzin 1989) and microlinguistic procedure (Kruse 2014) to reconstruct individual meaning-making, body–self relationships and social norms within the athletes' description of experience and behaviour. In order to identify normative patterns of dealing with pain, illnesses, injuries and the body, we compared the individual cases with one another (Kruse 2014). This comparison allowed us to identify understandings and descriptions of behaviour that challenged the orthodox masculine practices and indicated an unorthodox body–self relationship. Within the following presentation of results, we focus on two cases where athletes negotiate the orthodox masculine body culture by embracing greater body awareness and practices of self-care. This was not a dominant pattern within the group of young athletes. We thus choose one male and one female athlete who provided extensive data and in-depth reflections on the negotiation process. In order to highlight the process of gender boundary shifting, we start out by describing how orthodox health-related practices contribute to gender boundary constructions in young elite athletes.

Findings

'You try to play the tough guy'. Orthodox masculine health practices in youth athletes

The interviews provide in-depth and, in some cases, troubling accounts of pain, injury and illness experiences athletes can have in adolescence when aiming for a career in elite sport. While injury and illness experiences differ individually and between disciplines, going through and dealing with pain constitutes a collective experience. In the following section, we draw on quotes from both male and female biathletes, handball players, gymnasts and wrestlers to illustrate that taking bodily risks and ignoring pain constitute a normative practice in this group. The quotations further outline how embracing a 'tough guy' attitude, talk and practice contribute to the adolescents' construction of an athletic identity within the normative gender confines of elite sport.

For example, Lin,[6] a 15-year-old gymnast who trains about 20 h per week, explains:

> It [the pain] is just a part of it and when you can't handle it, then you are just a little too whiny for the sport. Because this ain't some kids' game where you never get hurt.

Lin has learnt to control bodily signs of pain and to mask her emotions, notably in competition:

> Nobody is interested in whether you suffer pain or not. You don't get extra points for clenching your teeth. That's why you don't tell anybody or show it but you try to play the tough guy.

In a similar way, Ron, a 17-year-old wrestler who lives at a boarding school and trains about as much as Lin, explains that the disrespect of pain is key, both to win but also to avoid being stigmatized:

> No, you usually don't say anything because then you'd be the sissy; that's just how it is. You have to swallow the pain … because if you have a small pain during the match and you get distracted, then that's it usually. That's an opening for your opponent. Then it's over.

Both Ron and Lin associate pain acceptance with characteristics that define traditional ideas of masculinity and at the same time construct this behaviour as a marker of 'real' athletehood. Simon, an 18-year-old handball player who trains about 9 h per week and has regular games at the weekend, also supports this notion. He describes pain tolerance as a necessary disposition:

> When you want to compete at the top, pain comes with the territory. You have to be ready to take the pain in order to make a goal.

The fact that the level to which an athlete embraces this 'tough guy' attitude does influence his or her in or exclusion from elite sport competitions, and practice is further supported by coach Nick, a former biathlete now in his 30s. He interprets both male and female youth athletes' willingness to embrace pain as the decisive selection criterion:

> The older they are, those who are not ready to torture themselves have already been sorted out or have already given up on their own or have been told that it might not be the right thing for them … so only the ones who are willing to suffer are in the game.

While the acceptance of bodily pain and suffering is constructed as the dividing line between those who are selected and those who are 'sorted out', this practice promotes a risky body–self relationship that includes bodily damage. Magnus, a 17-year-old gymnast who experiences chronic pain in his wrist and back but still trains more than 20 h per week, states:

> You can't do it without having pain. It just isn't possible to go so many years without an injury or to have everything work out perfectly. It doesn't work like that. Because the body is under such intense pressure that it just can't stand it ... It [pain] is just a part of it all.

The readiness to take bodily risks leads some athletes to think of painkillers as a legitimate way to avoid missing an important competition. For example, Carina, a 16-year-old handball player who lives at a boarding school, explains that she generally does not take painkillers, unless 'there is something big like a [national] championship coming up, then you just have to turn a blind eye to it [painkillers]'.

The above-cited quotations outline the wide acceptance of 'the pain principle' (Young, White, and McTeer 1994) in both male and female youth athletes. Furthermore, the interviewed athletes are aware of the symbolic power of orthodox masculine body strategies in elite sport (Kidd 2013; Malcom 2006; Pronger 1990). Risking bodily health and suppressing emotions seem to allow both boys and girls to acquire status and raise their chances for selection and promotion. Beyond its relevance for 'doing athlete', tolerating pain is also experienced as a strong symbolic gender marker (Lamont and Molnár 2002). Thus, some male athletes address the risk of being stigmatized as 'a sissy' when crossing gender boundaries by showing (too much) sensitivity to pain. The risk of stigmatization is directly linked to both the social construction of health-related practices as gendered (Evans et al. 2011; Meuser 2005) and the devaluation of so-called 'feminine' practices and attitudes in elite sport (Kidd 2013; Theberge 2008). This interrelation also affects female athletes but with a somewhat inverse dynamic. Some of them report, not without pride, experiencing themselves as different from girls outside of sport, which they link to the capacity to accept pain and take health risks. By explicitly rejecting a 'feminizing' fragility and sensitivity to body signals, they both negotiate and reproduce orthodox conceptions of femininity (Deutsch 2007; Lamont and Molnár 2002). This is illustrated by Silvia, a 17-year-old wrestler:

> I am not as sensitive as some other (laughs) girls. There are some who are more sensitive and some who are rougher and I belong to the rougher group. You just get used to the pain. It just somehow becomes a part of your life, having that pain.

The fact that pain is widely accepted as a part of elite sport practice also affects youth athletes coping with health problems (Schubring and Thiel 2014). Various athletes recount having adopted risky health behaviours (e.g. competing while injured, seeking medical help too late or not at all and taking pain killers when injured) that align with orthodox masculinity (see, e.g. Courtenay 2000; Lorber 2001; Messner and Sabo 1990; Meuser 2005). However, some athletes developed unorthodox body–self relationships, notably in the aftermath of career-critical injuries or illnesses. In the following section, two such cases are presented.

Negotiating gender boundaries through unorthodox health practices in elite sport

From pain ignorance to health awareness

Sina is a 16-year-old handball player who lives at a boarding school, trains in a first division club, and is a member of the national youth team. Prior to playing handball, she played football and had a horse that she rode regularly. Usually, she trains about 12 hours per week and has youth and women's team events on weekends. However, since her move to the first division club boarding school, Sina increasingly suffers from knee problems, which have forced her to take a longer break.

The handball player describes herself as dedicated:

> When I play handball, then I really do it and not halfway ... not even I can slow myself down then.

As a pivot, she is used to getting hit, bumped or pinched but nevertheless likes matches to be tough and challenging. Like many of the other athletes, Sina strongly adheres to the 'elite sport ethic' (Hughes and Coakley 1991). In order to win, she does not bother to protect herself:

> I go right into the gap. Even when my chance of somehow getting through is pretty slim, I still go there. I really throw myself into it and then I do land on the ground and it hurts, but I do it anyways.

While aggressive play was normal in her home club, Sina realizes that in the new club, some of the girls see this as a problem. Occasionally, she is even asked to play less toughly and some teammates give up defending her properly in order to not get hurt. Sina states:

> Many people say that I play too physically and that I attack so that it hurts. I can be a bit of a bully ... because that's just how we have learnt to do it [in the former club].

Sina's account outlines how she has been socialized to spare neither her body nor those of others in order to win the match. This 'disposition' (Bourdieu 1984) has become so deeply anchored in her that she finds it hard to control. Contrary to the critical reactions of some players at the new club, in the national youth team, Sina is encouraged to push her rather 'bully-like' playing style even further:

> It comes with time, I think, that you become more aggressive. For me, it came from the national team ... you have to play more aggressively, or they're going to run you over.

While her rather instrumental body–self relationship helps her to gain a place in the national youth team and to use orthodox masculine gender markers in her identity construction (Azzarito and Katzew 2010), it does not allow her to properly care for the knee problems she develops. Thus, at the time of the interview, Sina is taking a break because of overuse problems. The break forces the player to revaluate the body relationship she has acquired from elite sport as well as the health costs of identifying with its 'pain principle' (Young, White, and McTeer 1994). Accordingly, Sina also talks about ongoing changes in her body–self relationship:

> At first, I didn't care. Then it was still hurting and I played anyways because I really wanted to play no matter what. That is actually really pretty stupid ... and that's when I said to myself, okay, I can't go on now.

Sina describes how she started to pay attention to her feeling of pain instead of playing through it. Paradoxically, it is through her injury and the obligation to accept medical care that she questions the orthodox masculine ideals of toughness and stoicism (Anderson 2005; Messner 1990). One important person in this process is a physiotherapist who outlines the consequences of her risky body–self relationship and seeks to protect Sina from her own and others' expectations by defining the limits of training loading. In so doing, he represents a 'culture of precaution' (Safai 2003), which temporarily moderates the influence of the 'culture of risk' (Nixon 1992) Sina is a part of. This experience is very formative for the handball player. The health problems, the long break from training and her interaction with the physiotherapist change her views on health. While health, pain and injuries were previously 'not important' to her, she is 'now aware ... that if you don't pay attention, there can be big consequences later'. In Sina's case, the health problems lead to a re-negotiation of the instrumental body–self relationship and the health-compromising practices she adopted in constructing an orthodox masculine athletic identity:

> You can totally wear yourself out. My knees, for example, are worn out now and if I'm not careful, then I won't even need to think about maybe playing in the national league in five years ... or even playing like I can now ... And now, if I get even more injured then I won't develop either. That's why I think that it is important to make sure that you are always healthy.

In this account, the athlete recognizes the potential harm she can inflict on herself through 'too much' athletic engagement. Even though the ultimate goal of recovery is to perform, Sina begins to adopt a more caring body–self relationship (Meuser 2005). In embracing health-protecting strategies, the handball player challenges the gender boundaries of an orthodox masculine risk-culture by integrating practices and attitudes which are socially constructed as 'feminine' gender markers (Lorber 2001; Safai 2003). These also include elements of submission and compliance with medical recommendations (Connell and Messerschmidt 2005), which replace the earlier 'positive deviance' (Hughes and Coakley 1991) of not going to the doctor when injured.

Rejecting risk-taking and developing a complex health protection regime

Lars is an 18-year-old biathlete who lives at home and trains at a national training centre about 14 h per week. He just finished school, and, thanks to his membership in the national youth squad, he obtained a state-funded position. This allows him to train as part of the job but also puts pressure on him to deliver good results. Before focusing on biathlon, Lars was also involved in downhill and cross-country skiing. Besides being attracted to the shooting, he enjoyed biathlon more for several reasons:

> First of all, I always froze when I was skiing. Second of all, I was way too light for skiing because I was a real small fry ... I was always in the back in skiing, but in biathlon and cross-country skiing, I was always right up front.

Throughout adolescence, Lars experiences several ups and downs in performance and recalls 'no longer being that strong'. One difficult phase involves a mononucleosis[7] infection, which was diagnosed only after the actual illness. He remembers: 'I was pretty bad in the summer. We didn't know why. Never did anything about it either'. The difficulties dragged on into the next season, where he struggled to perform successfully. At times like these, Lars reports on receiving important emotional and practical support from his parents, who also introduced him to the alternative medical practitioner he then began to work with.

Lars states that he likes the feeling when he is 'done' with training or competition and can say to himself: 'Hey, I pushed past my limits again and pulled through ... I did it'. Nevertheless, he only 'now and then' has the 'ambition' to 'overcome' his 'weaker self'. In contrast to the health-sacrificing dedication most athletes incorporated through socialization in elite sport, Lars embraces the 'pain principle' to a much lesser degree. While he knows and feels the cultural expectation to 'give everything for success', he talks about, sometimes, giving in to pain. Furthermore, in his reasoning for choosing biathlon, he sketches both a body disposition and a mind-set that do not align with orthodox masculinity (Anderson 2005; Connell and Messerschmidt 2005; Courtenay 2000). On the contrary, his description of a light, ectomorph and cold-sensitive body coupled with his inferior position at downhill races challenges gendered conceptions of men being 'injury-proof' and women being 'injury prone' (Meuser 2005). Thus, in Lars' narrative both the dominant concepts of athletehood and socially constructed gender boundaries are negotiated (Evans et al. 2011; Kidd 2013; Lamont and Molnár 2002). This becomes particularly evident in the body–self relationship that Lars develops, as well as in a complex set of health-protecting and help-seeking practices he engages in:

> Well, I pay pretty close attention to hygiene now, to handshakes, and I won't let anyone from here drink out of my bottle because maybe he has mono [mononucleosis]. You never know … maybe he has bacteria, or he isn't sick but could become sick and that's when you're most contagious, and then I'll get sick too.

To protect his body from infections, Lars employs body strategies like regular hand washing, avoiding handles or having clothes 'as if for three' with him in order to be prepared for weather changes while most others 'just have a t-shirt, and one pair of underpants, trousers or socks'. This does not pass without reaction from peers in the training group. 'A lot of people ask: "Are you crazy?"' and 'the girls' ask him 'What is wrong with you?' Although Lars runs the risk of stigmatization for being overly sensitive, his focus is clear:

> For me it is just important to not get sick. That is just really the worst that can happen to an athlete. That he gets sick and is somehow incapacitated.

Lars' growing disregard of orthodox masculinity characteristics for the sake of being able to compete can be compared to a gender-specific pattern of help seeking identified in younger men (O'Brien, Hunt, and Hurt 2005). While generally reluctant to seek medical help because of gender norms, some of the young men did seek help in cases of ill health, 'when it was perceived as a means to *preserve* or *restore* another, more valued, enactment of masculinity' (503).

This may explain why Lars' sensitivity to his bodily vulnerability increases significantly with further integration into the high-performance system. Thus, while the cultural norms expect him to become tougher, his fear of falling ill and putting his body – the medium of performance – at risk leads him to develop a health care regime that can be seen to challenge established gender boundaries (Nixon 1992; Theberge 2008). This is also reflected by the gradual rejection of orthodox masculine risk behaviours such as drinking alcohol and using tobacco, paired with the adoption of more preventive practices such as checking blood values and periodically supplementing iron, magnesium and vitamin C in order to keep the immune system in good shape (Currie et al. 2012; Lee and Frayn 2008; Meuser 2005). Another dimension of Lars' unorthodox health regime is the use of alternative medicine and the rejection of conventional medicine, which is strongly supported by his parents:

> I don't really like going to the doctor because that always means antibiotics, some injection or a ton of pills and I don't really want antibiotics, because then I'm incapacitated for a week and you can't train or you're sick again right away. I don't think it's so healthy either. With the [homeopathic] globules, we can usually get it under control … or with drinks or poultices. There are a lot of things now.

In this shift, Lars calls orthodox masculine characteristics further into question. While conventional medicine has been associated with masculinity, complementary and alternative medicine is frequently gendered as being a 'feminine', and thus 'natural' and more 'careful' healing system (Lee and Frayn 2008; Sointu 2011). Two factors appear as critical preconditions to Lars' development of an unorthodox body–self relationship: on the one hand, his experience with infectious illnesses and body fragility has triggered reflections, learning and change (Denzin 1989; Pike 2005). On the other hand, his parents' health regime and their paramedical network is a powerful 'familial' heritage that shapes Lars' health concerns, as evidenced in the biathlete's following reflections:

> I pay relatively close attention to my health because my parents are also pretty fussy … and my sister and I are just like them now … because my parents raised me saying: "Hey, don't just shake everyone's hand, don't ever let them drink out of your bottle, pay attention to what you're touching".

This inclination gains further momentum from sensitization campaigns against infectious diseases in biathlon,[8] as well as from the professional pressures to show good results.

Discussion

The findings confirm, on the one hand, the dominance of an orthodox masculine body culture with health-compromising practices that are practiced as early as in youth elite sport. This culture sets boundaries to adolescent athletes' conceptions of identity, and, as a result of this, their body–self relationship and health practices. Thus, both male and female players were found to employ e.g. 'normalizing pain' as a symbolic strategy for embodying and communicating a form of orthodox masculine athletehood (Bourdieu 1984; Malcom 2006). On the other hand, in both the handball player Sina and the biathlete Lars, changes in body–self relationship and unorthodox health practices were found. While further integration into the high-performance system has frequently been described as leading to the embodiment of health-compromising practices (Malcom 2006; Schubring and Thiel 2011, 2014; Young, White, and McTeer 1994), these two athletes developed practices of care and health protection. These findings are of interest, as no attention has been paid so far to the question of how youth athletes challenge the hegemonic 'elite sport ethic' by caring for their health (Lee and Frayn 2008). Drawing on the Hughes and Coakley (1991) conception of playing hurt as 'positive deviance' in elite sport, the adoption of caring and health-protecting practices crosses the socially constructed gender boundaries and can be described as deviance in an orthodox masculine culture. While in the case of Sina and Lars, the health-related gender boundary crossing appears to be tolerated to a certain degree by the sporting communities they occupy; they nevertheless address the danger of being stigmatized e.g. when taking a break because of pain or when visiting a natural health professional (O'Brien, Hunt, and Hart 2005; Sointu 2011). Within this process, both critical events, such as injuries and illnesses, and alternative social networks were found to promote the health-related gender boundary crossing in elite sport (Pike 2005; Safai 2003). These factors appear to make alternative identity conceptions available for athletes and may provide them with 'social capital' (Bourdieu 1984) to challenge and cross orthodox masculine gender boundaries in elite sport. However, one may also suspect that the crossing of gender boundaries in elite athletes constitutes a temporary strategy to '*preserve* or *restore* another, more valued, enactment of masculinity' (O'Brien, Hunt, and Hart 2005), namely that of being an elite performer. To fully understand this interrelationship and the conditions that allow athletes to challenge or cross gender boundaries with regard to health, further research is needed.

Ahead of questioning the homogenizing effect of the culture of risk on youth athletes' body–self relationships, the cases of Lars and Sina also give insight into ongoing identity constructions in adolescence. Their accounts stress that, even within a social system that strongly clings to and continually reproduces both symbolic and social gender boundaries, different masculinities and femininities coexist, and within both boys and girls gendered norms are negotiated differently (Azzarito and Katzew 2010). For some girls, for example, as for Sina initially, embracing pain and suppressing bodily signs of fragility had become a part of their identity. Thus, in 'doing athlete', those athletes also challenged stereotypical conceptions of feminine fragility and distanced themselves from what Sina called 'being a gazelle'. While this shifting of 'gender boundaries' (Lamont and Molnár 2002) might not have been a conscious intention, the reactions she got even from some of the others players can be interpreted as a 'social order' to adjust to the gendering behavioural norms within the new club. The fact that Sina's orthodox masculine playing style is critiqued by peers but at the same time valued and even encouraged in the national team indicates that, also within female handball, double standards and conflicting constructions of gender boundaries and athletehood coexist. As in Sina's case, negotiating these conflicting norms in the process of identity construction can be troubling and may deter adolescent athletes from challenging normative social forces. So, while Lars gradually distances himself from orthodox masculine norms and develops a complex set of practices to protect and improve his health, some other boys' accounts indicate social pressures to display a stoic attitude towards pain (Connell and Messerschmidt 2005).

However, while criticizing the frequently health-compromising orthodox masculine practices in elite sport, we are aware that more caring health practices associated with orthodox femininity cannot necessarily be considered good per se. These practices are ambiguous because they are centrally based on practices of body control, monitoring and submission (Bordo 1990; Lee and Frayn 2008). Accordingly, Meuser (2005) stresses that the socially acquired orthodox feminine concern about the body, its health and grooming essentially constitutes a form of incorporated social control.

Conclusion

We started this article by summarizing the literature that stresses persisting gender differences in men and women's health behaviours (Bordo 1990; Currie et al. 2012, Evans et al. 2011; O'Brien, Hunt, and Hart 2005). The insights provided by our analysis of youth athletes' accounts at least partially challenge this generic statement. We point to context-bound dynamics, such as orthodox masculine athletic ideals, and critical health experiences that interact in shaping and changing gendered health practices in youth over time. Furthermore, the accounts outline how athletes can negotiate normative practices by crossing contextual gender boundaries in their relationship to health (Lamont and Molnár 2002). Thus, (gender) identity appears, as stated by Messner (1990, 5), not as a 'thing' that people have but as 'a process of construction that develops, comes into crisis, and changes as a person interacts with the social world'. In line with Messner's observation, the findings point to an array of interacting conditions that impact and alter gendered body–self relationships and health practices in youth.

Social constructions of gender boundaries and the socialization context are thus not the only influencing factors. Critical experiences such as the 'epiphany' (Denzin 1989) of an injury can profoundly alter body–self relationships and practices. Ahead of this, unorthodox bodily dispositions, such as sensitivity to cold or a muscular body disposition, obviously shape adolescents' gendered health practices. Another important factor appears to be familial 'somatic practices' (Boltanski 1976) and the interactions with caretakers in the paramedical sector, which 'may introduce' youth athletes to unorthodox health practices (Gerbing and Thiel 2015). In light of this, further understanding of the conditions that contribute to changes in adolescents' gendered body–self relationship are key and may provide starting points for promoting more 'inclusive' (Anderson and McGuire 2013) and thus maybe more sustainable body–self relationships and athletic identity constructions in youth elite sport.

Notes

1. Anderson and McGuire (2010) draw on Pronger (1990) to characterize 'orthodox masculinity' as 'a form of masculinity that is predicated on homophobia, misogyny, physicality, and bravado' (250). We will use the term 'orthodox' to characterize an archetypical from of masculinity (or femininity) and the behaviours and mind-sets related to it. We do this with a focus on health-related body management.
2. The concept of physical culture draws together a broad variety of activities (Hargreaves and Vertinsky 2007). Based on a sociocultural understanding of movement forms, physical culture is first and foremost seen as an arena of individual and / or collective physical identity construction and embodiment.
3. The HBSC study is a large-scale survey that began in 1983. The aim is to monitor health outcomes and behaviours in 11–15-year olds in Europe and North America. Despite alignments, the latest studies still state gender differences (Currie et al. 2012).
4. The terminology with regard to different forms of masculinity and femininity is somewhat unclear. In an attempt to summarize Robert Connell's theory, Howson (2006) distinguishes in 'the masculinities schema' (59) between 'hegemonic masculinity', 'subordinate masculinities' and 'marginalised masculinities' as well as 'emphasised femininity', 'ambivalent femininities' and 'protest femininities'. Focusing on masculinity alone, Anderson and McGuire (2013) differentiate between 'inclusive masculinity' and 'orthodox masculinity'.
5. The German Young Olympic Athletes' Lifestyle and Health Management Study contained several sub-studies. Herein, we only refer to the qualitative study. All interviews were conducted by the first author with the help of a student for the discipline wrestling.
6. All names given are pseudonyms.
7. Mononucleosis is a virus infection caused by the Epstein-Barr virus. Symptoms, may differ individually, are easily misdiagnosed as a heavy flu (fever, muscle aches and drowsiness) and can last for weeks. Contact sport and vigorous activities should be avoided in order to recover without harm (Ebell 2004).
8. As a response to the swine flu epidemic and the upcoming Winter Olympics in Vancouver, the German skiing federation increased efforts to educate winter sport athletes about the risks of infectious diseases and methods of prevention.

Acknowledgements

We particularly thank the participants in this study for sharing their experiences with us. We acknowledge Elizabeth Dickie for her translation and proofreading work. We also thank our colleagues from the GOAL Study Group (Jochen Mayer, Alexia Schnell, Sven Schneider, Katharina Diehl, Stephan Zipfel, Katrin Giel and Anne Werner).

Disclosure statement

No potential conflict of interest was reported by the authors.

Funding

This work was supported by the Federal Institute of Sport Science (BISp) [grant number IIA1-081907/09-14].

References

Amis, J. 2005. "Interviewing for Case Studies." In *Qualitative Methods in Sports Studies*, edited by David L. Andrews, Daniel S. Mason, and Michael L. Silk, 104–138. London: Berg.

Anderson, E. 2005. "Orthodox and Inclusive Masculinity: Competing Masculinities among Heterosexual Men in a Feminized Terrain." *Sociological Perspectives* 48 (3): 337–355.

Anderson, E., and R. McGuire. 2013. "Inclusive Masculinity Theory and the Gendered Politics of Men's Rugby." *Journal of Gender Studies* 19 (3): 249–261.

Azzarito, L., and A. Katzew. 2010. "Performing Identities in Physical Education." *Research Quarterly for Exercise and Sport* 81 (1): 25–37.

Barker-Ruchti, N., and A. Schubring. 2015. "Moving into and out of High-Performance Sport: The Cultural Learning of an Artistic Gymnast." *Physical Education and Sport Pedagogy*. Advanced online publication. doi:10.1080/17408989.2014.990371.

Barker-Ruchti, N., K. Grahn, and E.-C. Lindgren. 2015. "Shifting, Crossing and Transforming Gender Boundaries in Physical Cultures." *Sport in Society*. Advanced online publication. doi:10.1080/17430437.2015.1073942.

Berg, E. C., T. A. Migliaccio, and R. Anzini-Varesio. 2013. "Female Football Players, the Sport Ethic and the Masculinity-Sport Nexus." *Sport in Society* 17 (2): 176–189.

Boltanski, L. 1976. "Die soziale Verwendung des Körpers [The Social Usage of the Body]." In *Zur Geschichte des Körpers*, edited by Dietmar Kamper and Volker Rittner, 138–183. München: Hauser.

Bordo, S. 1990. "Eating Disorders: The Feminist Challenge to the Concept of Pathology." In *The Body in Medical Thought and Practice*, edited by Drew Leder, 197–213. London: Kluwer.

Bourdieu, P. 1984. *Distinction: A Social Critique of the Judgement of Taste*. 7th ed. Cambridge, MA: Harvard University Press.

Charlesworth, H., and K. Young. 2006. "Injured Female Athletes. Experiental Accounts from England and Canada." In *Pain and Injury in Sport. Social and Ethical Analysis*, edited by Sigmund Loland, Berit Skirstad, and Ivan Waddington, 89–106. London: Routledge.

Chase, S. E. 2011. "Narrative Inquiry: Still a Field in the Making." In *The Sage Handbook of Qualitative Research*, edited by Norman K. Denzin and Yvonna Lincoln, 421–432. Thousand Oaks, CA: Sage.

Connell, R. W., and J. W. Messerschmidt. 2005. "Hegemonic Masculinity: Rethinking the Concept." *Gender and Society* 19 (6): 829–859.

Courtenay, W. H. 2000. "Constructions of Masculinity and their Influence on Men's Well-being: A Theory of Gender and Health." *Social Science & Medicine* 50: 1385–13401.

Currie, C., C. Zanotti, A. Morgan, D. Currie, M. De Looze, C. Roberts, O. Samdal, O. R. F. Smith, and V. Barnekow. 2012. *Health Behaviour in School-aged Children (HBSC) Study: International Report from the 2009/2010 Survey*. Copenhagen: WHO Regional Office for Europe.

Denzin, N. K. 1989. *Interpretive Biography*. Newsbury Park, CA: Sage.

Deutsch, F. M. 2007. "Undoing Gender." *Gender and Society* 21 (1): 106–127.

Drummond, M. 2010. "The Natural: An Autoethnography of a Masculinized Body in Sport." *Men and Masculinities* 12 (3): 374–389.

Ebell, M. H. 2004. "Epstein-Barr Virus Infectious Mononucleosis." *American Family Physician* 70 (7): 1279–1287.

Evans, J., B. Frank, J. L. Oliffe, and D. Gregory. 2011. "Health, Illness, Men and Masculinities (HIMM): A Theoretical Framework for Understanding Men and their Health." *Journal of Men's Health* 8 (1): 7–15.

Gerbing, K.-K., and A. Thiel. 2015. "Handling of Medical Knowledge in Sport: Athletes' Medical Opinions, Information Seeking Behaviours and Knowledge Sources." *European Journal of Sport Science*. Advanced online publication. doi:10.1080/17461391.2014.989278.

Hargreaves, J., and P. Vertinsky, eds. 2007. *Physical Culture, Power, and the Body*. London: Routledge.

Howson, R. 2006. *Challenging Hegemonic Masculinity*. London: Routledge.

Hughes, R., and J. Coakley. 1991. "Positive Deviance among Athletes – The Implications of Overconformity to the Sport Ethic." *Sociology of Sport Journal* 8 (4): 307–325.

Hurrelmann, K. 2007. *Lebensphase Jugend: Eine Einführung in die sozialwissenschaftliche Jugendforschung* [Adolescence as Phase of Life]. 9th ed. Weinheim: Juventa.

Kidd, B. 2013. "Sports and masculinity†." *Sport in Society* 16 (4): 553–564.

Kolip, P., and J. Bucksch. 2012. "Gesundheitsriskantes Verhalten im Jugendalter [Health-risky Behaviour in Adolescence]." *Monatsschrift Kinderheilkunde* 160 (7): 657–661.

Kruse, J. 2014. *Qualitative Interviewforschung. Ein integrativer Ansatz* [Qualitative Interview Research. An Integrative Approach]. Weinheim: Beltz Juventa.

Lamont, M., and V. Molnár. 2002. "The Study of Boundaries in the Social Sciences." *Annual Review of Sociology* 28: 167–195.

Lee, E., and E. Frayn. 2008. "The 'Feminisation' of Health. A Sociology of Health." In *A Sociology of Health*, edited by David Wainwright, 115–133. London: Sage.

Loland, Sigmund, Berit Skirstad, and Ivan Waddington, eds. 2006. *Pain and Injury in Sport. Social and Ethical Analysis*. Abingdon: Routledge.

Lorber, J. 2001. "Gender." In *Encyclopedia of Sociology*, edited by E. Borgatta and R. J. Montgomery, 1057–1066. New York: Macmillan Reference USA.

Malcom, N. L. 2006. "'Shaking It Off' and 'Toughing It out' – Socialization to Pain and Injury in Girls' Softball." *Journal of Contemporary Ethnography* 35 (5): 495–525.

McKay, J. 2000. *Masculinities, Gender Relations, and Sport Research on Men and Masculinities*. London: Sage.

Messner, M. A. 1990. "When Bodies are Weapons: Masculinity and Violence in Sport." *International Review for the Sociology of Sport* 25 (3): 203–220.

Messner, M. A., and D. F. Sabo, eds. 1990. *Sport, Men, and the Gender Order: Critical Feminist Perspectives*. Champaign, IL: Human Kinetics.

Meuser, M. 2005. "Frauenkörper - Männerkörper. Somatische Kulturen der Geschlechterdifferenz [Women's Bodies – Men's Bodies: Somatic Cultures of Gender Differences]." In *Soziologie des Körpers*, edited by Markus Schroer, 271–294. Frankfurt am Main: Suhrkamp.

Moegling, K. 2006. "Zum Umgang mit Sportverletzungen bei jugendlichen Handballspielern [On Dealing with Sport Injuries among Adolescent Handball Players]." In *Über die Grenzen des Körpers hinaus*, edited by Klaus Moegling, 154–202. Immenhausen: Prolog.

Nixon, H. L. 1992. "A Social Network Analysis of Influences on Athletes to Play with Pain and Injuries." *Journal of Sport and Social Issues* 16 (2): 127–135.

O'Brien, R., K. Hunt, and G. Hart. 2005. "'It's Caveman Stuff, but that is to a Certain Extent how Guys Still Operate': Men's Accounts of Masculinity and Help Seeking." *Social Science & Medicine* 61: 503–516.

Pfister, G. 2013. "Developments and Current Issues in Gender and Sport from a European Perspective." In *Gender Relations in Sport*, edited by Emilya Roper, 163–180. Rotterdam: Sense.

Pike, E. C. J. 2005. "'Doctors Just Say "Rest and Take Ibuprofen"': A Critical Examination of the Role of 'Non-Orthodox' Health Care in Women's Sport." *International Review for the Sociology of Sport* 40 (2): 201–219.

Pronger, B. 1990. *The Arena of Masculinity: Sports, Homosexuality and the Meaning of Sex*. New York: St. Martin's Press.

Richartz, A. 2000. *Lebenswege von Leistungssportlern. Anforderungen und Bewältigungsprozesse der Adoleszenz* [Life Journeys of Elite Athletes. Demands and Coping Processes in Adolescence]. Aachen: Meyer & Meyer.

Safai, P. 2003. "Healing the Body in the 'Culture of Risk': Examining the Negotiation of Treatment between Sport Medicine Clinicians and Injured Athletes in Canadian Intercollegiate Sport." *Sociology of Sport Journal* 20 (2): 127–146.

Schubring, A. 2014. *Growth as a Challenge. A Sociological Analysis of the Growth Management of Youth Elite Athletes, and their Coaches*. PhD diss., University of Tübingen, Tübingen, Germany.

Schubring, A., and A. Thiel. 2011. "Growth as Crisis Potential in Elite Youth Sports – Origins and Construction of Growth Problems in Young Elite Athletes from a Sociological Perspective." *Sport und Gesellschaft* 8 (3): 259–286.

Schubring, A., and A. Thiel. 2014. "Coping With Growth in Adolescent Elite Sport." *Sociology of Sport Journal* 31 (3): 304–326.

Selting, M., P. Auer, B. Barden, J. Bergmann, E. Couper-Kuhlen, S. Günthner, C. Meier, U. Quasthoff, P. Schlobinski, and S. Uhmann. 1998. "Gesprächsanalytisches Transkriptionssystem (Gat) [Conversational Analytic Transcription System]." *Linguistische Berichte* 173: 91–122.

Sointu, E. 2011. "Detraditionalisation, Gender and Alternative and Complementary Medicines." *Sociology of Health & Illness* 33 (3): 356–371.

Sparkes, A. C. 1996. "The Fatal Flaw: A Narrative of the Fragile Body-Self." *Qualitative Inquiry* 2 (4): 463–494.

Theberge, N. 2008. "'Just a Normal Bad Part of What I Do': Elite Athletes' Accounts of the Relationship between Health and Sport." *Sociology of Sport Journal* 25 (2): 206–222.

Thiel, A., J. Mayer, and H. Digel. 2010. *Gesundheit im Spitzensport* [Health in elite sports]. Schorndorf: Hofmann.

Thiel, A., K. Diehl, K. E. Giel, A. Schnell, A. Schubring, J. Mayer, S. Zipfel, and S. Schneider. 2011. "The German Young Olympic Athletes' Lifestyle and Health Management Study (GOAL Study): Design of a Mixed-Method Study." *BMC Public Health* 11 (410): 1–10. doi: http://dx.doi.org/10.1186/1471-2458-11-410.

West, C., and D. Zimmerman. 1987. "Doing Gender." *Gender and Society* 1 (2): 125–151.

Young, K., P. White, and W. McTeer. 1994. "Body Talk: Male Athletes Reflect on Sport, Injury, and Pain." *Sociology of Sport Journal* 11 (2): 175–194.

Hanging up the shirt: an autoethnographic account of disengaging from a social rugby culture

D. Barker and N. Barker-Ruchti

Department of Food and Nutrition, and Sport Science, University of Gothenburg, Gothenburg, Sweden

ABSTRACT
Violent practices are a common feature of homosocial sporting environments. The objective of the current paper is to explore how one individual disengaged from a sporting community characterized by such practices. An autoethnographic approach involving recollection and interactional exchanges is used to create a realist narrative account which offers insight into the process of disengagement. The narrative focuses on the: (1) ongoing nature of cultural participation; (2) agency and the restriction of ways of being in sports teams and (3) the durable nature of personal characteristics that are learned in sporting environments. These issues are discussed in light of cultural learning theory and specifically, the analytic concept, 'becoming'. The paper concludes with methodological reflections and a consideration of directions for future research.

Introduction

There exists a substantial body of literature on masculinity and homosocial sport environments (Anderson, McCormack, and Lee 2012; Messner 1992; Sabo, Messner, and Mackay 2000). Many scholars have investigated the symbolic and at times, physical violence that groups of males unleash on themselves and others within and around sporting contexts (Pringle 2008; Sparkes, Partington, and Brown 2007). Aggression, self-harm and a variety of risk-taking behaviours have been associated with these environments (Drummond 2002; Grossbard et al. 2009; Murnen and Kohlman 2007). The current paper contributes to existing research by providing an account of one individual *disengaging* from a sporting community characterized by violent practices. It further adds to existing literature by relating this disengagement to women's roles in challenging homosocial cultures. By relying on an autoethnographic methodology (Carless 2012) and interactional exchanges (Allen-Collinson and Hockey 2001), a realist account (Smith and Sparkes 2009) of the first author's participation in, and disengagement from, a social rugby community is constructed. This narrative raises issues related to gender and boundary crossing, which, following a dialogical form of narrative analysis (Douglas and Carless 2014), are discussed in conversational format (Clough 2002; Jones 2007) in the second part of the paper.

Sport and masculine subcultures

Male sporting cultures have attracted much attention over the years (Anderson 2009; Muir and Seitz 2004; Sabo et al. 2000). While some scholars have provided counter-narratives and evidence of change (Anderson and McGuire 2010), many have shown that when groups of young men get together to play or watch sport, anti-social practices can co-occur. Scholars investigating fields such as collegiate sport and physical education teacher education have shown how groups of men entering adulthood establish and maintain highly complex and encompassing codes of behaviour based on sporting involvement (Grossbard et al. 2009; Muir and Seitz 2004; Sparkes, Brown, and Partington 2010). These codes frequently privilege dominant, heterosexual and masculine orientations and involve misogyny, the objectification of women, binge drinking, competition, hierarchies, adulation of physical prowess (and the devaluing of intellectualism) and homophobia (Connell 1995).

Violence is a recurring theme across investigations. Violence takes various forms ranging from non-verbal marginalization and exclusion to verbal, physical or sexual abuse and humiliation. Victims of violence include women (Brown, Sumner, and Nocera 2002; Murnen and Kohlman 2007) and men who do not conform to an 'orthodox' masculinity (Carless [2010]; see also Anderson [2008], for a detailed discussion of orthodox masculinity). Even those most willing to embrace the tenets of orthodox masculinity are often harmed by, for instance, continuing to participate in sport when they are injured, drinking excessive amounts of alcohol or denying themselves meaningful relationships with others (Anderson 2008; Drummond 2010).

Much of the existing research highlights negative aspects of team sports (Anderson et al. 2012), while at the same time countering more popular, positive readings. Some of this work is presented in non-traditional ways (see, e.g. Pringle [2008]; Sparkes et al. [2007]). A number of scholars have suggested that various strands of interpretivist research have the capacity to rouse emotions and empathy in an academic context where reason and rationality are normally foregrounded (Carless 2010; Pringle 2001). We agree. It is difficult to read stories of hazing and assault for example, without *feeling* the suffering that occurs in these contexts. Indeed, one of the first questions to come to mind when considering violent sporting environments is: Why do people continue to participate in communities when violence is pervasive? Even if we accept that strong discourses positively frame team sport participation, why do individuals not leave?

Several studies have shed light on this question. Anderson and colleagues (2012) for example, discuss the relevance of initiation activities noting that rituals are often used to test recruits' masculinity and willingness to adopt a near agentic-less state. Kirby and Wintrup (2002) point to the importance of consensus in groups where initiation involves sorting the ones willing to share norms and values from the ones that are unwilling. For the willing, a degree of investment, as well as a belief in the collective good is enough to ensure that members stay in the group. Finally, Anderson (2009) posits that as in other male-dominated institutions, individuals in team sports face stigmatization if they quit.

In accounts of why people stay, men are constructed in particular ways. They suspend moral or ethical judgement and robotically follow team rules at least until they are experienced enough to enforce these same rules. They buy into and enjoy enacting aggressive and competitive codes. They are caught up in the team culture, playing their part for fear of social repercussions. This paper contributes to existing literature by focusing on the process of an individual disengaging from such practices. In doing this though, we want to propose an alternative account of participation. In line with others that have explored negotiations of masculinity (Douglas and Carless 2010; Drummond 2010), we want to put forward a picture of a reflective actor interacting with cultural narratives. Further, we want to focus on how that actor changes over time, or *learns*, and how this is at once a personal and cultural process. In order to capture this process, we have adopted a theoretical framework based on cultural learning.

Becoming someone else

To understand the first author's disengagement from a homosocial environment, we use the notion of 'becoming' (Hodkinson 2005; Hodkinson et al. 2007; Sparkes and Bloomer 2000). For Hodkinson, Biesta, and James (2008), becoming describes 'the ways in which individuals learn through participation in many different situations, both simultaneously and successively' (40). It is a holistic and continuous perspective on learning that encompasses both embodied construction and social participation and shares similarities with Bourdieu's concept habitus. The idea of becoming attempts to collapse any theoretical distinction between individuals and cultures.[1] Rather than focusing on the texture of cultures and/or learners' identities or selves, it posits a reflexive relationship between culture and individual.

From this perspective, culture is constituted by 'actions, dispositions and interpretations [that exist] in and through interaction and communication' (Hodkinson et al. 2008). A focus on individuals' thinking and doing is adopted to conceptually merge the physical and psychological world and to allow for intelligent human action in the form of anticipation, embodied judgement and intelligible decision-making. In accordance with this view, Hodkinson and colleagues (2008) acknowledge that cultural traditions and histories have degrees of endurance, and create and maintain differences in position and power. Individual interpretations, as well as possibilities for interaction and communication, are both socioculturally structured and structuring. However, as these structures exist in conduct, they can be negotiated through intelligible sense-making and practical action (Hodkinson et al. 2007).

In this issue, 'boundaries' has been adopted as an analytic concept to think about how individuals and groups of individuals understand, negotiate and break limitations associated with gender (Barker-Ruchti, Grahn, and Lindgren, forthcoming). For most intents and purposes, the idea of 'boundaries' offers quite a neat way of thinking about how someone moves from one culture to another, or crosses cultural boundaries. In this paper, we are going to re-frame boundaries as dialogic; existing in individuals and culture simultaneously and visible through practices. It is thus a particular set of cultural practices adopted by a sporting community that this paper examines.

Research methods

The current project emerged from long-running conversations between the authors about Dean's shift from enthusiastic member of a male sporting community to one who questioned the community and disengaged from its practices. As the project progressed, conversations became more in line with autoethnographic/self-ethnographic research (Alvesson 2003). Similar to Allen-Collinson and Hockey's (2001) work, interactional exchanges constituted a significant part of the research process and while we do not claim that these exchanges allowed Natalie to 'enter into the experience of the other', we do believe that they provided us with a degree of intersubjectivity (Allen-Collinson and Hockey 2001).

Data production

Data production involved two main phases. Dean began by systematically recording 'headnotes' (Sanjek 1990) that reflected phenomenological experiences of engaging with a social rugby community in New Zealand in the late 1990s. In 2007, Dean began using these notes to produce a self-ethnographic account (Alvesson 2003). Dean and Natalie then began a phase of interaction work alluded to above (Allen-Collinson and Hockey 2001), where further notes, generated through collaborative introspections and retrospective discussions, were made in an attempt to reconstruct and refine the account of the experiences that appear below (for a similar methodology, see Carless [2012]; Smith [1999]). For both authors, remembering specific events was not difficult and although there were undoubtedly tracts of experience that did not come to mind, the events described were vivid enough to re-create the following narrative with a sense of attachment and closeness.

Narrative

Writing a series of connected accounts served as an analytic procedure (Richardson 2000) and writing in combination with reading other accounts of male sporting environments helped us to reconsider how masculine selves/cultures are created, sustained and changed. It is useful to note that multiple-author, autoethnographic scholarship is still relatively rare and the methodological strategy raises interesting questions about representation and voice. In this case, the narrative section that follows was constructed by both authors but is told by, and is primarily about, Dean (Natalie enters the narrative towards the end). In our discussion, we have avoided reverting to a collective 'we'. In order to illustrate the reflexive nature of our discussion, we have adopted a conversational structure where we use reported speech to show how each of us thought about the story we had created. This fits quite well with Frank's (2005) notion of a dialogic approach[2] as well as the idea that narratives themselves are interactional achievements (Allen-Collinson and Hockey 2001).

Context

The narrative focuses on a period of Dean's life in which he was completing a sport science degree in New Zealand. Over four years (1995–1998), Dean was a member of the Pullers[3] social rugby team. Rugby holds a celebrated position in New Zealand and is regularly associated with the country's national identity (Pringle 2008). The Puller members came from around the country to a university town and most were living away from home for the first time. Many social activities were structured around participation in the rugby team. The majority of the approximately 25 members were studying sport science. Neither the University nor the sport science programme explicitly supported a 'jock culture' (Sparkes et al. 2007) and efforts were being made to prevent initiation activities within the sport science programme from taking place. Some of the social scientific courses in the programme incorporated socially critical perspectives and dealt with gender issues in sport. In this respect, the homosocial environment was created and practiced beyond formal institutional boundaries (Skelton [1993] noted a similar situation in British PE teacher education).

Playing the game

Eleven young men are gathered in a rough circle in the front yard of Tosher, Muzza, Rats, and Robbo's flat. They are all aged eighteen or nineteen. It is Wednesday afternoon and an aluminum keg of cheap beer has almost been drained. Soon everyone will be expected to put in ten dollars for a second keg.

"A cameo 50 is way better than a hard fought century," insists Macca.

"Yeah mate. A quick 50 takes much more skill. Who wants to watch a boring century," adds Handy.

"Yeah, but what about winning the game?" offers Foreskin. "A century is more important in the bigger picture. Centuries win tests."

Sport is a typical topic of conversation. Foreskin is not going to win this argument. He may have more cricket experience. He is a superior cricketer but none of the other boys have entered into the discussion to assist Foreskin, and supporters are crucial in these situations.

"How many points are you on Bazza?"[4] asks Robbo, a tall, athletically-built basketballer, from the other end of the circle. *Barry, or Bazza, is my nickname from the previous year in the student hostel. Some of the Pullers are not aware that my name is Dean.*

I leave the cricket discussion and turn to Robbo.

"Ah, 8 or 9." *I respond, trying to sound modest. I am actually pretty proud for this tally so early in the year.*

"What about you Brownie?"

"10"

"Hey, who's leading the points table?" *Robbo poses the question more loudly, marking it as a public dialogue.*

"It must be Thompson," *asserts Rog enthusiastically.*

"Yeah, Tommo's been getting three pointers all over the place. He rooted three or four chicks just during orientation. First year slappers at the hostel. And then he went home with Kaz last weekend." *While Dazza is often quiet, he holds relevant information and is happy to share it with the group.*

"Where is Tommo?" *asks Robbo, as if just realizing that Tommo is not actually here to talk for himself.*

"Probably at the gym." *Dazza volunteers.*

"Soft cunt. Why isn't he here drinking?"

The discussion of points finishes almost as quickly as it started as Tosher makes an announcement to the entire group.

"I think it's almost time for a plucked chicken rodeo."

"What the fuck is a plucked chicken rodeo?" *obliges Macca.*

There is no answer as Muzza cuts in, "Not yet. Do it later. It's too early."

Tosher has signaled his intent for the afternoon. You can count on Tosher to liven things up. In fact, he is starting to build a reputation as a larrikin. He has taken his singlet off. When he makes his announcement, there is an air of expectation.

"What's a plucked chicken rodeo?" *I ask Brownie quietly as conversations start anew.*

"Well, you know what a plucked chicken is, don't you?"

"No." I reveal my ignorance and thus amateurishness in this game. It's only to Brownie though.

"You'll see."

"Whose is this jug?" shouts Muzza from the keg.

Oh, shit. "Ah, that's mine." I catch the jug after Muzza throws it to me, getting some of the dregs on my shirt and arms.

"You don't want to lose it Barry. You've already lost two of our jugs."

I am not keen to make a reputation as someone a bit absent-minded. I already feel like I am a bit soft. For one, I cannot drink as much or as quickly as the others. I am not a real rugby player, even if I have played at fly half for the Pullers. I have started to gain a modest level of credibility by engaging in raucous behaviour. Relating amusing anecdotes is important. At some level I know what is involved. Rog slept in a rubbish container. He also brought a girl home and had sex with her six times (emphasis on the six). After receiving oral sex, Rats was locked in a girl's car for a night. Too drunk to get out. Each of the guys have built reputations for 'disgraceful' behaviour (used as a positive adjective) and hence earned a place within the group.

The sun has dipped behind the hill. Tosher disappears into the flat to urinate. When he returns he has on his singlet, but has removed his shorts and underwear. He has also acquired a broom stick which he is holding between his legs with one hand behind his back. In the other hand he stretches his penis upwards.

"Yee hahhh!" he shouts and gallops off up the road. Not stopping when he gets to the rise in the road, he charges up the incline until we see only his silhouette on the crest.

The laughing does not stop but is punctuated by short comments.

"Fuck he's a clown."

"How far is he going to go?"

"Look he's going past those chicks. Oh No."

"What a good cunt."

Tosher returns breathless to the admiration of the other Pullers and goes inside to put his shorts on.

Liz and I are sitting at a small square table. Lucky to have found one actually, but that is the benefit of getting to the pub early. Liz arrived with her girlfriends not long ago. The Pullers are all there in new rugby jerseys. Just as Gibbo said, we are dominating the pub. Even if Tosher had not sent a call around reminding everyone to wear their jerseys, I would have put mine on. The shirts look smart.

Liz and I are talking. It is pleasant. I feel relaxed. I have known Liz for a couple of years. We were in the same hostel. We hitch hiked together one time when she did not want to go alone and I wanted to visit my uncle and aunt. Otherwise we have not had much to do with each other. It is a bit of a shame because she and her friends are actually ok.

"Barry! Barry!"

Rats is calling to me urgently while standing with his index finger on the ceiling. It takes me a moment to realize what he is doing. I jump to my feet and balance on my stool and press my index finger to the ceiling. The others already have their fingers in contact with the ceiling, most of them leisurely reaching up with one hand. I am not fond of this game as I am reminded of my diminutive stature. All the guys have their fingers on the ceiling now, all except Handy, who has had more to drink than anyone else and is flayed out on one of the couches.

"What are you doing?" Liz asks, not really puzzled but playing along with the game.

"Oh, it's just a game we play." I reply with a degree of pride.

"Ahh, scull Handy!" commands Muzza from the pool table. Muzza is now the vice-captain of the Pullers and has taken on the job of enforcing little games like this. Handy, already the most inebriated, takes his empty glass from the table, fills it unsteadily with beer and takes it to his lips. If he drinks the contents of the glass quickly he will, under the gaze of the team, be seen to be playing his part. If he has to stop to get his breath, he will lose face, be seen as soft. I know the shame of this because I have done it a number of times. There is no question that he will finish the glass.

The whole scene takes less than a minute. Conversations pick up where they left off but all the Pullers are aware that this will not be the last time they are reminded of their belonging. The evening wears on to the sounds of Green Day, Bob Marley, Radiohead. I continue talking with Liz.

I am not breaking etiquette. I am talking to a chick but I am still with my mates. I am wearing the jersey, playing the games, drinking beer. I am still one of the boys.

"I'll be back in minute." I say as I slide off the stool and head to the toilets. As I relieve myself, I study the poster of the Southern Man[5] above the urinal. "Everything you'll ever need to know about drinking, dressing, talking, driving and thinking Southern Man style" says the caption above a rugged guy dressed in a blue Swandri jacket with a beer logo. He is New Zealand's answer to the Marlboro Man and is meant to embody the positive characteristics of the country's early colonials: tough, silent, hardworking.

I return to the table. But why? Why talk to Liz? It is not like she finds me attractive – I am shorter than her and she is into Frank, that Maori guy that plays basketball. If we are not going to go home with each other, what is the point in even talking? I mull it over reminding myself of other times I have hit on girls and been rejected. I slowly build myself into a quiet rage and if anything, feel more sober than before.

"Why are you talking to me?" My tone is abrupt. My face is clenched. I have changed.

A look of astonishment. Even somewhat anticipated, her look catches me off guard. Still, I continue.

"You don't even like me. There's no way you'd come home with me so why are we even talking?"

Nothing.

"Admit it. You're not interested in me." I would like her to argue but even in my state of agitation realize that in the circumstances, she is not going to.

"I don't know. Do you like me? Is that...?"

I pause. I had not really thought about it.

"Well that's a bit irrelevant isn't it." A safe retreat into sarcasm.

I push it further. I have started now, feeling anger and spitting the words at her.

"Just piss off. I don't even want to talk to you."

She gets up. Goes slowly back to her friends. I head over to Foreskin.

"Are you going to O'Leary's soon?"

"Yeah. We'll just wait for Robbo to finish his jug. Here, you can help."

"Cheers."

I wake early and while the rest of the house is asleep, shame slowly, but completely, envelops me. This is what it feels like to drown. How do I fix this? What can I say? Geez. I will never do that again. But I do. More drinking, more depressive aggressive episodes. Sometimes aimed at women that I know, sometimes women that I do not know, sometimes my mates. I do not know what is happening or why. Only that I am becoming increasingly unpopular and that the harder I try to gain acceptance, the more I feel like an outsider.

"Why don't you come home? Just for a few weeks?"
"I can't mum, I've only got eight weeks left and then I'm finished. What would people think?" I have locked myself away in my bedroom with the phone on the extended cable.
"What's wrong?"
Silence.
"It's just hard."
Silence.
"Why don't you go and see a counselor. That's what they're there for."
"I might go and see a doctor."

The doctor had not been that helpful. He had said that he thought a counselor could probably be of more use in this instance, even if I was experiencing nauseousness. In the corridor to the counselor's room, I run into a guy, Greg, that I know from courses. I am embarrassed that I am about to enter a counseling session. Greg is at the medical centre for a knee injury. I am not sure if he buys my explanation of a "stomach bug or something" but take comfort in the fact that I probably will not see him after finishing university.

As I sit in the waiting room, I go over what I am going to say. In fact, I have not thought about much else in the last few days. Problems scoring chicks. On the couple of occasions that I have managed to get chicks into bed, I have performed terribly. I do not fit in with my friends. There is only one explanation.

"Ah, Dean?" A man in jeans and a neat short sleeved shirt calls into the waiting room.
"Yeah."
I follow him to his room.
"Hi. Dean is it? My name is Richard. How can I help?" a man, forty-odd, an easy manner that suggests that he knows what he is doing. Not that it matters. I am ready to talk to just about anyone now, as long as they do not know me too well. There are pamphlets and small posters covering much of the wall behind the counselor. Men's issues. I suppose I am in the right place.
"Right, what can I help you with?"
"I think I'm gay."
"Oh, ok. And is this a problem?"
"Yeah ... Well, yeah."
"And what brought you to this conclusion?"
"Ah I'm not really sure." It's true, I am not sure. I am not even sure how I would know I was gay. That's the reason I am here.
"Ok, let me start with a fairly direct question. When you fantasize do you think about men or women or both?"
"Ah, women."
"Ok, look. It's like this." The counselor's tone is almost irritated. It is not what I expected. I feel almost like I am being admonished.
"When it comes to sexuality, things are quite gray." The counselor talks for several minutes. He talks about spectrums, diversity, 'normal behavior' and even touches on customs in ancient Greek societies.

"Look, if you do have feelings about men, I suggest you don't try to ignore them. Try exploring them. See where your thinking takes you. See how these thoughts make you feel."

I am not sure that he realizes what being gay would mean in my life, but somehow his talk makes me think beyond my situation anyway.

"There's one question that I have to ask you. Have you thought about suicide or self-harm in the last few weeks?"

This signals the end of the session. I was expecting a protracted discussion where I would be able to talk at length about myself and my problems. Feeling like an outcast. Having a different point of view to everyone else. Not measuring up.

"Oh, not really. I mean I have, but not seriously." Is this a lie? What does thinking about suicide *seriously* mean?

Hurry up Natalie, I think to myself. I don't want to be here when they arrive. The Pullers will not be impressed that I have decided to spend the afternoon with my girlfriend instead of watching the test match on television. I am sitting on a small concrete retaining wall outside a flat that is occupied by some of the Pullers. It is 1.45 pm. The match starts at 2.20 pm. The guys have gone to get beer but they will be back soon to settle in to old couches and armchairs and enjoy the build-up to the game.

Why I have chosen this particular time and place to meet with Natalie is a mystery. I regret the decision and I do not want to be here. In the previous weeks, I have invited this girl to gatherings with the team and it has been uncomfortable for both of us. At one point, she got all agro with Reido and told him to piss off. After a few more minutes of anxious waiting, she comes into view, pushing her bike up the steep slope. She is a small figure dressed warmly. I have not known her long but I recognize her clothes. More importantly, she is a few minutes late. The guys will surely not be far behind her. A few more seconds of hope and then sure enough, they round the corner and trail her up the hill. When she arrives, we embrace, exchange a few words. My thoughts are elsewhere as the Pullers approach. They come within talking distance. As I have told Natalie, most of them are decent guys. When they are alone. I should know because I have spent the last four years with these guys.

The boys arrive and their pace does not slow. No one makes eye contact with Natalie or me. They are almost past us before one of them speaks. As they funnel through the gate, Reido, who I have lived with for three years, mutters: "Don't you know there's a rugby match on Barry?" They disappear into the flat. I do not know what to say. I know that Natalie does not like these guys. But they are still friends.

"Why don't you write something about the Pullers?" Natalie gently urges, not for the first time. "This is exactly the kind of stuff that you read about in sociology journals and you have experienced it."

"I'm not turning my life into some academic project. That was my life. This is my life." Besides, I think, it was not that bad. We had a lot of good times. Everyone knows that those university years are the best years of your life.

Natalie does not persist. We have moved in together. I am at teachers' training college. Natalie is writing a Master's thesis. Sometimes I envy her, but I am immersed in a different set of activities. I have unit plans, assessment tasks and practicum to concern me. I have little to do with my old friends. Many shifted from the university town to the city in which I now live. We kept in touch for a while. Gradually though, I stopped calling to find out what was *going on. I could not have kept up with the drinking and the parties with those guys, I reason. Better that I finished up with those guys and moved on. They will all do the same sooner or later. But did I really make a choice? Did I leave the group on my own accord? Was that how it happened? Or did I get banished from the group? Too many indiscretions. Too soft. Not enough of a good cunt. I am living what most of the Pullers would call a 'married life'. That is incompatible with being in the team.*

Discussion

Presentation of empirical material as narrative is not always accompanied by separate 'analysis'. It is usually clear that theoretical tenets have shaped the account (and the account is therefore already analytic) and authors often want to invite interpretation(s). Given this aim, it may not be desirable to provide a 'preferred' reading. In our case, a discussion *is* useful because it affords both of us a voice and offers a sense of how we are able to tell the story *now*. The challenge of incorporating both our voices in analysis led us to a conversational format (Jones 2007; Frank 2005). While we have done a significant amount of 'tidying up', this form of presentation lets us demonstrate reflexivity and at the same time, show some of the methodological messiness (and fun) of shared meaning making.

D: Mm. OK, so how do we start this?

N: Not sure. There are still some parts of the story that make me really angry. When you write that your time with the Pullers wasn't all that bad. Maybe for you, but for me, it was intimidating. I also remember doubting your commitment towards me.

D: Yeah, I know, but we should focus on the narrative that we have presented.

N: Alright. How does cultural learning and becoming help us to take readers beyond the story?

D: Mmm.

N: Well, we could start by picking up Hodkinson, Biesta and James' (2007) idea that learning is social, embodied and practical.

D: Yeah, and use those ideas to give a bit of structure to our discussion … Well, the Pullers rugby team didn't exist until we made it. The idea of a social rugby team and the cultural scripts that went with it pre-dated us. We 'breathed' life into those scripts, if you like.

N: Yes, Sparkes and colleagues (2007) have written about activating cultural scripts – drinking games and stories of bad behaviour are quite good examples of this. We showed this at the beginning of the paper. 'Activation' involved social learning in that you were finding out what was acceptable through participation and communication with one another (see Hodkinson, Biesta, and James 2007).

D: Mmm, and through these practices, we became certain kinds of people. This was relational in the sense that our actions meant something to the members of the group. And non-members like you, for that matter. The positioning and status that Anderson (2008) and Pringle (2001) have talked about was achieved in and through these interactions. Those who developed particular styles of interaction, what Bourdieu would call habitus, were positioned in particular ways within the community.

N: Yeah, like the guy doing the chicken rodeo. He climbed the ladder. But you didn't really interact in that kind of extreme way.

D: No, not for the most part, I didn't feel like I could. As in other homosocial sporting environments, drinking large quantities of alcohol and displays of physical size and strength were explicitly valued. I couldn't really push limits in either of these areas.

N: It's probably worth mentioning that you were quite academic and had had meaningful social relations outside of the Pullers culture and maybe this made it easier for you to move out?

D: Mm, anti-intellectualism has been linked with these kinds of cultures. But leaving was probably easier for me than for some of the other Pullers because I participated in other communities. And maybe being physically different also made it easier to become someone else.

N: But I mean … the rugby team was a restrictive community that closed down other possibilities for being. But since you had had other horizons (see Sparkes and Bloomer 2000), you could still see other ways of being.

D: Yeah, that's true, but I think other Pullers also had other horizons.

N: OK, so, how was learning embodied? Would you agree that the Pullers culture was ingrained in you? Some theorists have used the term 'durability' to talk about the influence of culture (Sayer 2005). You had become a Puller, even though you also participated in other settings. Your description of how it felt to wear the Pullers jersey is, I would say, a good example of this deep identification.

D: I think some things were durable and some weren't. A couple of years after leaving, I remember not wanting to wear my rugby shirt. But in terms of embodied learning … and we haven't really focused on this in the narrative – not compared to Carless (2010), for example – I would say that I was often conscious of my body. I haven't talked about the extreme pleasure of running around on the rugby field, the pain of dislocating my knee several times, the despair of having a small body in a context where strength and size were being valued, or the embodied pleasure of having a girlfriend after a long period of (mainly talking about) short-lived sexual exploits.

N: Well, I'm not sure that we need to go into all of that for this paper.

D: No?

N: But getting back to the idea of durability, many aspects relating to your context changed, which affected who you became. For one, the Pullers culture was bound by a time frame. It was a particular phase and once you moved away from university, you were geographically removed from the Puller practices.

D: Yes, but thinking about the spatial or temporal boundaries of cultures seems to mask the ways in which culture becomes embodied which we were talking about. The geographic move did not mean that I no longer called myself a Puller.

N: Agreed. Bloomer and Hodkinson (2000) talk about learning as an ongoing process, characterized by stops and starts, moments of significant transformation and reversion to old ways of being. I think that fits quite nicely here.

D: So what about the practical aspect of learning?

N: Well, Hodkinson and colleagues (2007) propose that learning relates to intelligent action, including anticipation, foresight, and embodied judgement. This is where they acknowledge that although culture encourages particular ways of being, people have opportunities for agency, even when they're not completely aware of the motives or consequences of their actions. Like when you suggested meeting me despite the rugby game. You knew that the Pullers wouldn't approve of you missing the event. But you still agreed to meet me.

D: Yeah. I can see that. And there were other occasions where I chose to do stuff with you instead of with the Pullers. In this respect, Kirby and Wintrup's (2002) notion of a 'choice of one' (56) along with Anderson and colleagues' (2012) suggestion of non-agency doesn't fit that well. I would add though that possibilities for action *emerged*. For example, meeting you opened up quite a range of possibilities.

N: But are we downplaying structure here? How limited was your choice?

D: That question goes beyond this paper, surely. How limited is anyone's agency?

N: OK ... But to be able to resist the culture, you needed to fully become a part of it first (see also Douglas and Carless [2014]). Otherwise it's difficult to explain your frustration and anger. And I would say that by moving out, you also challenged the culture.

D: I'm not sure. I moved out and the culture went on, just without me. That's not particularly challenging or transformative.

N: Well, this relates to the 'social' aspect of learning we talked about before. If we think of learning as relational, then your disengagement probably did have effects. You can't assume that the Pullers remained the same. Frank (2005) suggests that, 'any person takes responsibility for the other's becoming, as well as recognizing that the other's voice has entered one's own' (967). It may be difficult to identify the effects your actions had on the Pullers. But as much as their actions affected you, your actions would have left an impression on them.

Concluding thoughts on narrative becoming

In this paper, we have explored disengagement from orthodox masculine practices revolving around sport participation and one woman's involvement in this process. By drawing on autoethnographic material that was produced through interactional exchanges, we have constructed a realist narrative that describes one of our experiences in a social rugby team and the process of discontinuing participation in this team. With the help of cultural learning theory, we have suggested that this move can be understood as: (1) a form of border crossing; and (2) a reflexive process involving personal and cultural transformation.

The account itself is of personal-cultural change, yet, writing the account also facilitated transformation. As Smith and Sparkes (2009) have proposed, the telling of narratives provides opportunities for reflection and narrative re-framing. The account describes a life stage that occurred in the late 1990s, the narrative section was constructed mainly in 2007 and 2008, and the scientific account was developed and theorized in 2014 and 2015. There is – somewhat like the structure of Christopher Nolan's film *Inception* – an experience that is embedded within a narrative embedded within an analysis. Importantly, in 2008, almost 10 years after leaving the Pullers, it was still unclear to us how to tell the story. The end of the narrative has been left as it was and a draft title of the paper was 'Escape or exile: Leaving the hegemonic masculine'. Obviously, the two possible stories had very different consequences for how the first author understood himself, alternating between escape artist and social outcast, as well as the second author's role in this process. Neither provided the heroic tale of 'man challenging violent practices and bringing about social justice' that might have accompanied a more traditional independent position. Seven years on, writing and theorizing has enabled us to re-tell (and extend) the story but it is still not heroic: Dean engaged in violent practices that supported orthodox masculinity in a situation where these practices had a historical precedent. Disengaging from these practices and becoming someone different was difficult and resulted in a period of doubt. Disengagement was part of the twin process of learning and becoming, a process that continues today.

As well as providing insight though, we hope that the account has raised some questions. It would be useful to know how other men disengage from violent sporting practices. Males across a variety of age ranges drop out of sport every day. How often is retirement a result of violent cultural practices? What kinds of stories do these men tell? What implications does disengagement have for these men's sense of self? Disengaging is obviously not simply a question for sports theorists and risk taking, aggression and misogyny are not limited to sporting contexts (Connell 1995). Scholars might investigate how men cease participation in violent practices in other fields. Finally, it is crucial to locate women in this picture. We have made a small but potentially important step in showing how women's voices *are* and can be included in stories of and about men. If gender is relational, then we might well explore further the roles women can play in curbing violent practices.

Notes

1. It is important to keep in mind that cultures involve learning. Messner (2002) notes that sports teams provide homosocial contexts in which boys and men can learn about violence, drinking, sexism and so forth. Muir and Seitz (2004) also describe rugby deviance as 'learned behavior' (311).
2. Frank (2005) suggests that a dialogic approach acknowledges that 'any person takes responsibility for the other's becoming, as well as recognizing that the other's voice has entered one's own' (967).
3. 'Pullers' is a pseudonym, as are all other names given to individuals included in this article's narrative account.
4. The 'points table' refers to an informal system through which the Pullers kept track of sexual conquests.
5. The 'Southern Man' was a character used in an advertising campaign by a beer brewery in the 1990s.

Acknowledgements

The authors would like to thank Richard Pringle and Anne Flintoff for their encouragement during the preparation of this paper.

References

Allen-Collinson, J., and J. Hockey. 2001. "Runners' Tales: Autoethnography, Injury and Narrative." *Auto/Biography* 9 (1&2): 95–106.

Alvesson, M. 2003. "Methodology for Close Up Studies: Struggling with Closeness and Closure." *Higher Education* 46 (2): 167–193.

Anderson, E. 2008. "'I Used to Think Women were Weak': Orthodox Masculinity, Gender Segregation, and Sport." *Sociological Forum* 23 (2): 257–280.

Anderson, E. 2009. "The Maintenance of Masculinity among the Stakeholders of Sport." *Sport Management Review* 12 (1): 3–14.

Anderson, E., M. McCormack, and H. Lee. 2012. "Male Team Sport Hazing Initiations in a Culture of Decreasing Homohysteria." *Journal of Adolescent Research* 27 (4): 427–448.

Anderson, E., and R. McGuire. 2010. "Inclusive Masculinity Theory and the Gendered Politics of Men's Rugby." *Journal of Gender Studies* 19 (3): 249–261.

Barker-Ruchti, N., K. Grahn, and E.-C. Lindgren. Forthcoming. "Shifting, Crossing and Transforming Gender Boundaries in Physical Cultures." *Sport in Society*.

Bloomer, M., and P. Hodkinson. 2000. "Learning Careers: Continuity and Change in Young People's Dispositions to Learning." *British Educational Research Journal* 26 (5): 583–597.

Brown, T. J., K. E. Sumner, and R. Nocera. 2002. "Understanding Sexual Aggression against Women: An Examination of the Role of Men's Athletic Participation and Related Variables." *Journal of Interpersonal Violence* 17 (9): 937–952.

Carless, D. 2010. "Who the Hell was That? Stories, Bodies and Actions in the World." *Qualitative Research in Psychology* 7 (4): 332–344.

Carless, D. 2012. "Negotiating Sexuality and Masculinity in School Sport: An Autoethnography." *Sport, Education and Society* 17 (5): 607–625.

Clough, P. 2002. *Narrative and Fictions in Educational Research*. Buckingham: Open University Press.

Connell, R. 1995. *Masculinities*. Berkeley, CA: University of California Press.

Douglas, K., and D. Carless. 2010. "Restoring Connections in Physical Activity and Mental Health Research and Practice: A Confessional Tale." *Qualitative Research in Sport and Exercise* 2 (3): 336–353.

Douglas, K., and D. Carless. 2014. "Sharing a Different voice: Attending to Stories in Collaborative Writing." *Cultural studies – critical methodologies* 14 (4): 303–311.

Drummond, M. 2002. "Sport and Images of Masculinity: The Meaning of Relationships in the Life Course of 'Elite' Male Athletes." *The Journal of Men's Studies* 10 (2): 129–141.

Drummond, M. 2010. "The Natural: An Autoethnography of a Masculinized Body in Sport." *Men and Masculinities* 12 (3): 374–389.

Frank, A. W. 2005. "What is Dialogical Research, and Why Should We Do it?" *Qualitative Health Research* 15: 964–974.

Grossbard, J. R., I. M. Geisner, N. R. Mastroleo, J. R. Kilmer, R. Turrisi, and M. E. Larimer. 2009. "Athletic Identity, Descriptive Norms, and Drinking among Athletes Transitioning to College." *Addictive Behaviors* 34 (4): 352–359.

Hodkinson, P. 2005. "Learning as Cultural and Relational: Moving Past Some Troubling Dualisms." *Cambridge Journal of Education* 35 (1): 107–119.

Hodkinson, P., G. Biesta, and D. James. 2007. "Understanding Learning Cultures." *Educational Review* 59 (4): 415–427.

Hodkinson, P., G. Biesta, and D. James. 2008. "Understanding Learning Culturally: Overcoming the Dualism between Social and Individual Views of Learning." *Vocations and Learning* 1 (1): 27–47.

Hodkinson, P., G. Ford, R. Hawthorn, and H. Hodkinson. 2007. "Learning as Being." *Learning Lives: Learning, Identity and Agency in the Life Course*. Leeds: The University of Leeds.

Jones, R. L. 2007. "Coaching Redefined: An Everyday Pedagogical Endeavour." *Sport, Education and Society* 12 (2): 159–173.

Kirby, S. L., and G. Wintrup. 2002. "Running the Gauntlet: An Examination of Initiation/Hazing and Sexual Abuse in Sport." *Journal of Sexual Aggression* 8 (2): 49–68.

Messner, M. 1992. *Power at Play: Sports and the Problem of Masculinity*. Boston, MA: Beacon Press.

Messner, M. 2002. *Taking the Field: Women, Men and Sports*. Vol. 4. Minneapolis, MN: University of Minnesota Press.

Muir, K. B., and T. Seitz. 2004. "Machismo, Misogyny, and Homophobia in a Male Athletic Subculture: A Participant-Observation Study of Deviant Rituals in Collegiate Rugby." *Deviant Behavior* 25 (4): 303–327.

Murnen, S. K., and M. H. Kohlman. 2007. "Athletic Participation, Fraternity Membership, and Sexual Aggression among College Men: A Meta-analytic Review." *Sex Roles* 57 (1–2): 145–157.

Pringle, R. 2001. "Competing Discourses: Narratives of a Fragmented Self, Manliness and Rugby Union." *International Review for the Sociology of Sport* 36 (4): 425–439.

Pringle, R. 2008. "'No Rugby—No Fear': Collective Stories, Masculinities and Transformative Possibilities in Schools." *Sport, Education and Society* 13 (2): 215–237.

Richardson, L. 2000. "Writing: A Method of Inquiry." In *Handbook of Qualitative Research*, edited by N. K. Denzin and Y. S. Lincoln, 516–529. Thousand Oaks, CA: Sage.

Sabo, D. F., M. A. Messner, and J. Mackay. 2000. *Masculinities, Gender Relations, and Sport*. Thousand Oaks, CA: Sage.

Sanjek, R. 1990. *Fieldnotes: The Makings of Anthropology*. Ithaca, NY: Cornell University Press.

Sayer, A. 2005. *The Moral Significance of Class*. Cambridge: Cambridge University Press.

Skelton, A. 1993. "On Becoming a Male Physical Education Teacher: The Informal Culture of Students and the Construction of Hegemonic Masculinity." *Gender and Education* 5 (3): 289–303.

Smith, B. 1999. "The Abyss: Exploring Depression through a Narrative of the Self." *Qualitative Inquiry* 5 (2): 264–279.

Smith, B., and A. Sparkes. 2009. "Narrative Analysis and Sport and Exercise Psychology: Understanding Lives in Diverse Ways." *Psychology of Sport and Exercise* 10 (2): 279–288.

Sparkes, A., and P. Bloomer. 2000. "Learning Careers: Continuity and Change in Young People's Dispositions to Learning." *British Educational Research Journal* 26 (5): 583–597.

Sparkes, A., D. Brown, and E. Partington. 2010. "The 'Jock Body' and the Social Construction of Space: The Performance and Positioning of Cultural Identity." *Space and Culture* 13 (3): 333–347.

Sparkes, A., E. Partington, and D. Brown. 2007. "Bodies as Bearers of Value: The Transmission of Jock Culture via the 'Twelve Commandments.'" *Sport, Education and Society* 12 (3): 295–316.

Gender and the 'cultural turn' in the study of sport and physical cultures

Susan J. Bandy

Department of Human Sciences, Ohio State University, Columbus, OH, USA

ABSTRACT
The study of gender, as it pertains to sport and physical cultures, began with the study of female athletes in the 1960s. With the increased participation of women in sport, scholars in North America and Western Europe began to study female athletes as they challenged the patriarchal ideology upon which sport was based, provoked questions about ideas concerning femininity and masculinity, and eventually raised questions about the basic nature and purpose of modern sport. In the humanities and social sciences, researchers began to explore the subject of the female athlete from a variety of disciplinary perspectives in sports studies, most notably in sport history and sport sociology. With the inclusion of gender in the research in the 1980s, the focus shifted away from the female athlete to a critique of culture and sporting culture. The 'cultural turn' in the humanities and social sciences in the 1980s was concurrent with changing perceptions of gender as scholars embraced interdisciplinary and later transdisciplinary perspectives to further examine sport and to incorporate the concept of physical cultures. It is in this historical context that the shifting, crossing, and transforming of gender boundaries can be situated and understood as critical to the ongoing research concerning gender. Indeed, the focus on physical cultures – rather than sport – suggests yet another 'turn' in the research and a point of view that seems worthy of consideration.

Introduction

The study of gender, as it pertains to sport and physical cultures, began with the study of female athletes in the 1960s. Scholars in North America and Western Europe began to study female athletes as more and more females crossed the boundaries of sport into what later came to be regarded as 'contested terrain' (Messner 1988). With their increased participation in sport, women challenged the patriarchal ideology upon which sport was based, provoked questions about ideas concerning femininity and masculinity and eventually raised questions about the basic nature and purpose of modern sport. In the humanities and social sciences in particular, researchers began to explore the subject of the female athlete as the DeBeauvorian 'other' from a variety of disciplinary perspectives in sports studies, most notably sport history and sport sociology. With the inclusion of gender in research in the 1980s, the focus shifted away from the female athlete to a critique of culture and sporting culture (Birrell 1988; Hall 1988; Bandy 2004a, 2005, 2006, 2010, 2014). The 'cultural turn' in the humanities and social sciences in the 1980s was concurrent with changing perceptions of gender as scholars embraced interdisciplinary and later transdisciplinary perspectives to further examine sport and to incorporate the concept of physical cultures (Andrews 2008; Andrews and Silk 2011). It is in this historical context that the shifting, crossing and transforming of gender boundaries explored in this volume can be situated and understood as critical to the ongoing research concerning gender. Indeed, the focus on physical cultures – rather than sport – suggests yet another 'turn' in the research and a point of view that seems worthy of consideration.

Disciplinary perspectives of the female athlete

The earliest work concerning the female athlete was based on the assumption that women are indeed different from men and have different experiences than men, which leads to a writing of 'her-story', as sport historians noted (Howell 1982). Some of the earliest work was done in sport philosophy and sport psychology. Philosophers argued for sex equality in sport and questioned the ideological, symbolic and mythic nature of sport, which, in retrospect, anticipated the feminist critique of sport that would eventually emerge (Metheny 1965; English 1978; Young 1979; Postow 1980, 1983; Wentz 1981). In the realm of sport psychology, researchers explored concepts such as the female apologetic and the notion of psychological androgyny in the sporting context (Harris 1971, 1972, 1973; Gill 1991, 1995). In particular, the concept of androgyny, the combination of masculine and feminine characteristics, can be considered as a transitional concept relating to the fluidity of sexual identity that would ultimately enable a consideration of 'gender' as relevant to the study of the female athlete. Finally, scholars began to offer a feminist critique of the social construction of woman and femininity that would further move the discourse closer to the view that sport was a social construction that privileged men and excluded women (Felshin 1974).

In 1978, Ann Hall introduced the concept of gender into the discourse in sport sociology in a monograph entitled *Sport and Gender: A Feminist Perspective on the Sociology of Sport*. With the work of Hall and other sport sociologists, gender displaced 'sex' as scholars rejected biological determinism and adopted the view that the behavioural, cultural or psychological traits typically associated with one sex were socially constructed. The inclusion of gender would then destabilize concepts such as sex and sex roles.

Sport historians from Canada, the United Kingdom, the United States and a number of Continental European scholars, joined sport sociologists by providing additional feminist critiques of sport and advocated the use of frameworks of an inclusive, relational nature rather than frameworks based on the notion of sexual difference. Historians called for the inclusion of gender as a 'fundamental historical variable' that should lie 'at the center of theoretical debates and methodological innovations' in sport history (Struna 1984; see also Struna 1991; Parratt 1994; Vertinsky 1999). Historians also forged ideas concerning the social production of gender *in* and *through* sport, linking social constructivist theories to the patriarchal character of modern sport.

The assumption of difference, upon which the majority of this early research was based, was problematic, yet productive for future research. On the one hand, it presented the notion of sexual difference and reinforced essentialist ideas concerning women, which had prevented their entry into sport and would later be addressed as a political issue concerning equality in sport. It also raised the age-old question about dualistic views that both feminism and postmodernism would address, and such considerations were productive in understanding the exclusion of women from sport. On the other hand, these reigning assumptions and persistent dualisms evoked important questions that could only be addressed through the inclusion of a revised concept of 'gender' into the scholarly discourse. Accompanying this revision was a cultural studies approach, a concern with sociological and historical issues that brought a critique of modern sport and society and the introduction of deconstructionist, feminist and postmodern theories.

The cultural turn: interdisciplinary and relational perspectives

In the early 1970s, scholars in the humanities and social sciences began to focus on culture and this brought forth a 'cultural turn' that embraced a vast array of new theories in these fields of knowledge with particular attention to language, symbols and systems of representation. The 'cultural turn' had a considerable influence on research in sports studies as historians and sociologists in particular, began to examine the cultural dimensions of sport with the perspective that sport is a reflection or mirror of culture and a product of social processes. As sport historian Amy Bass (2014) noted when considering the impact of the cultural turn in history upon sport history, with the focus upon sport' symbolic, historical, social and political significance, the cultural significance of sport 'transcends the game itself'. It was within the context of the 'cultural turn' that the concept of gender began to transform research in the humanistic and social scientific study of sport, most particularly within the sub-disciplines of sport sociology and sport history in which scholars embraced a transitional and evolving view of gender.

This new perspective of gender brought an examination of women and men in relation to one another in sport and began to destabilize the discourse, moving it away from a focus on sex and binary modes of thought towards an interdisciplinary focus in the various sub-disciplines (Costa and Guthrie 1994). In a turn from 'categoric' to 'relational' research, gender then came to be regarded as a process and a relational concept (Hall 1988), and scholars began to approach research from interdisciplinary and cultural studies perspectives incorporating a number of theories from a variety of disciplines in their analyses. Using the work of Foucault, Gramsci and postmodern and feminist theories, sport scholars began to deconstruct modern sport, arguing that 'sporting practices are historically produced, socially constructed, and culturally defined to serve the interests and needs of powerful groups in society,' as Hall (1996) claimed. Further, scholars turned their attention to concepts such as globalization, hegemony, masculinity, post-colonialism, power, the socially constructed body and the media.

Sport sociologists and historians challenged the anthropocentric definition of knowledge and began to critique the epistemology of modernity, specifically its rationalism and dualism as masculine modes of thought that serve to legitimate a patriarchal society. With new approaches to research, scholars also began to recognize the autonomy of sport in society and, therefore, its power of legitimation. According to this view, sport did not just reflect culture nor was it simply a product of social processes; rather, scholars argued that sport has a powerful effect upon culture. Using analytic cultural criticism or that which has been termed the sociology of culture in particular, sport was examined as a product of social processes, which enabled scholars to examine the ideological processes concerning gender differences in sport (Willis 1982). A focus on power and the processes of domination and subordination, as these relate to gender relations in sport – as well as critiques of the place of sport in cultural productions – brought the body into the discourse (Cole 1993).

A focus on gender as process also allowed scholars to further probe the relationship between sport and the construction of masculinity and femininity as well as sexual identity (Hall 1981; Lenskyj 2003) and to link sexuality in sport to a broader understanding of the relationship between sex and gender. Of critical importance is Brian Pronger's (1990) *The Arena of Masculinity: Sport, Homosexuality, and the Meaning of Sex*, in which the relationship between gender and sex and the non-elite level athlete are examined. Pronger's work foreshadowed the work that would be done somewhat later as scholars sought to deconstruct gender in an attempt to understand the relationships among sexuality, sex and gender, using a new feminist paradigm expressed as intersubjectivity.

Viewing 'gender' as a process also enabled scholars to critique the ongoing institutionalization of discrimination in modern sport (Hargreaves 1994). It became important to understand sport as an institution that developed, performed and rewarded discrimination against women in examining other institutions such as the media and politics that promoted similar ideologies of difference.

The feminist, interdisciplinary and cultural studies approach of this period encouraged a movement across the borders of traditional disciplinary configurations, and transformed the methodological approaches as well as the concerns of the discipline. Issues pertaining to 'gender' contributed as well to the need for an alternative view of gender – the interrelational (Park 1991). Such a view required a new focus as well as the introduction of new paradigms and methodologies. The interconnectedness and interrelational nature of gender, therefore, became apparent and the basis for changing views of gender that informed the scholarly discourse in sport as well as requiring different methodological approaches.

Gender as interrelational and intersubjective: transdisciplinary perspectives

Beginning in the 1970s, there were debates among feminists concerning the universalizing and uniformity of 'mainstream' feminism that did not allow for differences within feminist thought as women of colour, lesbians and working-class feminists gave voice to the debate. The response to such claims was the introduction of an analytical tool known as 'intersectionality', a paradigm for theorizing identity and oppression and combating exclusivity, hegemony and hierarchy (within feminism also). According to Nash (2008), intersectionality serves a few theoretical and political purposes that enable scholars to create new paradigms for a revisioning of gender. A number of important feminist critiques of gender also pointed towards a need for an intersectional analysis, most notably Lorber's (2005) view that 'gender is a binary system of social organization that creates inequality'. There was then a need to 'degender' which means:

> to recognize that the two genders are not at all homogenous categories since they are intersected by other major social statuses—racial ethnic group, social class, national identity, religious affiliation—and by individual variations such as age, sexual orientation, relational and parental statuses, and physical status. (Lorber 2005)

In other words, multiplicities of gender – gender diversity and gender freedom – suggest a living outside of the binary sex/gender system. Further, Lorber advocates that individuals should be open to intersexuality, sexual fluidity, transgender queering and deliberately ambiguous non-gendered presentations of self.

This paradigmatic shift towards intersectionality in feminist research also appeared in sports studies research concerned with gender. As early as 1990, sports studies scholars embraced the work of feminist scholars such as Judith Butler, Elizabeth Grosz and Judith Lorber. Following the work of Roberta Park in the early 1990s, sport historians began to recognize that gender was not monolithic; rather, it intersects with a number of other dimensions of human experience and identity in sport. Reflecting a trend towards intersectionality, scholars approached the study of gender in innovative ways, including the use of concepts or themes (rather than theories) and an admixture of methodologies and sources of knowledge, most particularly the use of narratives (Sparkes and Silvennoinen 1999; Bal 2002; Denison and Markula 2003; Markula 2005; Bandy 2004b).

With a recent interest in the transnational – as that which exists between nations or perhaps between people – the concept of difference brought new insights into the research as scholars sought to deconstruct gender, viewing gender (and race, social class and ethnicity) from an interrelational and intersectional point of view. An interest in the transnational also brought transdisciplinary views and methodologies into the research, and, thus, researchers adopted approaches that 'decentre' hierarchical organizations and patterns of knowledge in search of new knowledge that exist between structured disciplines of knowledge (Nicolescu 2002).

In this context, gender becomes fluid and multiple and serves as an interconnecting concept in understanding multiple points of view, resulting in the simultaneous inclusion of a gendered perspective among connecting and multiple perspectives. Although much research that has recently been published fails to incorporate a gender perspective, some research points to transdisciplinary perspectives in sports studies (Bandy, 2004b), and a few of these present us with new and alternative views and treatments of gender and sport.

Among the more important of these include an interrelational perspective of gender that recognizes multiplicities of gender as well as the intersections between other aspects of identity such as sexuality and race that brought forth an interest in 'other' women – women of colour, lesbians and those outside the margins of mainstream sport theory and practice – that entered the discourse, most notably in the sociological approach to sport. Cahn's work (1994) concerning the 'Cinderellas' of sport, for example, included histories of women of colour as well as lesbians in sport. Similarly, Hargreaves (2000) recognized the 'others' in sport in a study of Aboriginal, disabled, Muslim and lesbian women. Hargreaves looks from a transnational point of view and uses an admixture of methods and sources to examine the relationship between sporting experiences and identity of 'others' from different parts of the world. Informed by Foucault's notions of power, she examines power relations among women, using concepts of inclusion and exclusion, power and privilege, and the relationship between the local and the global. In this context, gender is seen as a shared and universal experience, while at the same time is an experience of difference (according to nationality, sexuality, physical ability, religion and social class) and individual identity in sport. With an interest in the transnational, Hargreaves' work examines both the simultaneity of multiple oppressions and the complexity of identity.

The introduction of 'queer theory' also supplied a theoretical framework that has recently been used to advance intersectional and transdisciplinary investigations of gender and sport. Introduced by de Lauretis (1991), 'queer theory' provoked a critique of sexual identity and postmodernism's suspicion of fundamental truths and categories and altered the way we think about gender, sexuality, desire and the body in sports studies. On a theoretical level, scholars have noted the absence of queer theory in sport – as is the case of the academy in general – and further that this absence has worked against a more expansive, comprehensive, interrelational and intersectional analysis of sport.

The most recent theoretical development in sports studies has been a focus on sexuality from an intersectional point of view. Influenced by expanding notions of gender and the influence of queer theory, researchers have begun to focus on the control and containment of female sexuality and the expression of sexuality in women's sport, turning their attention to sex testing and gender verification by sport organizations and transsexual and transgender policies in sport (Ritchie 2003; Caudwell 2006; Cavanagh and Sykes 2006; Sykes 2006; Parks Pieper 2012, 2014).

As I have argued thus far, the concept of gender, indeed, the lens of gender, has profoundly influenced the study of sport in recent decades. Its inclusion has moved the perspective of the study of sport from a disciplinary point of view to that of interdisciplinarity and transdisciplinarity, which incorporates a cultural sociology of sport. Instead of viewing culture as a product of social processes, the perspective of cultural sociology incorporates cultural analysis and critical theory and envisions culture as autonomous in shaping social life (Alexander 2003). Sport can thus be seen as a component of explanations of social phenomena and of shaping social life. Within this perspective, the concept of boundaries, 'boundary-work' and perhaps 'supra-disciplinary' conversations have surfaced (Lamont 2014), as is evidenced in the essays of this volume.

Towards a cultural sociology and a reconceptualization of gender boundaries in movement cultures

Originating in science studies, 'boundary-work' investigates the way in which boundaries, demarcations or other divisions between fields of knowledge are created, advocated, attacked or reinforced. Implicit in this work is the view that boundaries are socially constructed and therefore malleable. Following the work of Pierre Bourdieu, a contemporary proponent of such analysis is Michèle Lamont, a student of Bourdieu, whose work, with Virág Molnár (2002), has been incorporated into the essays in this collection. Lamont has distinguished between 'symbolic' and 'social' boundaries, as Barker-Ruchti, Grahn and Lindgren suggest in the introduction to this volume. 'Symbolic' boundaries are being understood as conceptual distinctions made by social actors that separate people into groups and generate feelings of similarity and group membership. Conversely, 'social' boundaries are objectified forms of social differences manifested in unequal access to unequal distribution of resources and social opportunities. When symbolic boundaries are widely agreed upon, they take on a constraining character and become social boundaries (Lamont and Molnár 2002). In her most recent work (2014), Lamont includes a variety of methods necessary for sociologists to work: content analysis, ethnographic fieldwork, historical and archival research, interviews and focus groups, mixed methods, statistical analysis and survey research. Further, according to Lamont, there is a need to study various elements in culture that she considers the 'building blocks of culture': norms, values, attitudes and beliefs; frames and symbolic boundaries; repertoires and rituals; ideas, arts and cultural capital; discourse and narratives; and institutions and identities (Lamont 2014).

It can be argued that sport has been ideal for studying the way in which symbolic boundaries become social boundaries and the way in which sport further genders social realities and social identities and thereby creates inequalities between participants, leaders and communities, as Barker-Ruchti, Grahn and Lindgren suggest in the introduction. To date, the majority of research in the field of sports studies has focused on sport and most often elite or high-performance sport. This focus, however, has not led to a consideration of a fluid movement through the boundaries of sport that successfully relieves sport of its gendered nature and state. A focus on elite-level sport has created a hierarchical structure in sport research, one that gives the principal voice to the natural sciences and privileges quantitative, objective analysis of sport. Or, as Andrews (2008) proposed, this epistemological hierarchy 'privileges positivist over postpositivist, quantitative over qualitative, and predictive over interpretive ways of knowing.' In addition to privileging hegemonic masculinity, this focus creates a hierarchical structure that precludes the various forms of human movement and settings in the analysis. It therefore leads to what Barker-Ruchti, Grahn and Lindgren maintain is a deficit approach, one that focuses on gender inequalities and disadvantages. Thus, they have proposed a positivist approach that enables a shifting, crossing and transforming of boundaries in a variety of movement forms and settings.

The boundary-work that these authors propose approximates a transdisciplinary point of view with its incorporation of multiple and varied methodologies to investigate the various aspects of culture and knowledge that exist across disciplines of inquiry. Barker-Ruchti, Grahn and Lindgren have astutely proposed a way to do 'boundary-work' in their introductory essay by envisioning three levels – shifting, crossing and transforming – that may build on each other progressively. Within their framework, they further envision future research in examining boundary transformation of physical cultures by exploring: the properties of boundaries, mechanisms of shifting and crossing boundaries, and the perceptions of those included or excluded by boundaries. The use of physical cultures, an all-inclusive and umbrella term in the plural form without specific and explicit attention to sport implies a different orientation to a variety of movement cultures in addition to sport, without excluding it.

The focus on physical cultures 'mobilize[s] alternative objects and modes of inquiry' (Andrews and Silk 2011) as clarified by the selection of papers included in this volume. They conform as well to Lamont's acknowledgement of a multiplicity of methodologies that can be used in cultural sociology by employing interviews, auto-ethnography, a linguistic genealogy and analyses of language and media coverage. Furthermore, these papers use an admixture of theories: feminist theory, postcolonial theories, discursive analysis, embodiment, symbolic and social boundaries (boundary-work), feminist cultural studies perspective and identity theory. Additionally, the perspectives of the authors propose that physical cultures are an important area in which to investigate the fluid character of sexuality, its social construction and its flexibility, and, further, they suggest that physical cultures shape multiple aspects of individual identity and social life.

As the editors of this collection suggest, these essays – taken as a whole – provide readers with a view of micro-level processes that encourage a better understanding of the way in which power relations affect individuals and groups of individuals in creating, maintaining, negotiating and transforming dominant ideologies and gender discourses in various forms of human movement cultures. Their work challenges the predominance of elite-level sport in the research of scholars, the preponderance of the natural sciences and its hegemonic grasp on our understandings of human movement, various physical cultures and sport.

Disclosure statement

No potential conflict of interest was reported by the author.

References

Alexander, J. 2003. *The Meanings of Social Life: A Cultural Sociology*. New York: Oxford University Press.
Andrews, D. 2008. "Kinesiology's Inconvenient Truth and the Physical Cultural Studies Imperative." *Quest* 60: 45–62.
Andrews, D., and M. Silk. 2011. "Physical Cultural Studies: Engendering a Productive Dialogue." *Sociology of Sport Journal* 28: 1–3.
Bal, M. 2002. *Traveling Concepts in the Humanities: A Rough Guide*. London: University of Toronto Press.
Bandy, S. 2004a. "Fra 'sex' til 'gender', fra kvinder og sport til kulturkritik og fra det nationale til det transnationale: En oversight over amerikansk, canadisk og britisk forskning I sport og køn [From 'sex' to 'gender', from women and sport to cultural critique and from the national to the transnational: An overview of American, Canadian, and British research on sport and gender]." *Dansk Sociologi* 2 (15): 125–135.
Bandy, S. 2004b. *Nordic Narratives in Sport and Physical Culture: Transdisciplinary Perspectives*. Aarhus: Center for Idræt.
Bandy, S. 2005. "From Women in Sport to Cultural Critique: A Review of Books about Women in Sport and Physical Culture." *Women's Studies Quarterly* 33 (1 & 2): 246–261.
Bandy, S. 2010. "Gender." In *The Routledge Companion to Sports History*, edited by S. Pope and J. Nauright, 129–147. London: Routledge.
Bandy, S. 2014. "Gender and Sports Studies: An Historical Perspective." *Movement & Sport Sciences – Science & Motricité* 86: 15–27.
Bandy, S. 2006. "Køn og idraetsforskning: Et historisk perspektiv." In *Kvinder, køn og krop – kulturelle fortaellinger, Idraetshistorisk Arbogi*, edited by Danish Sports Yearbook, 11–22. Odense, Denmark: University Press of Southern Denmark.
Bass, A. 2014. "State of the Field: Sports History and the 'Cultural Turn.'" *Journal of American History* 101 (1): 148–172.
Birrell, S. 1988. "Discourses on the Gender/Sport Relationship: From Women in Sport to Gender Relations." *Exercise and Sport Sciences Reviews* 16: 459–502.
Cahn, S. 1994. *Coming on Strong: Gender and Sexuality in Twentieth Century Women's Sport*. London: Harvard University Press.
Caudwell, J. 2006. *Sport, Sexualities and Queer/Theory*. London: Routledge.
Cavanagh, S., and H. Sykes. 2006. "Transsexual Bodies at the Olympics: The International Olympic Committee's Policy on Transsexual Athletes at the 2004 Athens Summer Games." *Body and Society* 12 (3): 75–102.
Cole, C. 1993. "Resisting the Canon: Feminist Cultural Studies, Sport, and Technologies of the Body." *Journal of Sport and Social Issues* 17: 79–97.
Costa, D., and S. Guthrie. 1994. *Women and Sport: Interdisciplinary Perspectives*. Champaign, IL: Human Kinetics.
de Lauretis, T. 1991. "Queer Theory: Lesbian and Gay Sexualities." *Differences: A Journal of Feminist Cultural Studies* 3 (2): iii–xviii.

Denison, J., and P. Markula. 2003. *Moving Writing: Crafting Movement in Sport Research*. New York: Peter Lang.

English, J. 1978. "Sex Equality in Sports." *Philosophy and Public Affairs* 7 (3): 269–277.

Felshin, J. 1974. "The Social View." In *The American Woman in Sport*, edited by E. Gerber, J. Felshin, P. Berlin, and W. Wyrick, 179–279. London: Addison-Wesley.

Gill, D. 1991. "Gender and Sport Behavior." In *Advances in Sport Psychology*, edited by T. Horn, 143–160. Champaign, IL: Human Kinetics.

Gill, D. 1995. "Women's Place in the History of Sport Psychology." *The Sport Psychologist* 9: 418–433.

Hall, A. 1996. *Feminism and Sporting Bodies: Essays on Theory and Practice*. Champaign Urbana, IL: Human Kinetics.

Hall, A. 1981. *Sport, Sex Roles, and Sex Identity*. Ottawa: Canadian Research Institute for the Advancement of Women.

Hall, A. 1978. *Sport and Gender: A Feminist Perspective on the Sociology of Sport*. Ottawa: Canadian Association of Health, Physical Education, and Recreation.

Hall, A. 1988. "The Discourse of Gender and Sport: From Femininity to Feminism." *Sociology of Sport Journal* 5: 330–340.

Hargreaves, J. 2000. *Heroines of Sport: The Politics of Difference and Identity*. London: Routledge.

Hargreaves, J. 1994. *Sporting Females: Critical Issues in the History and Sociology of Women's Sports*. London: Routledge.

Harris, D. 1971. *DGWS Research Reports: Women in Sports*. Washington, DC: AAHPER.

Harris, D. 1972. *Women and Sport: A National Research Conference*. State College: The Pennsylvania State University.

Harris, D. 1973. *DGWS Research Reports: Women in Sports*. Washington: AAHPERD.

Howell, R. 1982. *Her Story in Sport: A Historical Anthology of Women in Sports*. West Point: Leisure Press.

Lamont, M., and V. Molnár. 2002. "The Study of Boundaries in the Social Sciences." *Annual Review of Sociology* 28: 167–195.

Lamont, M. 2014. "Introduction." In *Cultural Sociology: An Introductory Reader*, edited by M. Wray, xiii–xxxvii. London: W.W. Norton.

Lenskyj, H. 2003. *Out on the Field: Gender, Sport, and Sexualities*. Toronto: Women's Press.

Lorber, J. 2005. *Breaking the Bowls: Degendering and Feminist Change*. New York: W.W. Norton.

Markula, P. 2005. *Feminist Sport Studies: Sharing Experiences of Joy and Pain*. Albany: State University of New York Press.

Messner, M. 1988. "Sports and Male Domination: The Female Athlete as Contested Ideological Terrain." *Sociology of Sport Journal* 5: 197–211.

Metheny, E. 1965. "Symbolic Forms of Movement: The Feminine Image in Sports." In *Connotations of Movement in Sport and Dance*, edited by E. Metheny, 43–56. Dubuque, IA: Brown.

Nash, J. 2008. "Re-thinking Intersectionality." *Feminist Review* 89: 1–15.

Nicolescu, B. 2002. *Manifesto of Transdisciplinarity*. Translated by Karen-Claire Voss. Albany: State University of New York Press.

Park, R. 1991. "Guest Editor's Introduction." *Journal of Sport History* 18 (1): 5–9.

Parks Pieper, L. 2012. "Gender Regulation: Renée Richards Revisited." *The International Journal of the History* 29 (5): 675–690.

Parks Pieper, L. 2014. "Sex Testing and the Maintenance of Western Femininity in International Sport." *The International Journal of the History* 31 (13): 675–690.

Parratt, C. 1994. "From the History of Women in Sport to Women's Sport History." In *Women and Sport: Interdisciplinary Perspectives*, edited by M. Costa and S. Guthrie, 5–14. Champaign, IL: Human Kinetics.

Postow, B. 1980. "Women and Masculine Sports." *Journal of the Philosophy of Sport* VII: 51–58.

Postow, P. 1983. *Women, Philosophy, and Sport: A Collection of New Essays*. Metuchen, NJ: Scarecrow Press.

Pronger, B. 1990. *The Arena of Masculinity: Sports, Homosexuality, and the Meaning of Sex*. New York: St. Martin's Press.

Ritchie, I. 2003. "Sex Tested, Gender Verified: Controlling Female Sexuality in the Age of Containment." *Sport History Review* 34: 80–98.
Sparkes, A., and M. Silvennoinen. 1999. *Talking Bodies*. Jyväskylä: University of Jyväskylä.
Struna, N. 1984. "Beyond Mapping Experience: The Need for Understanding in the History of American Sporting Women." *Journal of Sport History* 11 (1): 120–133.
Struna, N. 1991. "Gender and Sporting Practice in Early America, 1750–1810." *Journal of Sport History* 18 (1): 10–30.
Sykes, H. 2006. "Transsexual and Transgender Policies in Sport." *Women in Sport and Physical Activity Journal* 15 (1): 3–13.
Vertinsky, P. 1999. "Gender Relations, Physical Education and Sport History: Is It Time for a Collaborative Research Agenda?" In *Gender & Sport from European Perspectives*, edited by E. Trangbæk and A. Krüger, 13–27, Copenhagen: Institute of Exercise and Sport Sciences, University of Copenhagen.
Wentz, P. 1981. "Human Equality in Sports." *The Philosophical Forum, XII* 3: 238–250.
Willis, P. 1982. "Women in Sport and Ideology." In *Sport Culture and Ideology*, edited by J. Hargreaves, 117–135. London: Routledge and Kegan Paul.
Young, I. 1979. "The Exclusion of Women from Sport: Conceptual and Existential Dimensions." *Philosophy in Context* 9: 44–53.

Index

Note: **Boldface** page number refer to tables, page number followed by n denote endnotes.

aesthetic body 71–3, 76
AI *see* appreciative inquiry
androgyny, concept of 113
appreciative inquiry (AI) 56
Arena of Masculinity, The: Sport, Homosexuality, and the Meaning of Sex (Pronger) 115
ASA *see* Athletics South Africa
ASGF *see* Association Suisse de Gymnastique Féminine
Association of the Gymnastics Central Institute (Föreningen GCI) 28
Association Suisse de Gymnastique Féminine (ASGF) 40–3, **48**
athletic body ideal 77; beef-ideal *vs.* 74–5; top model ideal *vs.* 73–4
Athletics South Africa (ASA) 17

beef ideal 74–5
body and physicality 30–1
body-positive dance community: appreciative inquiry 56; Bourdieu's concept of habitus 55–6; data sources 56–7; Irreverent Dance *see* Irreverent Dance; overview of 53–5
body-self relationship 82–3, 85, 91–2; unorthodox 87, 90
boundary-work *see* gender boundaries
Bourdieu, Pierre 55–6

CDA *see* critical discourse analysis
co-education reform: Swedish physical education culture 32–3; swimming (training) groups 75–6
constructivist grounded theory 57
critical discourse analysis (CDA) 15
critically gender-sensitive approach 34
crossing boundaries 5, 56–9; *see also* health-related gender boundary crossing
'cultural turn': boundary-work 117–19; female athletes, disciplinary perspectives of 113–14; interdisciplinary and relational perspectives 114–15; overview of 112–13; queer theory 117; transdisciplinary perspectives 115–17

Dâmaso, Fernando 46–7
degender, notion of 115
demasculinization of physiotherapy 31–2
Digel, Helmut 18–19
disengagement from sporting community: 'becoming' someone else 99; data production, phases of 100; idea of 'boundaries' 99; masculine subcultures 98–9; narrative section 100; overview of 97, 106–9; social rugby culture 100–6

Ecole Fédérale de Gymnastique et de Sport (EFGS) 40
emphasised femininity 93n4

Falk, Elin 29–30
Fédération Suisse de Gymnastique (FSG) 49, 50
female athletes, disciplinary perspectives of 113–14
femininity: conformity test 12; emphasised 93n4; non-white 18, 20; orthodox 83, 87, 92, 93n1; physical capital in 61; real 20; selective 68
feminist theory 15
Foucault's concept of power 27, 116
French Olympic Committee 40
FSG *see Fédération Suisse de Gymnastique*
functional body 71–2, 76

gender boundaries: Bourdieuian theories 55–6; conceptualization of 3–4, 117–19; crossing 5, 57–9; *see also* health-related gender boundary crossing; negotiations of 73–6, 87–91; shifting 5, 62, 75–6; social 4, 27, 68–9, 83, 117–18; symbolic 4, 27, 68–9, 83, 117–18; transformation 5–6, 60–2
gendered body ideals: aesthetic body 71–3; beef ideal 74–5; co-ed swimming 75–6; functional body 72; overview of 66–7, 76–8; research on ideals 67–8; in sport and social culture 68; Swedish swimming context 69–71; symbolic and social boundaries 68–9; top model ideal 73–4

INDEX

gender inequalities 1–2, 115, 118
gender-neutrality 60–2
Gymnastik med lek och idrott (Falk) 30

habitus, Bourdieuian concept of 55–6
Hall, Ann 113
Health Behaviour in School-Aged Children (HBSC) 82, 93n3
health-related gender boundary crossing: data and in-depth analysis 85; health and gender constructions 82–3; high-performance sport 84; orthodox masculinity 86–7; overview of 81–2; sampling and data collection 84–5; unorthodox health practices 87–91
hetero-normative gender system 21
high-performance sport 81–2; health-related practices in 84

IAAF *see* International Association of Athletics Federations
ID *see* Irreverent Dance
IFG *see* International Federation of Gymnastics
International Association of Athletics Federations (IAAF) 12
International Federation of Gymnastics (IFG) 40
International Olympic Committee (IOC) 12–13
interpretative repertoires 67, 71–3, 76, 78
IOC *see* International Olympic Committee
Irreverent Dance (ID) 56; body positivity 60; crossing boundaries in 57–9; gender-neutrality 60–2; shifting boundaries of codified dance 62

Karolinska Institute (KI) 31

lightweight body 72
Ling gymnastics system 26–35
Ljungqvist, Arne 18

masculine subcultures 98–9
mononucleosis infection 89, 93n7
Moret, Charles 42

National Committee for Elite Sport 43

orthodox femininity 83, 87, 92, 93n1
orthodox masculinity 86–7, 93n1, 98; athletehood 91; athletic identity 89; high-performance sport and 81; risk behaviours 90

PETE programmes *see* physical education teaching education programmes
physical education (PE) culture, Swedish context 26–35
physical education teaching education (PETE) programmes 32–5
physiotherapy, demasculinization of 31–2
Pronger, Brian 115
psychological androgyny 113
Pullers social rugby team 100–6, 109n3, 109n4

queer theory 117

real femininity 20

selective femininity 68
Semenya, Caster 14, 17–21
SFG *see* Société Fédérale de Gymnastique
shifting boundaries 5, 62, 75–6
'slim- to-win' body 66, 72, 77
social boundaries 4, 27, 68–9, 83, 117–18
socialization effect 83
social rugby culture 100–6, 109n3
Société Fédérale de Gymnastique (SFG) 39, 40, 43, **48**
space-time configuration 27
Sport and Gender: A Feminist Perspective on the Sociology of Sport (Hall) 113
sport and social culture, (gendered) body ideals in 68, 71–3
Swedish competitive youth swimming 66–78
Swedish gender-divergent physical education (PE) culture 35n1; body and physicality 30–1; co-education reform 32–3; Falk's ideas and conceptions 29–30; gender-neutral culture 33–4; Ling gymnastics system 27–8; overview of 26–7, 34–5; physiotherapy, demasculinization of 31–2; professional platform, manifestation of 28–9; theoretical frame of reference 27
Swiss feminine gymnastics: barring women from competition 41–3; competitions and innovations 43–5; framework and hypothesis 40–1; on international scene 45–8; overview of 39–40; reunification and new boundaries 48–50
symbolic boundaries 4, 27, 68–9, 83, 117–18

top-level sports: contextualization of 13; critical discourse analysis 15–16; deconstructive research 16; discourse analysis methods 14; dispositive analysis 15–16; hetero-normative gender system 21; heterosexual matrix 19; intersexuality in 14; racism and sexism 20; real femininity 20; sports values and gender norms 18–19; theoretical approach 14–15; transgressive aesthetic of performance and display 17–18
top model ideal 73–4
'tough guy' attitude 86–7
transforming boundaries 5–6, 60–2

unorthodox health practices 87–91

Women First (Fletcher) 26
World Championships for Artistic Gymnastics 42

youth elite sport, health-related gender boundary crossing in 81–93

For Product Safety Concerns and Information please contact our EU representative GPSR@taylorandfrancis.com
Taylor & Francis Verlag GmbH, Kaufingerstraße 24, 80331 München, Germany

www.ingramcontent.com/pod-product-compliance
Lightning Source LLC
Chambersburg PA
CBHW080940300426
44115CB00017B/2889